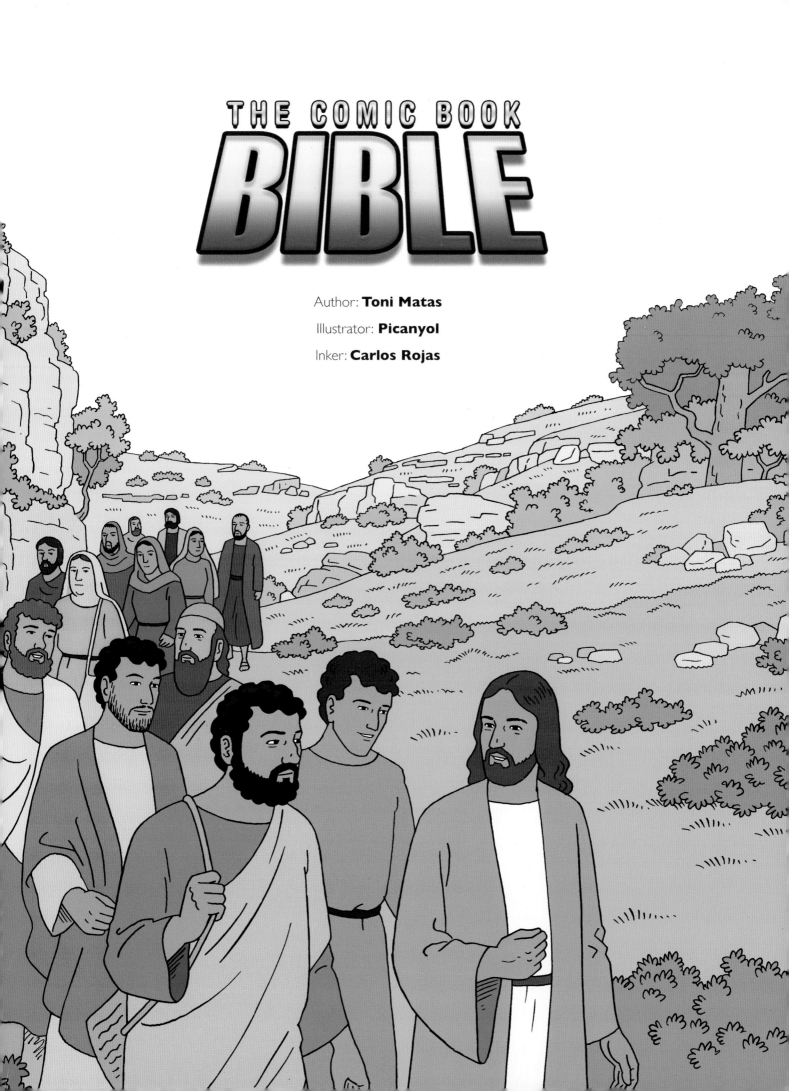

THE COMIC BOOK
BIBLE

Author: **Toni Matas**

Illustrator: **Picanyol**

Inker: **Carlos Rojas**

Silver Dolphin Books
An imprint of the Baker & Taylor Publishing Group
10350 Barnes Canyon Road, San Diego, CA 92121
www.silverdolphinbooks.com

ISBN-13: 978-1-60710-788-0
ISBN-10: 1-60710-788-0

First printing: January 2013

Printed in Shenzhen, China.

1 2 3 4 5 17 16 15 14 13

WOODSON

THE COMIC BOOK BIBLE

OLD TESTAMENT

NEW TESTAMENT

Old Testament

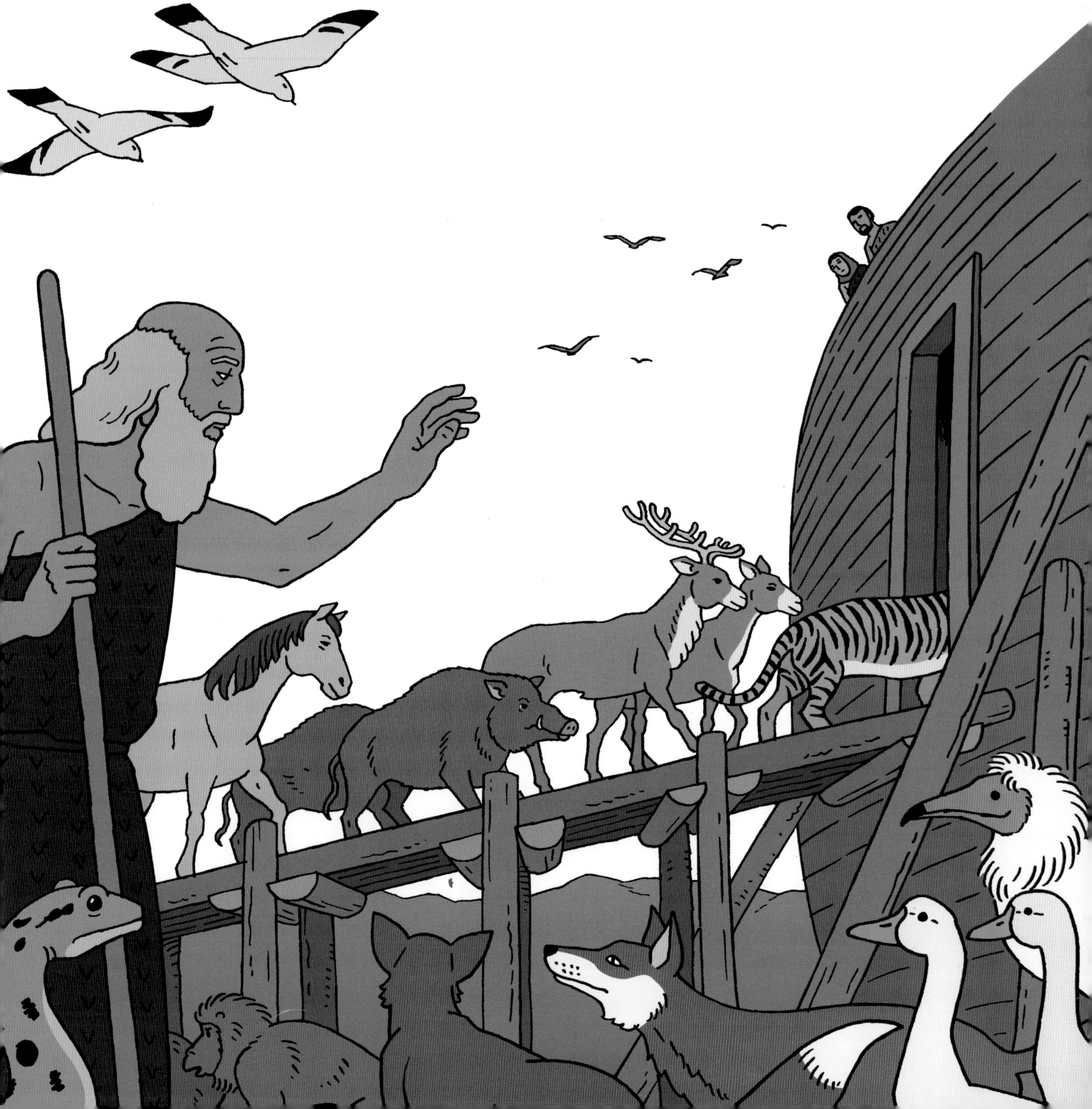

IN THE BEGINNING, WHEN GOD MADE THE UNIVERSE, THE EARTH WAS FORMLESS AND DESOLATE. THE OCEAN WAS ENGULFED IN TOTAL DARKNESS, AND THE SPIRIT OF GOD WAS MOVING OVER THE WATER.

LET THERE BE LIGHT.

AND LIGHT APPEARED. GOD WAS PLEASED WITH WHAT HE SAW, AND THEN HE SEPARATED THE LIGHT FROM THE DARKNESS.

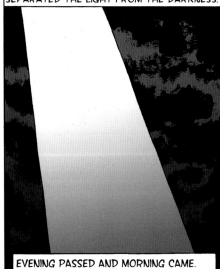

EVENING PASSED AND MORNING CAME. THAT WAS THE FIRST DAY.

LET THERE BE A DOME TO SEPARATE THE WATERS.

AND IT WAS DONE. HE NAMED THE DOME "SKY." EVENING PASSED AND MORNING CAME. THAT WAS THE SECOND DAY.

LET THE WATER BELOW THE SKY COME TOGETHER IN ONE PLACE SO THAT LAND WILL APPEAR.

AND IT WAS DONE. HE NAMED THE LAND "EARTH," AND THE WATER "SEA." AND GOD WAS PLEASED WITH WHAT HE SAW.

LET THE EARTH PRODUCE ALL KINDS OF PLANTS.

AND IT WAS DONE. EVENING PASSED AND MORNING CAME. THAT WAS THE THIRD DAY.

LET LIGHTS APPEAR IN THE SKY TO SEPARATE DAY FROM NIGHT AND TO SHOW THE TIME WHEN DAYS, YEARS, AND RELIGIOUS FESTIVALS BEGIN. THEY WILL SHINE IN THE SKY TO GIVE LIGHT TO THE EARTH.

AND IT WAS DONE. EVENING PASSED AND MORNING CAME. THAT WAS THE FOURTH DAY.

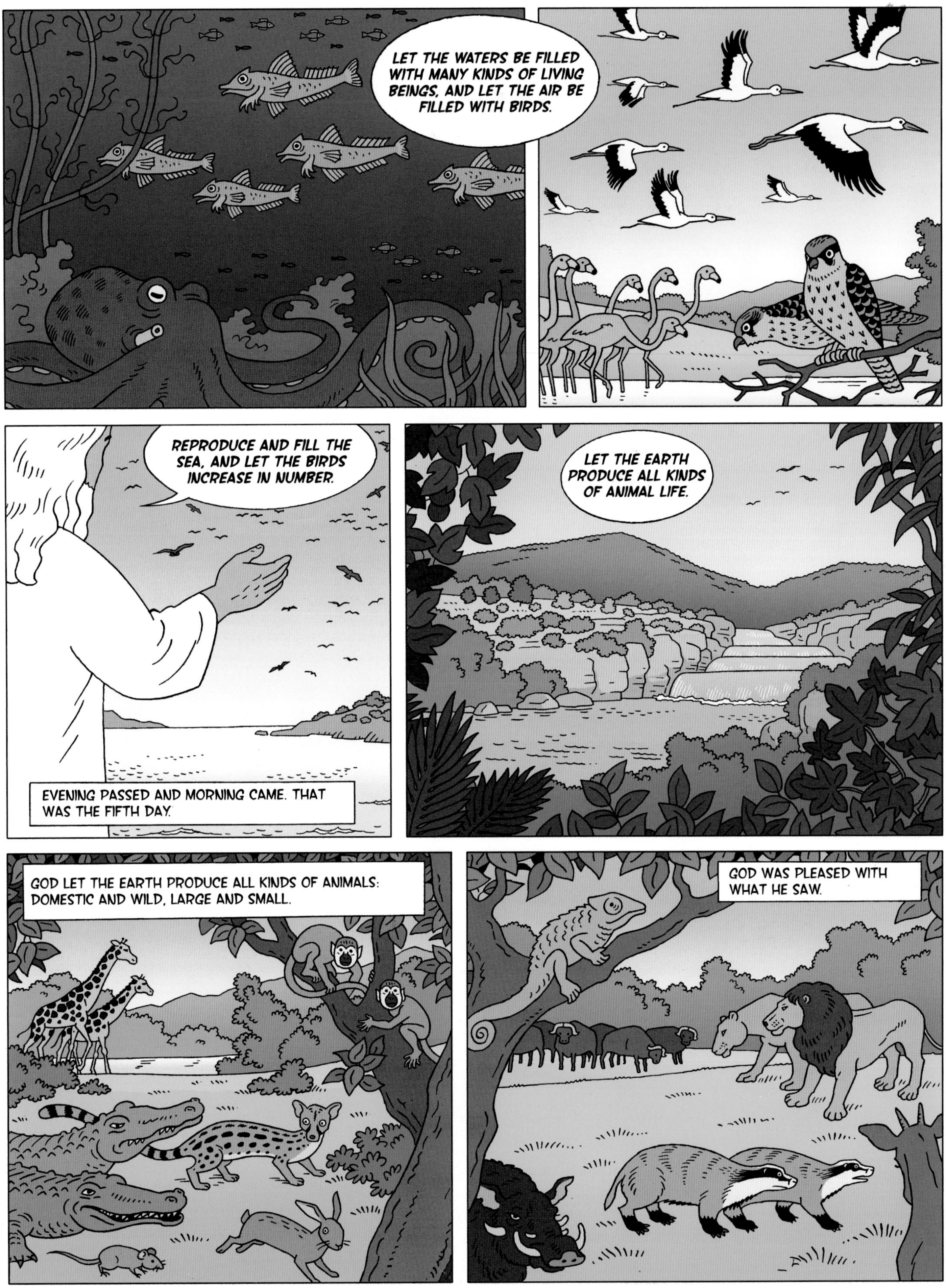
LET THE WATERS BE FILLED WITH MANY KINDS OF LIVING BEINGS, AND LET THE AIR BE FILLED WITH BIRDS.
REPRODUCE AND FILL THE SEA, AND LET THE BIRDS INCREASE IN NUMBER.
EVENING PASSED AND MORNING CAME. THAT WAS THE FIFTH DAY.
LET THE EARTH PRODUCE ALL KINDS OF ANIMAL LIFE.
GOD LET THE EARTH PRODUCE ALL KINDS OF ANIMALS: DOMESTIC AND WILD, LARGE AND SMALL.
GOD WAS PLEASED WITH WHAT HE SAW.

I WILL MAKE HUMANS, AND THEY WILL HAVE POWER OVER THE EARTH.

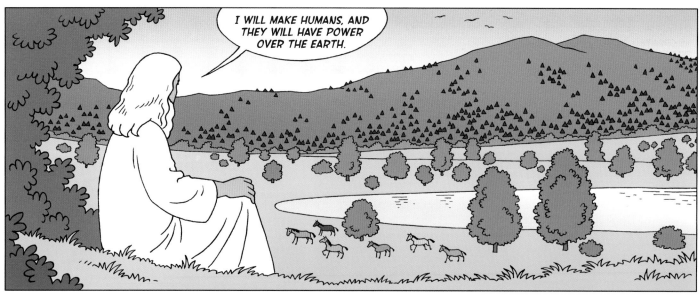

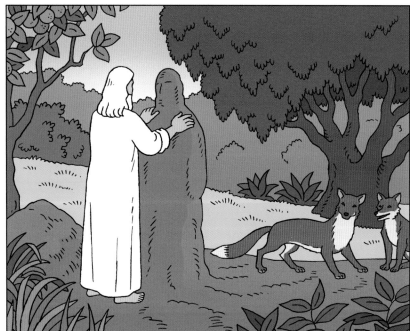

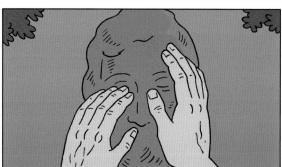

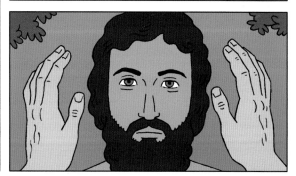

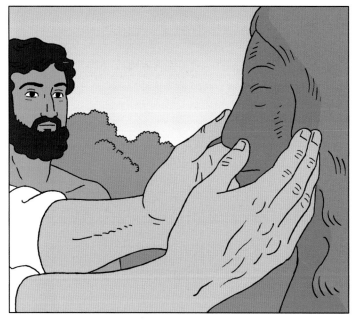

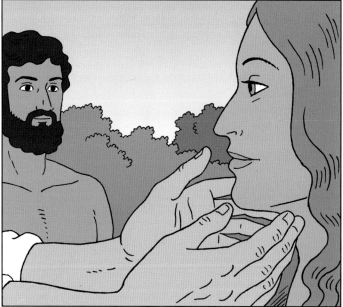

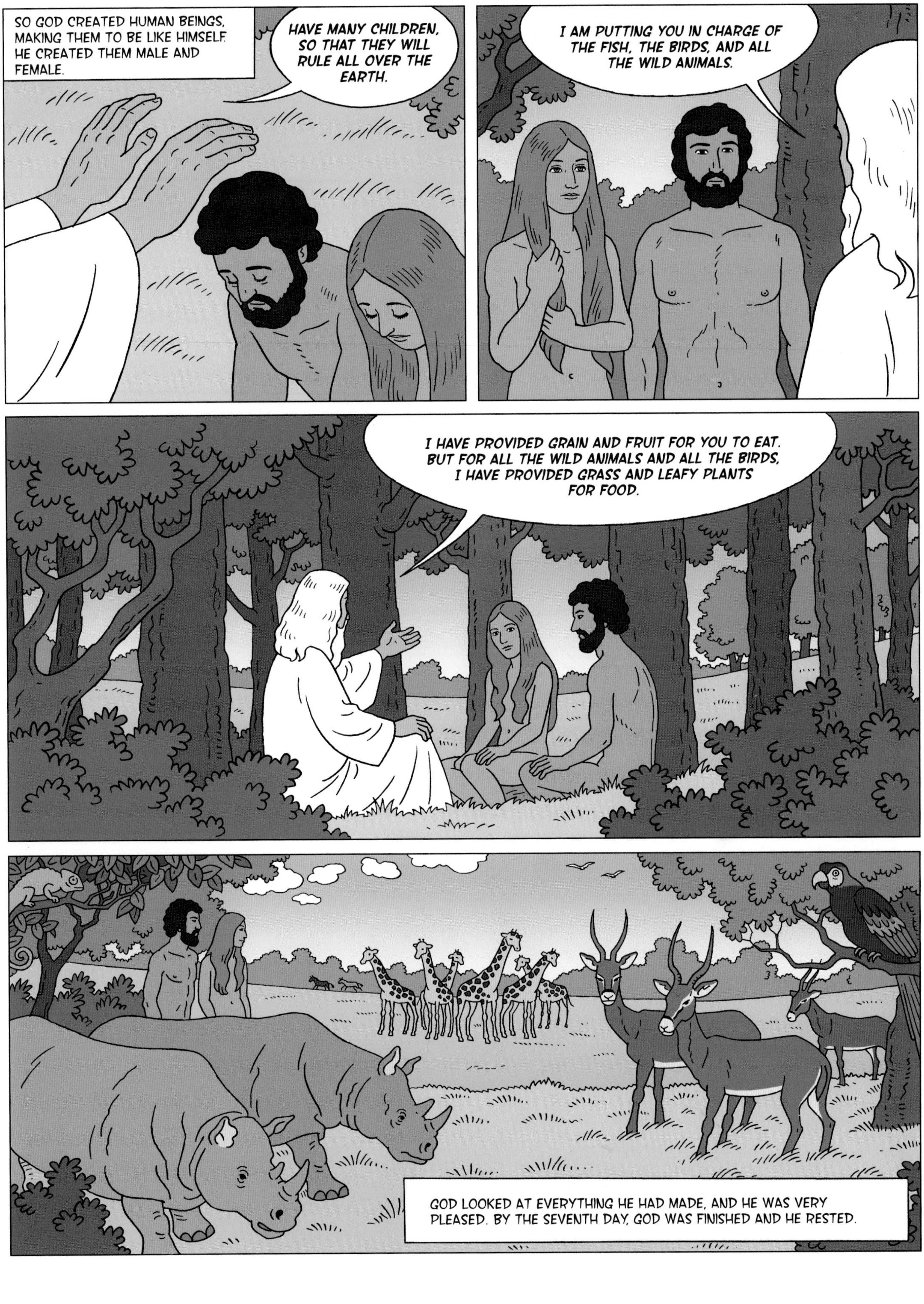
SO GOD CREATED HUMAN BEINGS, MAKING THEM TO BE LIKE HIMSELF. HE CREATED THEM MALE AND FEMALE.
HAVE MANY CHILDREN, SO THAT THEY WILL RULE ALL OVER THE EARTH.
I AM PUTTING YOU IN CHARGE OF THE FISH, THE BIRDS, AND ALL THE WILD ANIMALS.
I HAVE PROVIDED GRAIN AND FRUIT FOR YOU TO EAT. BUT FOR ALL THE WILD ANIMALS AND ALL THE BIRDS, I HAVE PROVIDED GRASS AND LEAFY PLANTS FOR FOOD.
GOD LOOKED AT EVERYTHING HE HAD MADE, AND HE WAS VERY PLEASED. BY THE SEVENTH DAY, GOD WAS FINISHED AND HE RESTED.

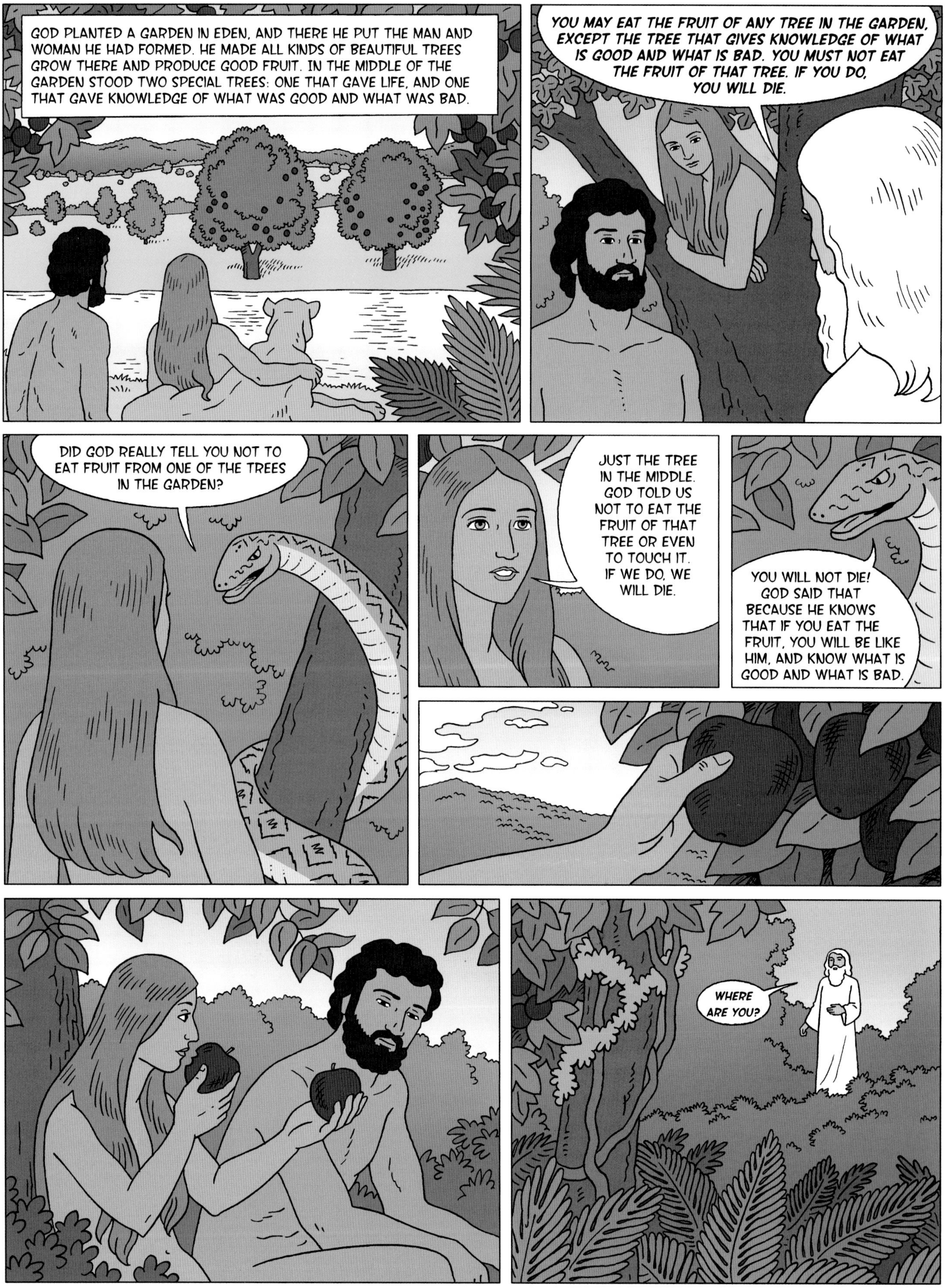
GOD PLANTED A GARDEN IN EDEN, AND THERE HE PUT THE MAN AND WOMAN HE HAD FORMED. HE MADE ALL KINDS OF BEAUTIFUL TREES GROW THERE AND PRODUCE GOOD FRUIT. IN THE MIDDLE OF THE GARDEN STOOD TWO SPECIAL TREES: ONE THAT GAVE LIFE, AND ONE THAT GAVE KNOWLEDGE OF WHAT WAS GOOD AND WHAT WAS BAD.
YOU MAY EAT THE FRUIT OF ANY TREE IN THE GARDEN, EXCEPT THE TREE THAT GIVES KNOWLEDGE OF WHAT IS GOOD AND WHAT IS BAD. YOU MUST NOT EAT THE FRUIT OF THAT TREE. IF YOU DO, YOU WILL DIE.
DID GOD REALLY TELL YOU NOT TO EAT FRUIT FROM ONE OF THE TREES IN THE GARDEN?
JUST THE TREE IN THE MIDDLE. GOD TOLD US NOT TO EAT THE FRUIT OF THAT TREE OR EVEN TO TOUCH IT. IF WE DO, WE WILL DIE.
YOU WILL NOT DIE! GOD SAID THAT BECAUSE HE KNOWS THAT IF YOU EAT THE FRUIT, YOU WILL BE LIKE HIM, AND KNOW WHAT IS GOOD AND WHAT IS BAD.
WHERE ARE YOU?

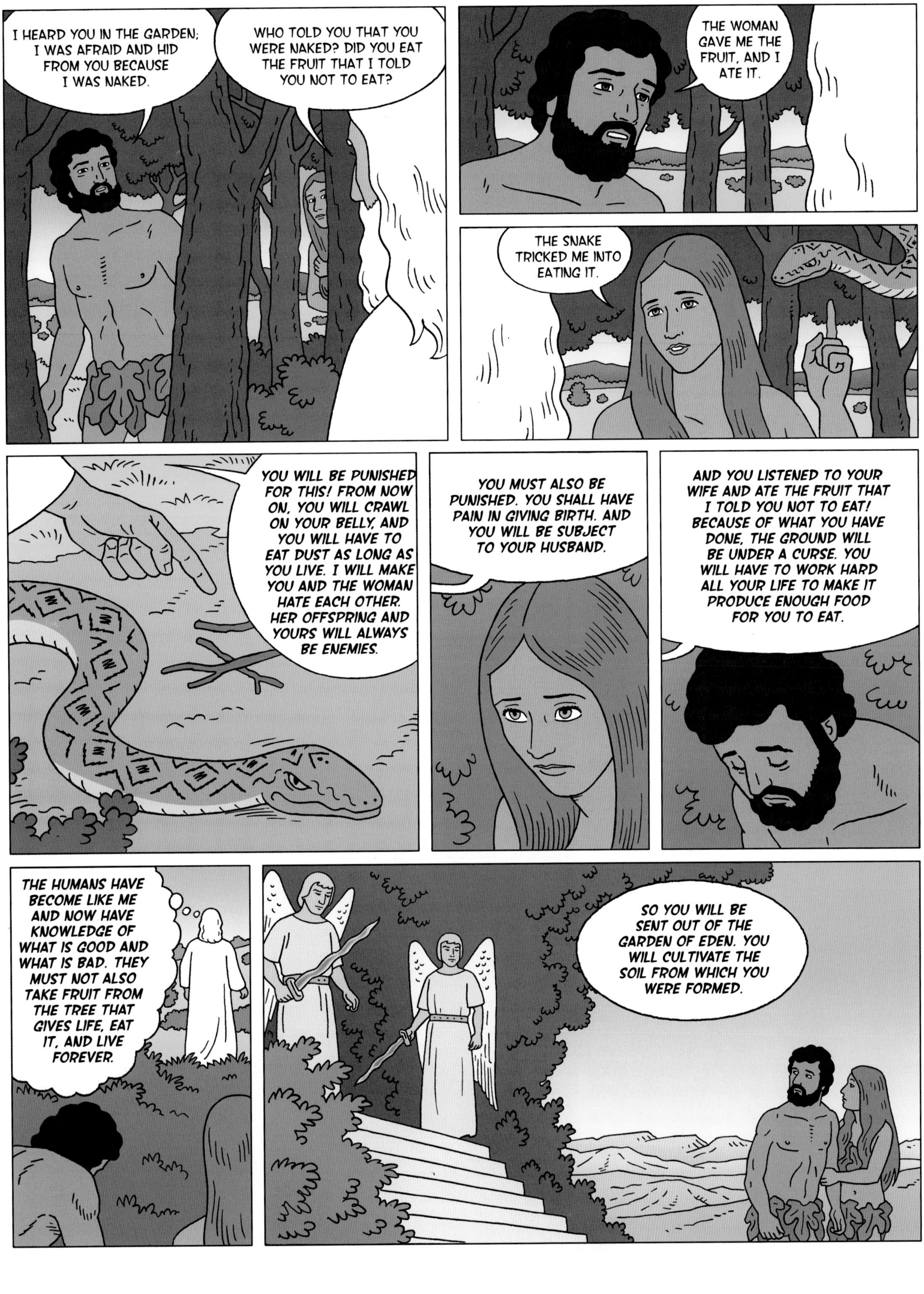
I HEARD YOU IN THE GARDEN; I WAS AFRAID AND HID FROM YOU BECAUSE I WAS NAKED.
WHO TOLD YOU THAT YOU WERE NAKED? DID YOU EAT THE FRUIT THAT I TOLD YOU NOT TO EAT?
THE WOMAN GAVE ME THE FRUIT, AND I ATE IT.
THE SNAKE TRICKED ME INTO EATING IT.
YOU WILL BE PUNISHED FOR THIS! FROM NOW ON, YOU WILL CRAWL ON YOUR BELLY, AND YOU WILL HAVE TO EAT DUST AS LONG AS YOU LIVE. I WILL MAKE YOU AND THE WOMAN HATE EACH OTHER. HER OFFSPRING AND YOURS WILL ALWAYS BE ENEMIES.
YOU MUST ALSO BE PUNISHED. YOU SHALL HAVE PAIN IN GIVING BIRTH. AND YOU WILL BE SUBJECT TO YOUR HUSBAND.
AND YOU LISTENED TO YOUR WIFE AND ATE THE FRUIT THAT I TOLD YOU NOT TO EAT! BECAUSE OF WHAT YOU HAVE DONE, THE GROUND WILL BE UNDER A CURSE. YOU WILL HAVE TO WORK HARD ALL YOUR LIFE TO MAKE IT PRODUCE ENOUGH FOOD FOR YOU TO EAT.
THE HUMANS HAVE BECOME LIKE ME AND NOW HAVE KNOWLEDGE OF WHAT IS GOOD AND WHAT IS BAD. THEY MUST NOT ALSO TAKE FRUIT FROM THE TREE THAT GIVES LIFE, EAT IT, AND LIVE FOREVER.
SO YOU WILL BE SENT OUT OF THE GARDEN OF EDEN. YOU WILL CULTIVATE THE SOIL FROM WHICH YOU WERE FORMED.

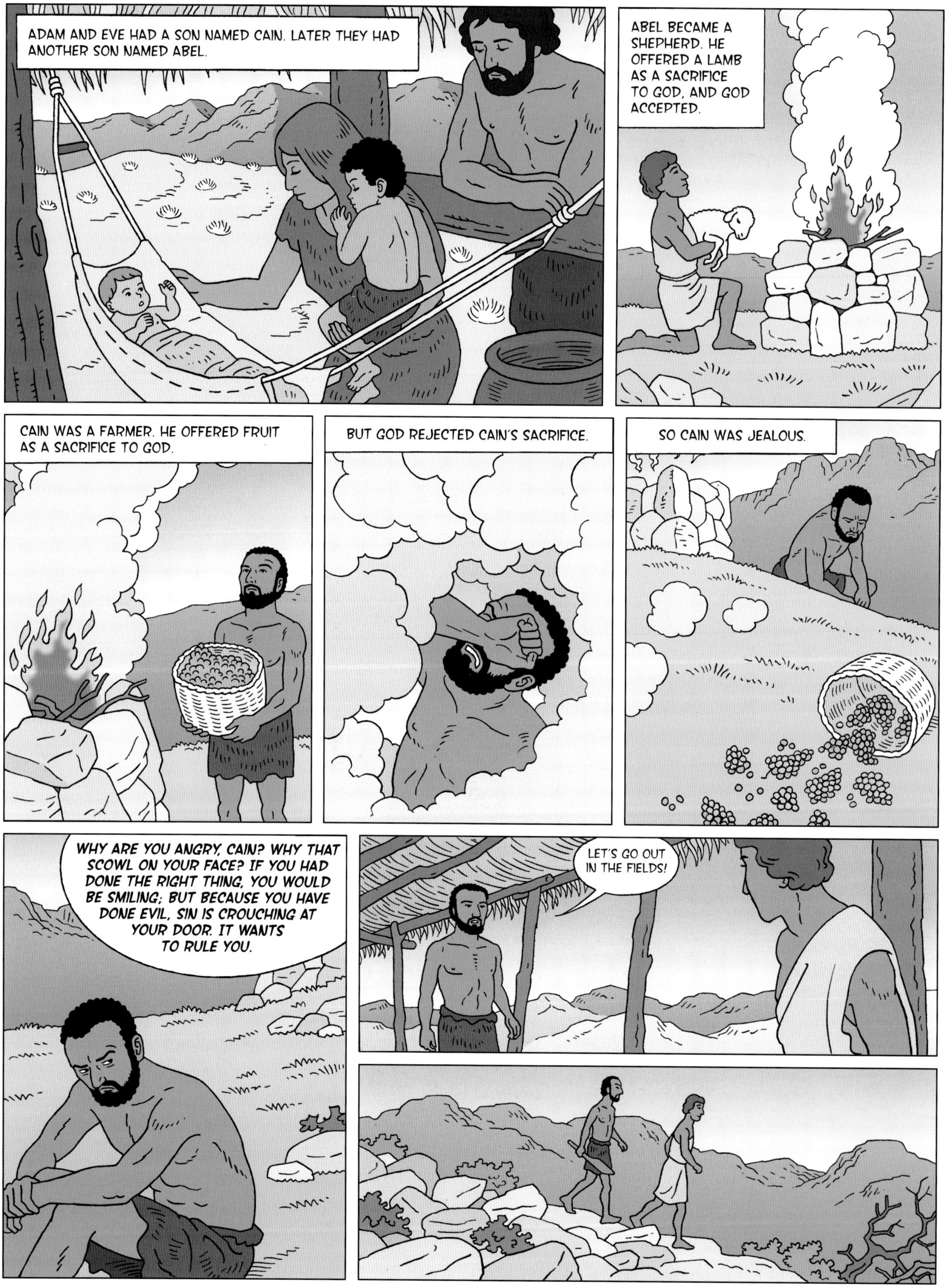
ADAM AND EVE HAD A SON NAMED CAIN. LATER THEY HAD ANOTHER SON NAMED ABEL.
ABEL BECAME A SHEPHERD. HE OFFERED A LAMB AS A SACRIFICE TO GOD, AND GOD ACCEPTED.
CAIN WAS A FARMER. HE OFFERED FRUIT AS A SACRIFICE TO GOD.
BUT GOD REJECTED CAIN'S SACRIFICE.
SO CAIN WAS JEALOUS.
WHY ARE YOU ANGRY, CAIN? WHY THAT SCOWL ON YOUR FACE? IF YOU HAD DONE THE RIGHT THING, YOU WOULD BE SMILING; BUT BECAUSE YOU HAVE DONE EVIL, SIN IS CROUCHING AT YOUR DOOR. IT WANTS TO RULE YOU.
LET'S GO OUT IN THE FIELDS!

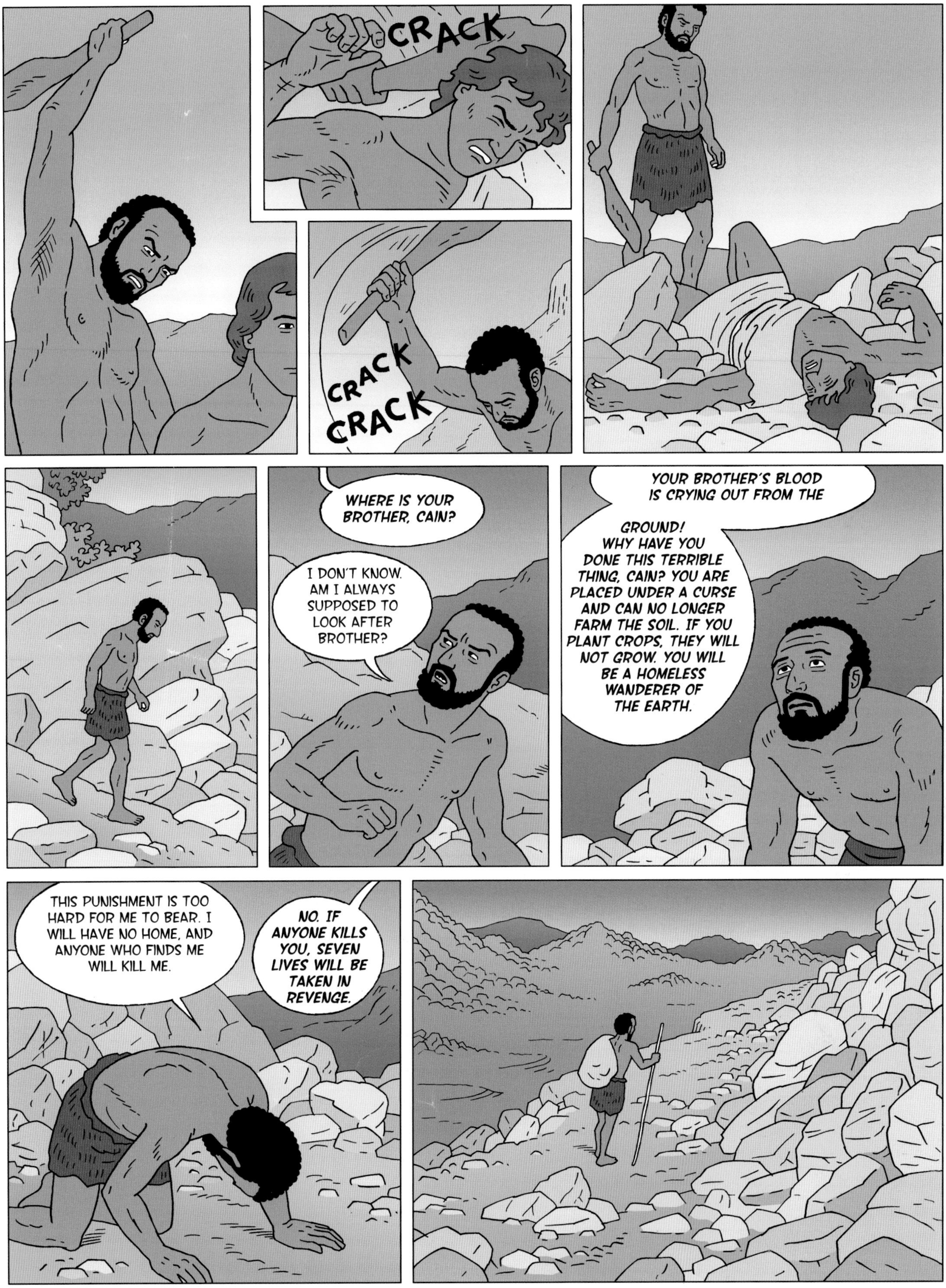
CRACK
CRACK
CRACK
WHERE IS YOUR BROTHER, CAIN?
I DON'T KNOW. AM I ALWAYS SUPPOSED TO LOOK AFTER BROTHER?
YOUR BROTHER'S BLOOD IS CRYING OUT FROM THE GROUND! WHY HAVE YOU DONE THIS TERRIBLE THING, CAIN? YOU ARE PLACED UNDER A CURSE AND CAN NO LONGER FARM THE SOIL. IF YOU PLANT CROPS, THEY WILL NOT GROW. YOU WILL BE A HOMELESS WANDERER OF THE EARTH.
THIS PUNISHMENT IS TOO HARD FOR ME TO BEAR. I WILL HAVE NO HOME, AND ANYONE WHO FINDS ME WILL KILL ME.
NO. IF ANYONE KILLS YOU, SEVEN LIVES WILL BE TAKEN IN REVENGE.

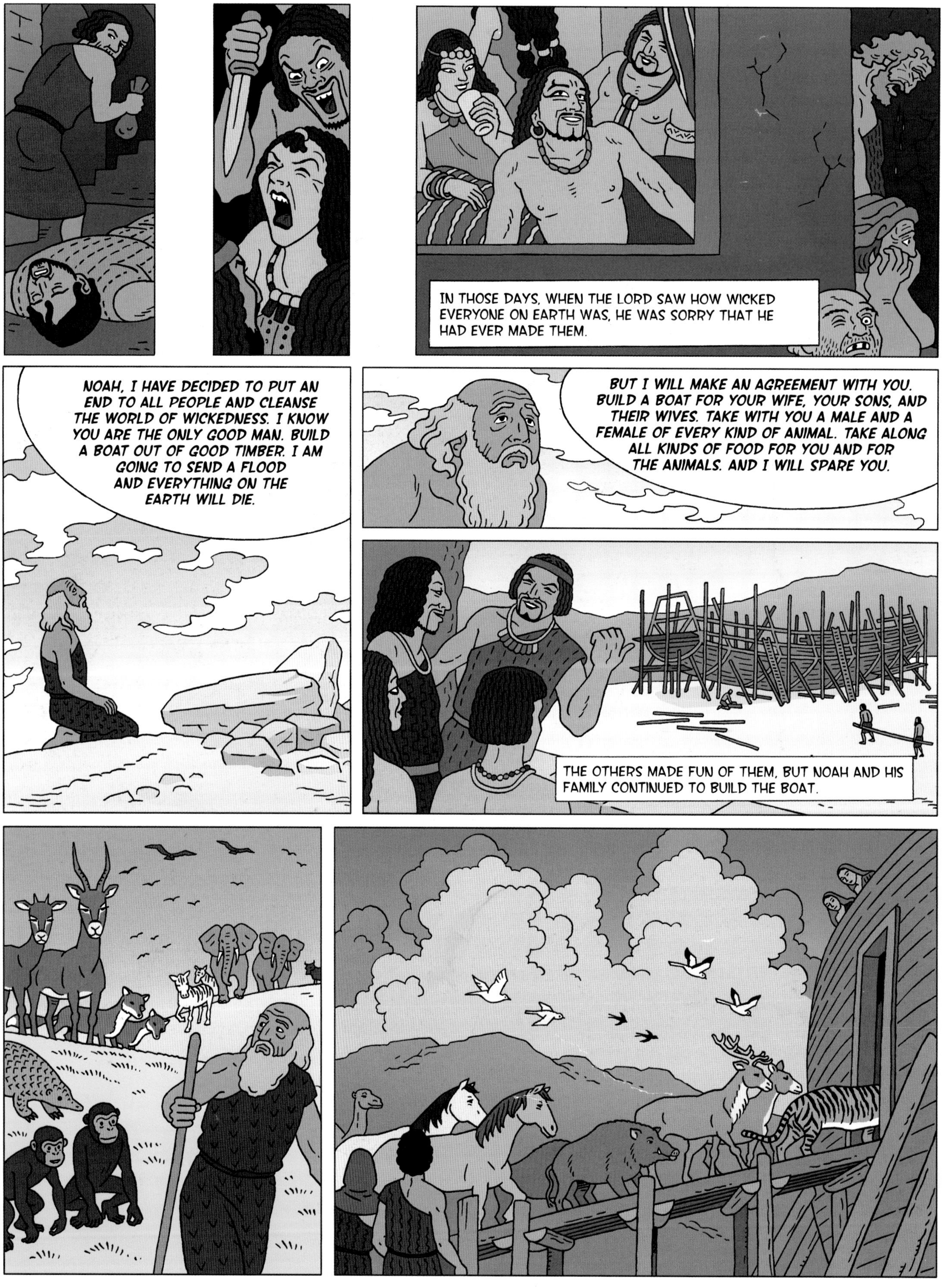
IN THOSE DAYS, WHEN THE LORD SAW HOW WICKED EVERYONE ON EARTH WAS, HE WAS SORRY THAT HE HAD EVER MADE THEM.
NOAH, I HAVE DECIDED TO PUT AN END TO ALL PEOPLE AND CLEANSE THE WORLD OF WICKEDNESS. I KNOW YOU ARE THE ONLY GOOD MAN. BUILD A BOAT OUT OF GOOD TIMBER. I AM GOING TO SEND A FLOOD AND EVERYTHING ON THE EARTH WILL DIE.
BUT I WILL MAKE AN AGREEMENT WITH YOU. BUILD A BOAT FOR YOUR WIFE, YOUR SONS, AND THEIR WIVES. TAKE WITH YOU A MALE AND A FEMALE OF EVERY KIND OF ANIMAL. TAKE ALONG ALL KINDS OF FOOD FOR YOU AND FOR THE ANIMALS. AND I WILL SPARE YOU.
THE OTHERS MADE FUN OF THEM, BUT NOAH AND HIS FAMILY CONTINUED TO BUILD THE BOAT.

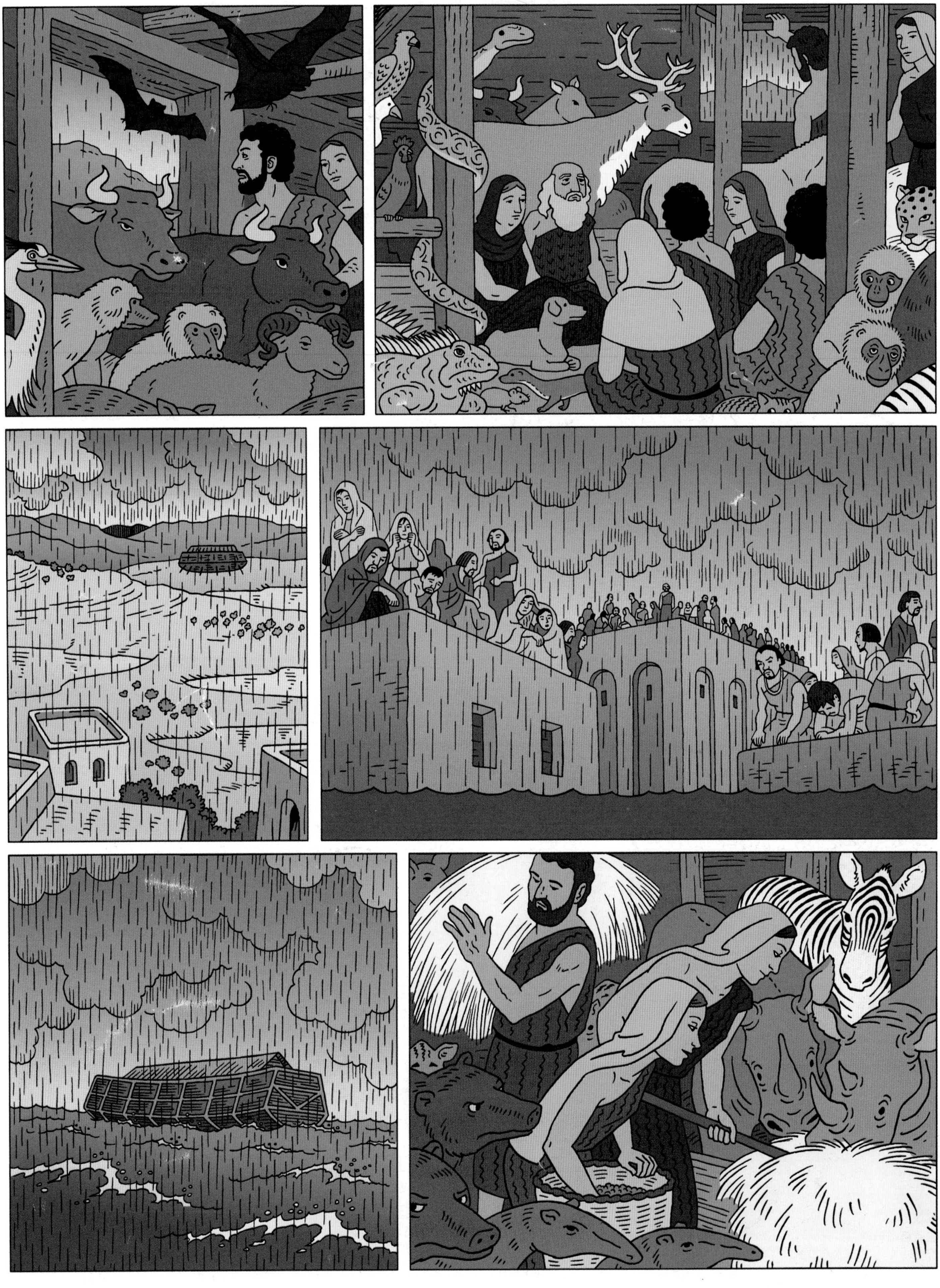

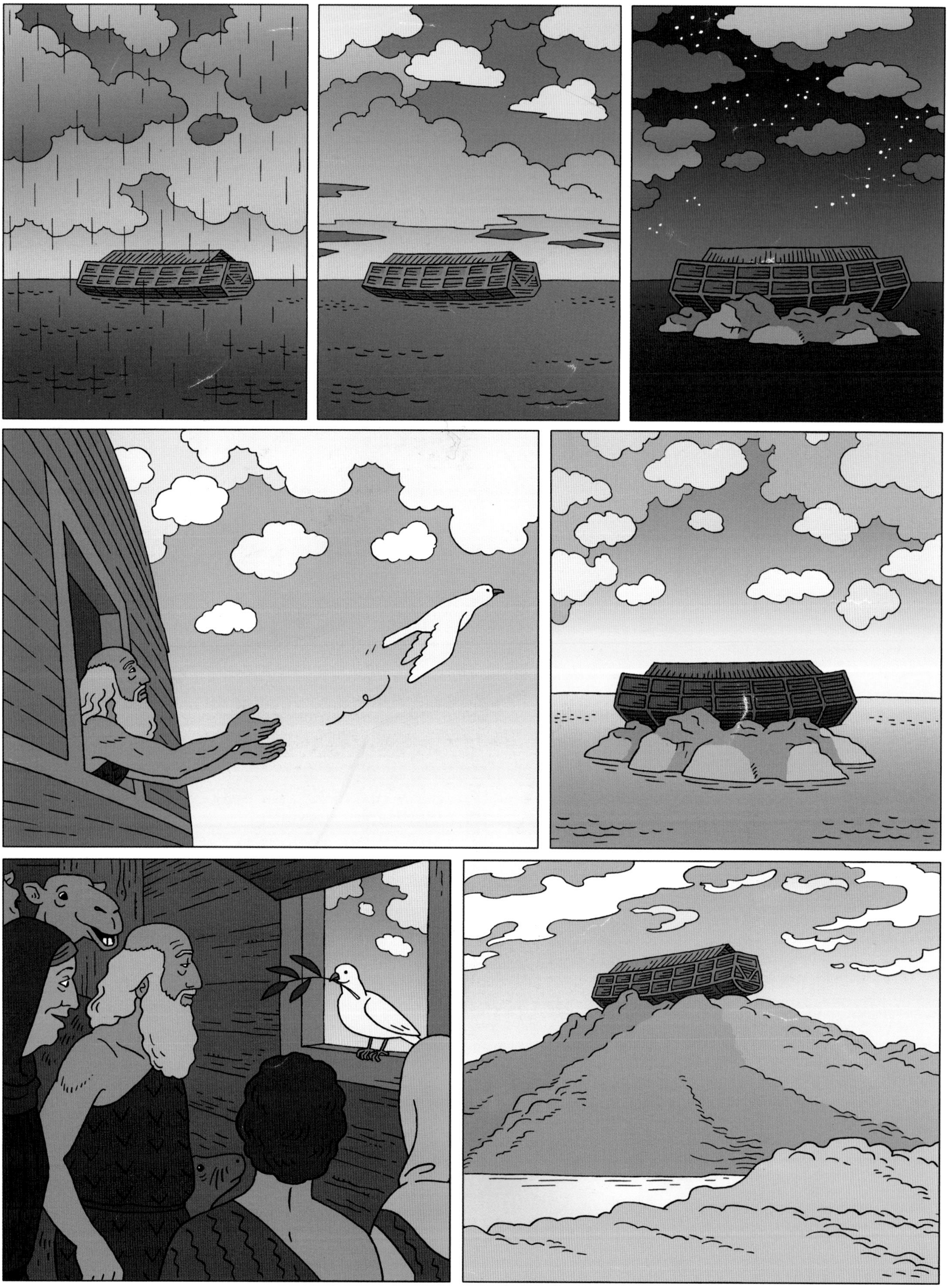

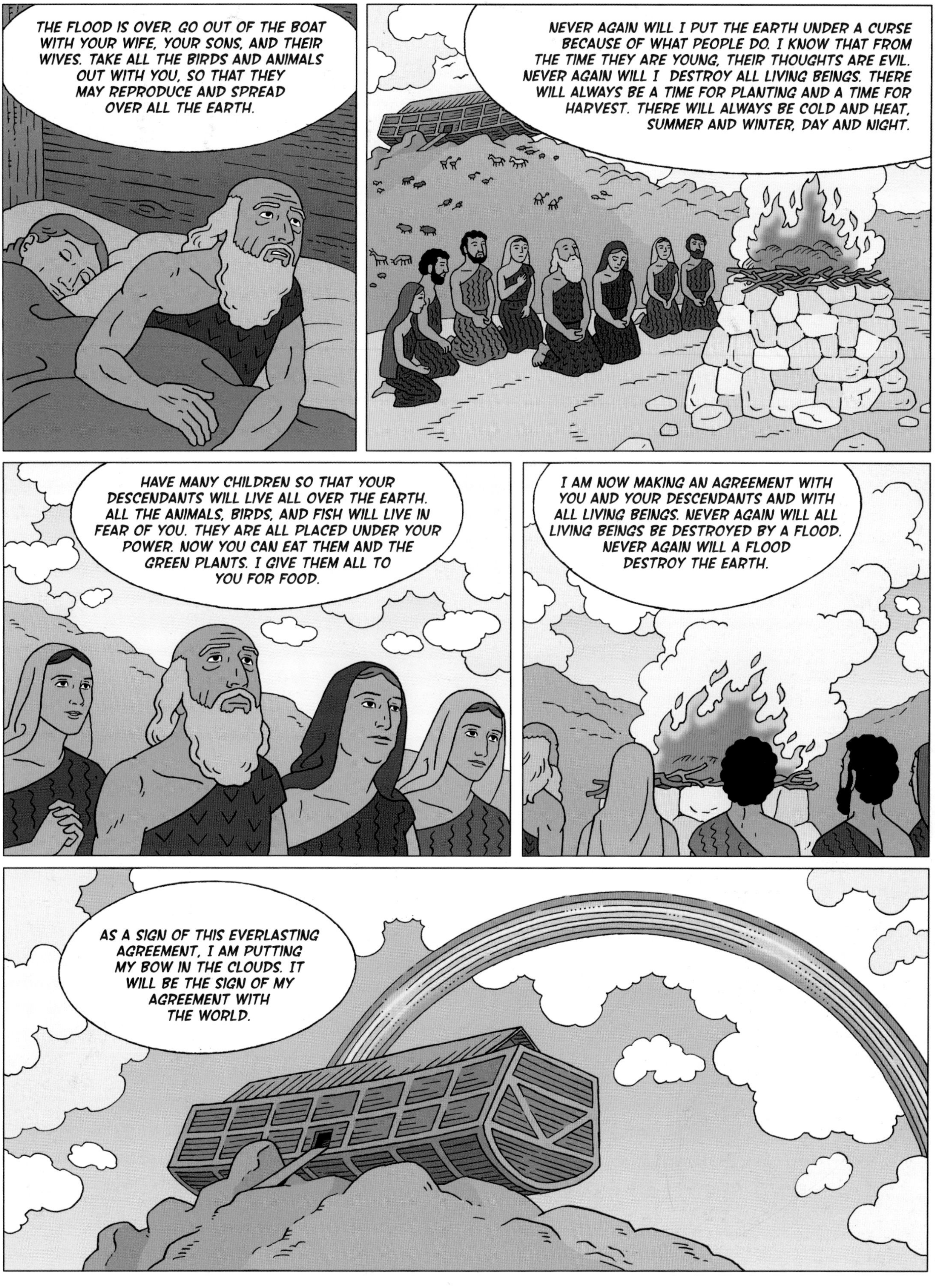
THE FLOOD IS OVER. GO OUT OF THE BOAT WITH YOUR WIFE, YOUR SONS, AND THEIR WIVES. TAKE ALL THE BIRDS AND ANIMALS OUT WITH YOU, SO THAT THEY MAY REPRODUCE AND SPREAD OVER ALL THE EARTH.
NEVER AGAIN WILL I PUT THE EARTH UNDER A CURSE BECAUSE OF WHAT PEOPLE DO. I KNOW THAT FROM THE TIME THEY ARE YOUNG, THEIR THOUGHTS ARE EVIL. NEVER AGAIN WILL I DESTROY ALL LIVING BEINGS. THERE WILL ALWAYS BE A TIME FOR PLANTING AND A TIME FOR HARVEST. THERE WILL ALWAYS BE COLD AND HEAT, SUMMER AND WINTER, DAY AND NIGHT.
HAVE MANY CHILDREN SO THAT YOUR DESCENDANTS WILL LIVE ALL OVER THE EARTH. ALL THE ANIMALS, BIRDS, AND FISH WILL LIVE IN FEAR OF YOU. THEY ARE ALL PLACED UNDER YOUR POWER. NOW YOU CAN EAT THEM AND THE GREEN PLANTS. I GIVE THEM ALL TO YOU FOR FOOD.
I AM NOW MAKING AN AGREEMENT WITH YOU AND YOUR DESCENDANTS AND WITH ALL LIVING BEINGS. NEVER AGAIN WILL ALL LIVING BEINGS BE DESTROYED BY A FLOOD. NEVER AGAIN WILL A FLOOD DESTROY THE EARTH.
AS A SIGN OF THIS EVERLASTING AGREEMENT, I AM PUTTING MY BOW IN THE CLOUDS. IT WILL BE THE SIGN OF MY AGREEMENT WITH THE WORLD.

AT FIRST, THE PEOPLE OF THE WORLD HAD ONLY ONE LANGUAGE AND THEY ALL USED THE SAME WORDS. AS THEY WANDERED ABOUT IN THE EAST, THEY CAME TO A PLAIN IN BABYLONIA AND SETTLED THERE.

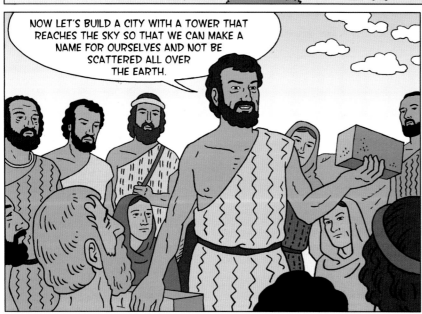

NOW LET'S BUILD A CITY WITH A TOWER THAT REACHES THE SKY SO THAT WE CAN MAKE A NAME FOR OURSELVES AND NOT BE SCATTERED ALL OVER THE EARTH.

THESE ARE ALL ONE PEOPLE AND THEY SPEAK ONE LANGUAGE. THIS IS JUST THE BEGINNING OF WHAT THEY ARE GOING TO DO. SOON THEY WILL BE ABLE TO DO ANYTHING THEY WANT! LET US GO DOWN AND MIX UP THEIR LANGUAGE SO THAT THEY WILL NOT UNDERSTAND EACH OTHER.

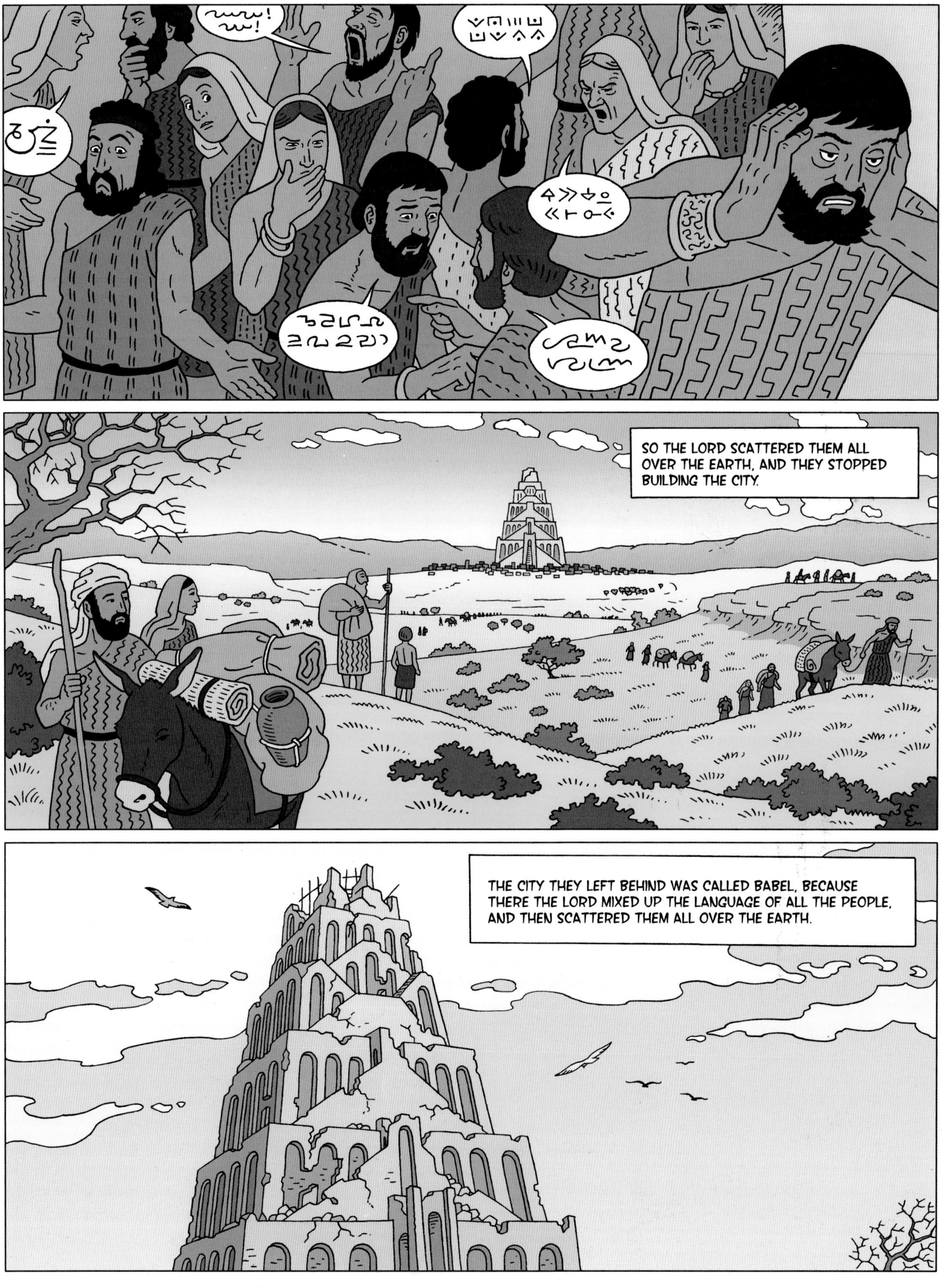
SO THE LORD SCATTERED THEM ALL OVER THE EARTH, AND THEY STOPPED BUILDING THE CITY.
THE CITY THEY LEFT BEHIND WAS CALLED BABEL, BECAUSE THERE THE LORD MIXED UP THE LANGUAGE OF ALL THE PEOPLE, AND THEN SCATTERED THEM ALL OVER THE EARTH.

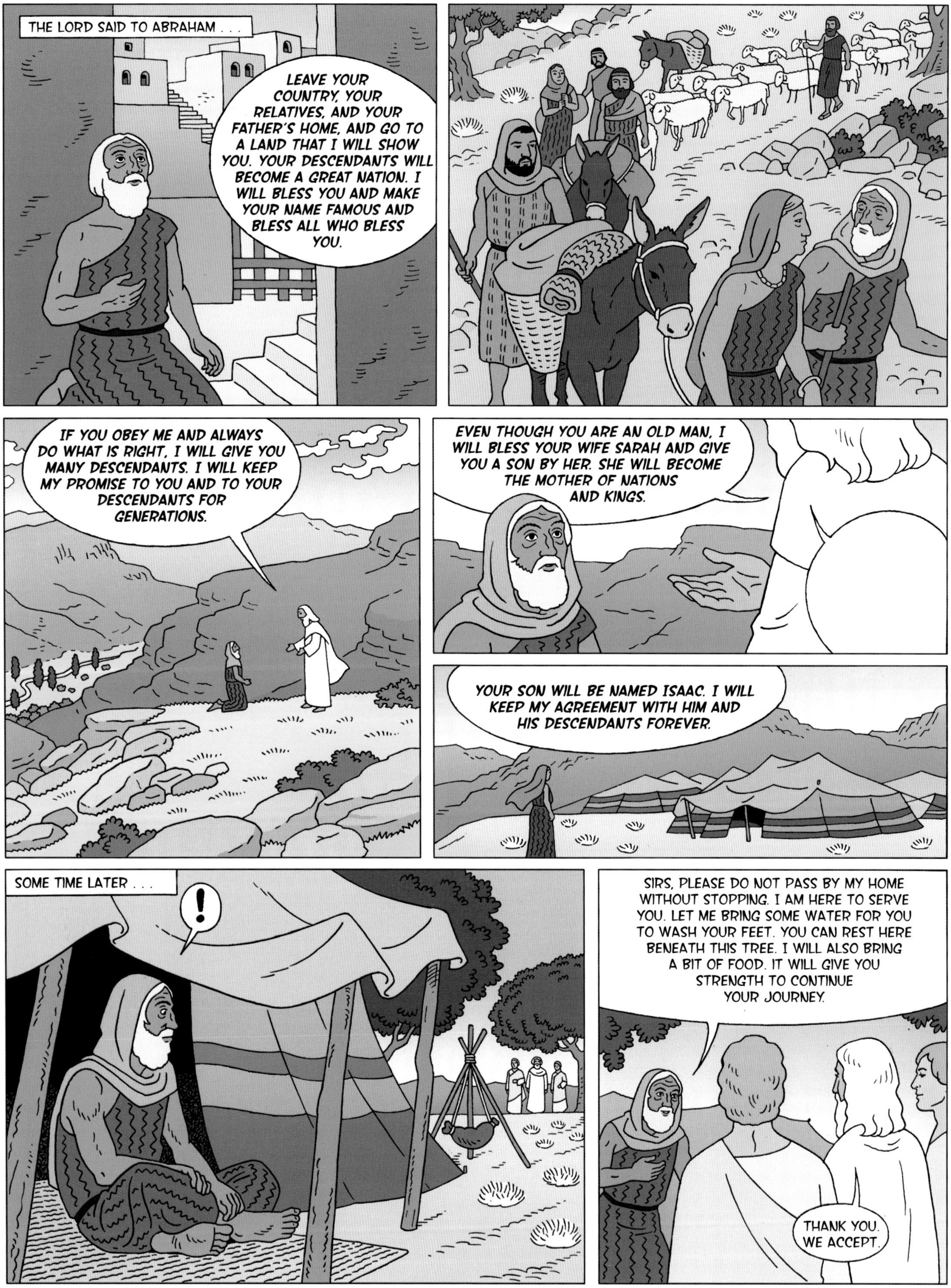
THE LORD SAID TO ABRAHAM . . .
LEAVE YOUR COUNTRY, YOUR RELATIVES, AND YOUR FATHER'S HOME, AND GO TO A LAND THAT I WILL SHOW YOU. YOUR DESCENDANTS WILL BECOME A GREAT NATION. I WILL BLESS YOU AND MAKE YOUR NAME FAMOUS AND BLESS ALL WHO BLESS YOU.
IF YOU OBEY ME AND ALWAYS DO WHAT IS RIGHT, I WILL GIVE YOU MANY DESCENDANTS. I WILL KEEP MY PROMISE TO YOU AND TO YOUR DESCENDANTS FOR GENERATIONS.
EVEN THOUGH YOU ARE AN OLD MAN, I WILL BLESS YOUR WIFE SARAH AND GIVE YOU A SON BY HER. SHE WILL BECOME THE MOTHER OF NATIONS AND KINGS.
YOUR SON WILL BE NAMED ISAAC. I WILL KEEP MY AGREEMENT WITH HIM AND HIS DESCENDANTS FOREVER.
SOME TIME LATER . . .
!
SIRS, PLEASE DO NOT PASS BY MY HOME WITHOUT STOPPING. I AM HERE TO SERVE YOU. LET ME BRING SOME WATER FOR YOU TO WASH YOUR FEET. YOU CAN REST HERE BENEATH THIS TREE. I WILL ALSO BRING A BIT OF FOOD. IT WILL GIVE YOU STRENGTH TO CONTINUE YOUR JOURNEY.
THANK YOU. WE ACCEPT.

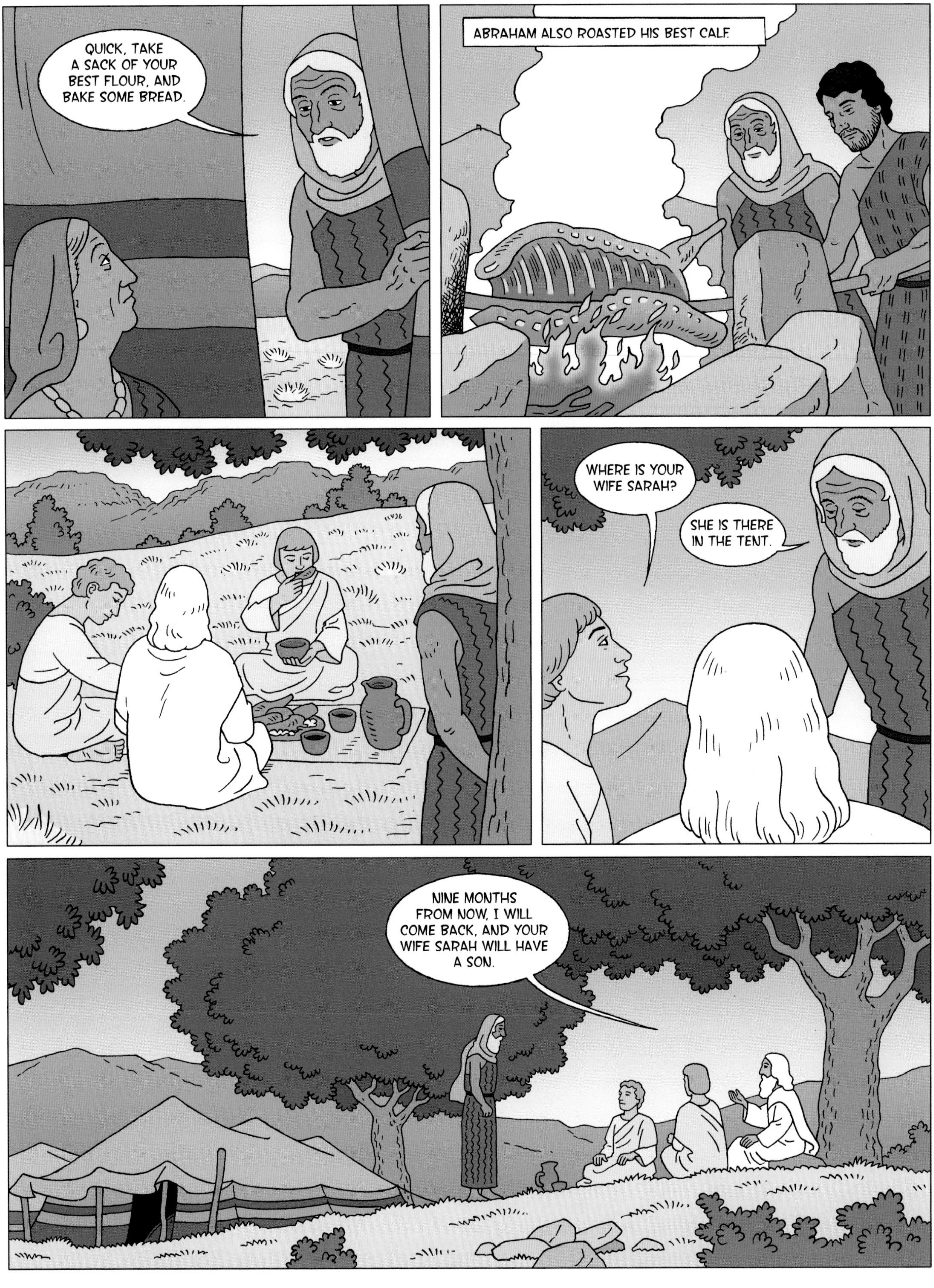
QUICK, TAKE A SACK OF YOUR BEST FLOUR, AND BAKE SOME BREAD.
ABRAHAM ALSO ROASTED HIS BEST CALF.
WHERE IS YOUR WIFE SARAH?
SHE IS THERE IN THE TENT.
NINE MONTHS FROM NOW, I WILL COME BACK, AND YOUR WIFE SARAH WILL HAVE A SON.

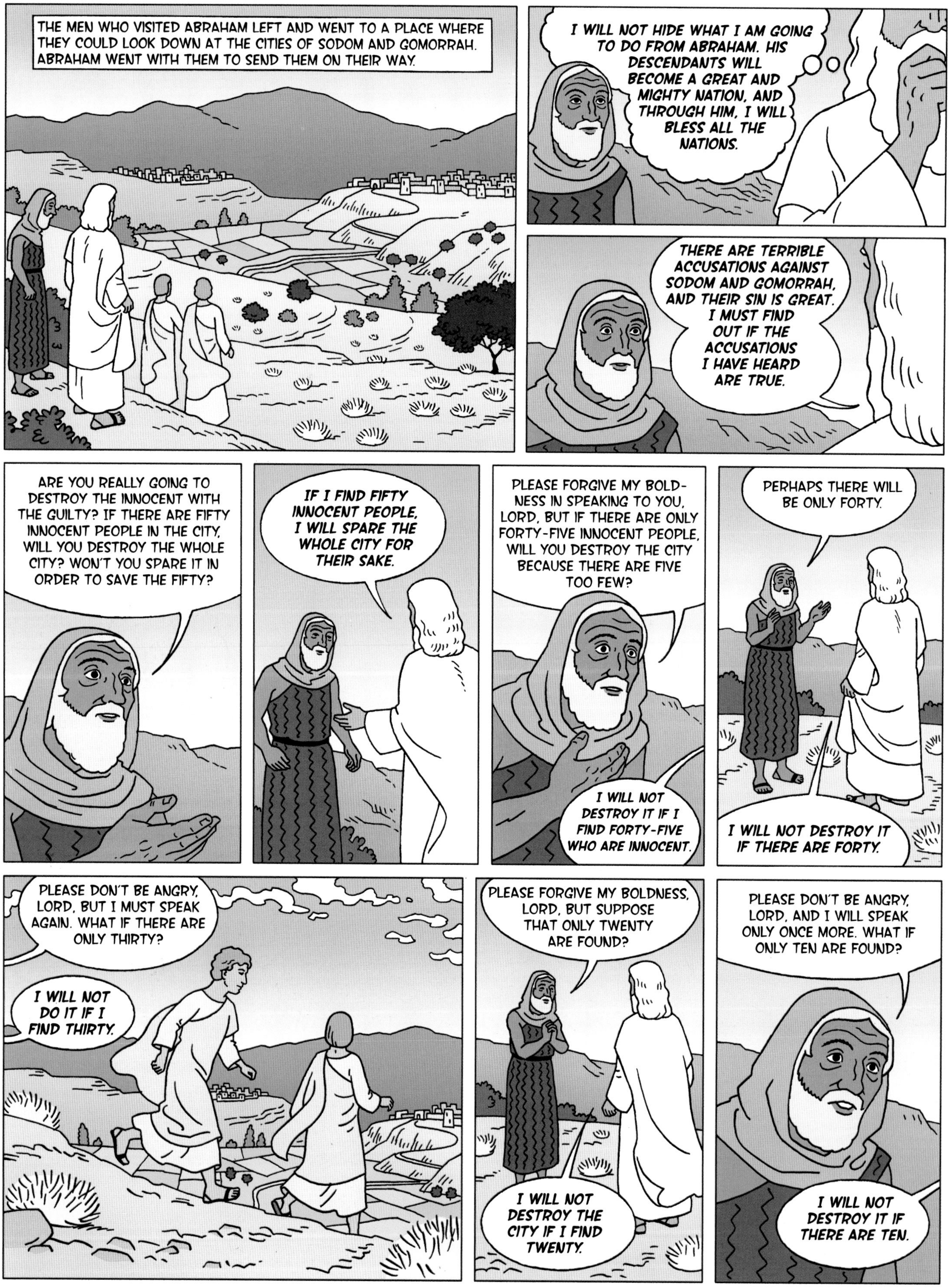
THE MEN WHO VISITED ABRAHAM LEFT AND WENT TO A PLACE WHERE THEY COULD LOOK DOWN AT THE CITIES OF SODOM AND GOMORRAH. ABRAHAM WENT WITH THEM TO SEND THEM ON THEIR WAY.
I WILL NOT HIDE WHAT I AM GOING TO DO FROM ABRAHAM. HIS DESCENDANTS WILL BECOME A GREAT AND MIGHTY NATION, AND THROUGH HIM, I WILL BLESS ALL THE NATIONS.
THERE ARE TERRIBLE ACCUSATIONS AGAINST SODOM AND GOMORRAH, AND THEIR SIN IS GREAT. I MUST FIND OUT IF THE ACCUSATIONS I HAVE HEARD ARE TRUE.
ARE YOU REALLY GOING TO DESTROY THE INNOCENT WITH THE GUILTY? IF THERE ARE FIFTY INNOCENT PEOPLE IN THE CITY, WILL YOU DESTROY THE WHOLE CITY? WON'T YOU SPARE IT IN ORDER TO SAVE THE FIFTY?
IF I FIND FIFTY INNOCENT PEOPLE, I WILL SPARE THE WHOLE CITY FOR THEIR SAKE.
PLEASE FORGIVE MY BOLDNESS IN SPEAKING TO YOU, LORD, BUT IF THERE ARE ONLY FORTY-FIVE INNOCENT PEOPLE, WILL YOU DESTROY THE CITY BECAUSE THERE ARE FIVE TOO FEW?
I WILL NOT DESTROY IT IF I FIND FORTY-FIVE WHO ARE INNOCENT.
PERHAPS THERE WILL BE ONLY FORTY.
I WILL NOT DESTROY IT IF THERE ARE FORTY.
PLEASE DON'T BE ANGRY, LORD, BUT I MUST SPEAK AGAIN. WHAT IF THERE ARE ONLY THIRTY?
I WILL NOT DO IT IF I FIND THIRTY.
PLEASE FORGIVE MY BOLDNESS, LORD, BUT SUPPOSE THAT ONLY TWENTY ARE FOUND?
I WILL NOT DESTROY THE CITY IF I FIND TWENTY.
PLEASE DON'T BE ANGRY, LORD, AND I WILL SPEAK ONLY ONCE MORE. WHAT IF ONLY TEN ARE FOUND?
I WILL NOT DESTROY IT IF THERE ARE TEN.

LOT WATCHED AS THE TWO ANGELS ENTERED SODOM.

SIRS, I AM HERE TO SERVE YOU. PLEASE COME TO MY HOUSE. YOU CAN WASH YOUR FEET AND SPEND THE NIGHT, AND IN THE MORNING YOU CAN RISE EARLY AND BE ON YOUR WAY.

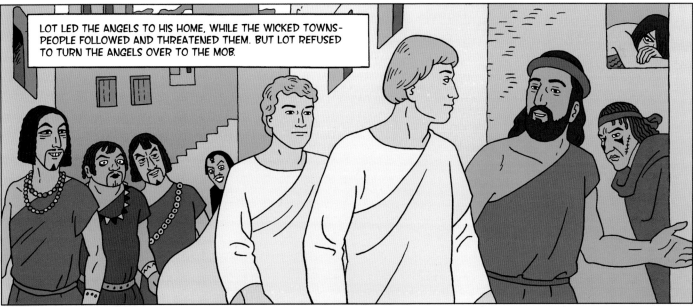

LOT LED THE ANGELS TO HIS HOME, WHILE THE WICKED TOWNSPEOPLE FOLLOWED AND THREATENED THEM. BUT LOT REFUSED TO TURN THE ANGELS OVER TO THE MOB.

THE LORD HAS HEARD THE TERRIBLE ACCUSATIONS AGAINST THESE PEOPLE AND HAS SENT US TO DESTROY SODOM AND GOMORRAH!

QUICK, LOT! TAKE YOUR WIFE AND YOUR DAUGHTERS AND GET OUT SO THAT YOU WILL NOT LOSE YOUR LIVES WHEN THE CITIES ARE DESTROYED.

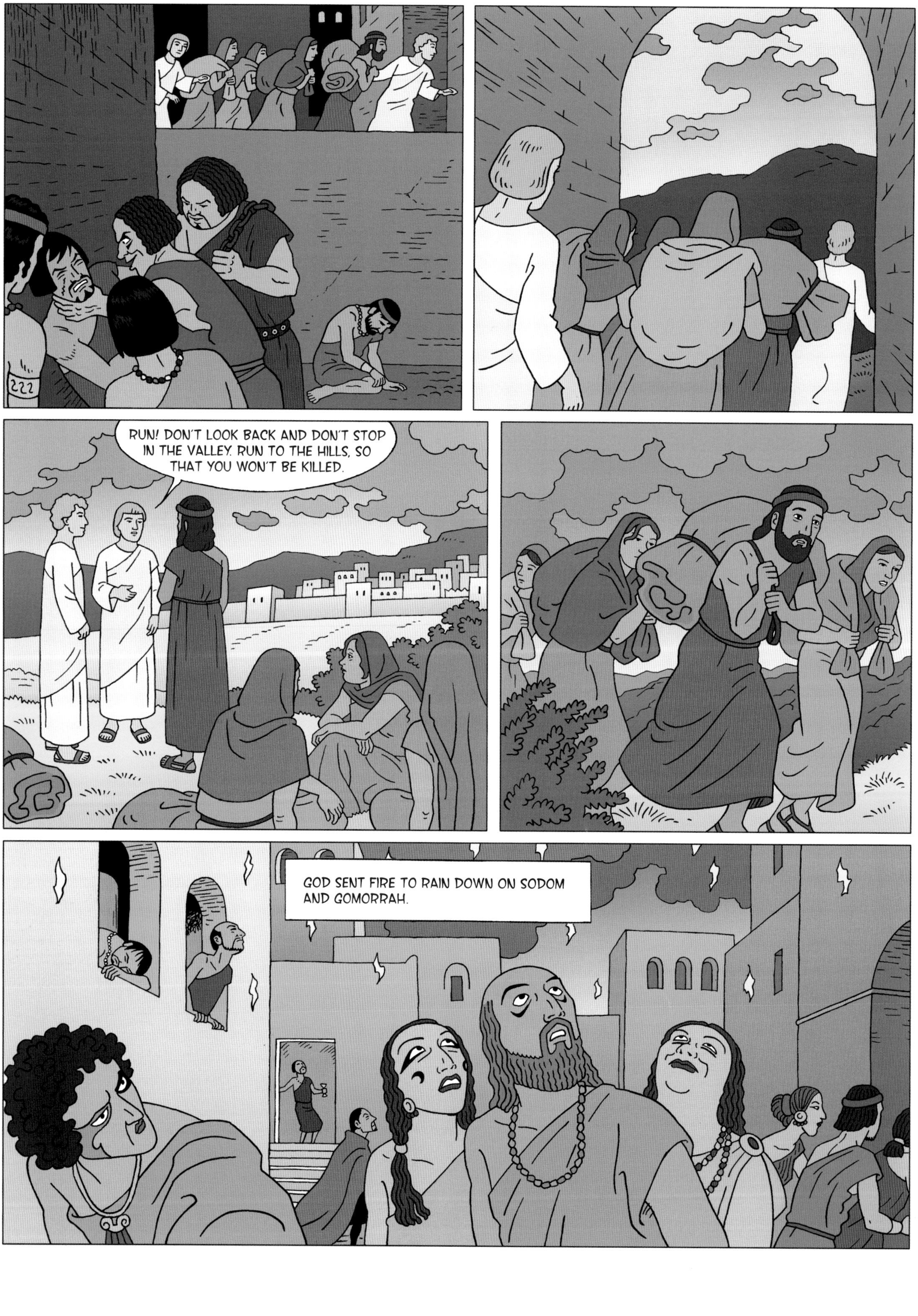
RUN! DON'T LOOK BACK AND DON'T STOP IN THE VALLEY. RUN TO THE HILLS, SO THAT YOU WON'T BE KILLED.
GOD SENT FIRE TO RAIN DOWN ON SODOM AND GOMORRAH.

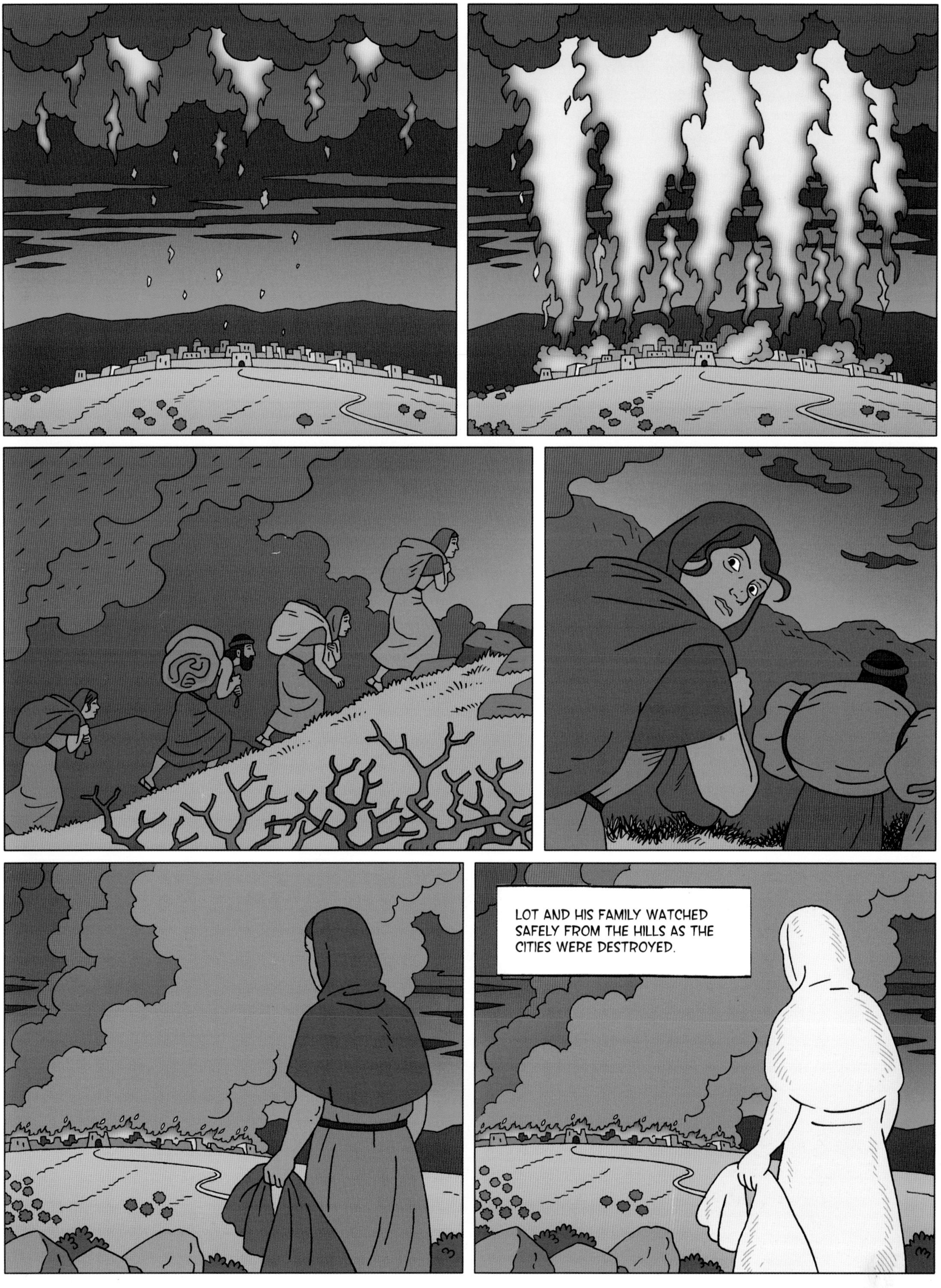
LOT AND HIS FAMILY WATCHED SAFELY FROM THE HILLS AS THE CITIES WERE DESTROYED.

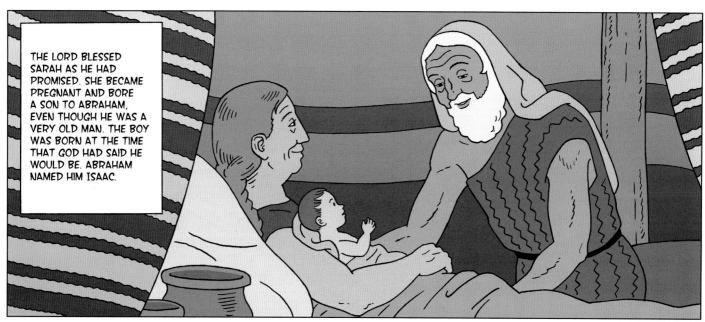

THE LORD BLESSED SARAH AS HE HAD PROMISED. SHE BECAME PREGNANT AND BORE A SON TO ABRAHAM, EVEN THOUGH HE WAS A VERY OLD MAN. THE BOY WAS BORN AT THE TIME THAT GOD HAD SAID HE WOULD BE. ABRAHAM NAMED HIM ISAAC.

SOME TIME LATER, GOD TESTED ABRAHAM.

ABRAHAM!

YES, HERE I AM!

TAKE YOUR ONLY SON, ISAAC, WHOM YOU LOVE SO MUCH, AND GO TO THE LAND OF MORIAH.

THERE, ON A MOUNTAIN, OFFER HIM AS A SACRIFICE TO ME.

FATHER?

YES, MY SON?

I SEE YOU HAVE THE COALS AND THE WOOD, BUT WHERE IS THE LAMB FOR THE SACRIFICE?

GOD HIMSELF WILL PROVIDE ONE.

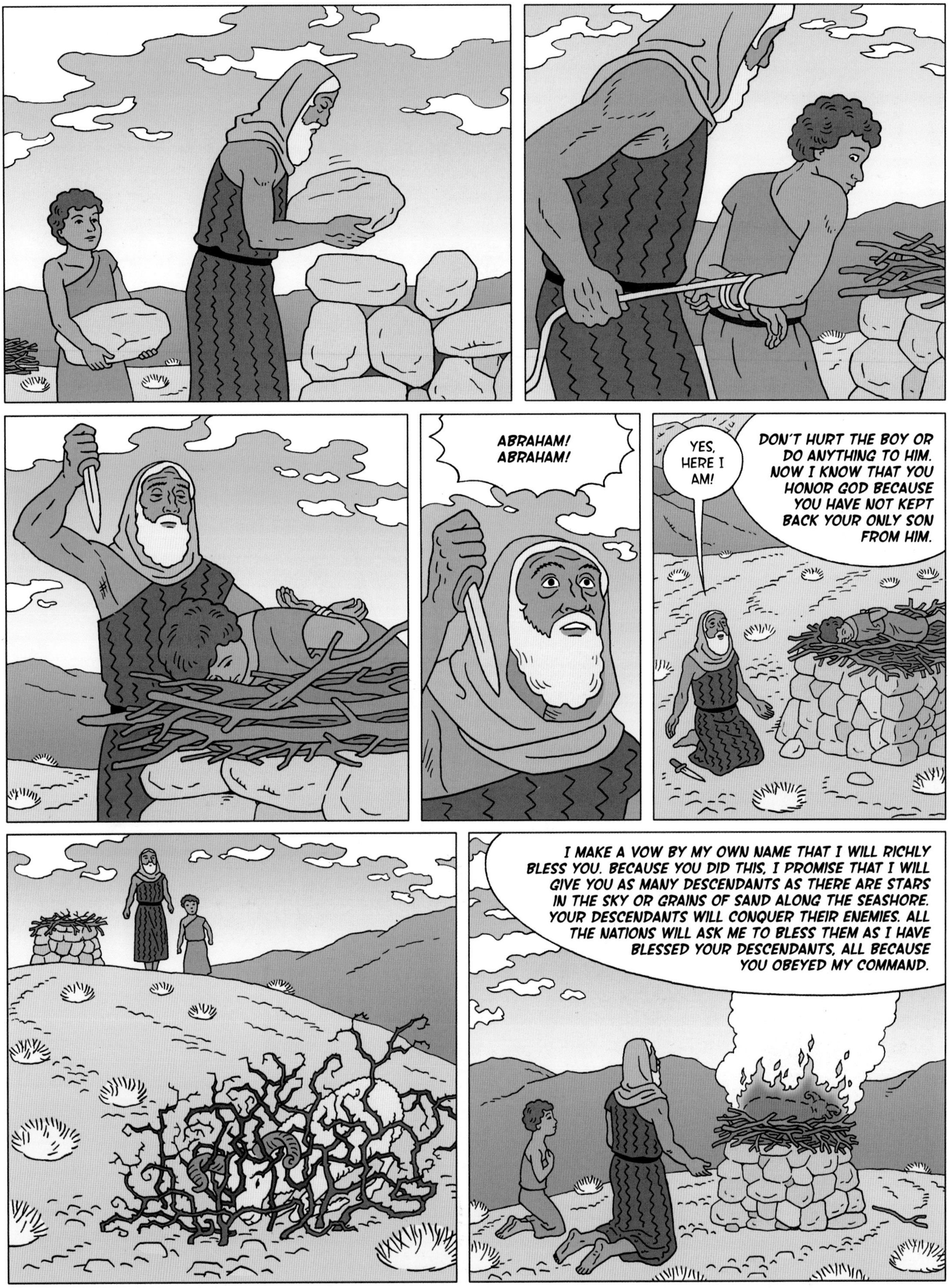
ABRAHAM!
ABRAHAM!
YES, HERE I AM!
DON'T HURT THE BOY OR DO ANYTHING TO HIM. NOW I KNOW THAT YOU HONOR GOD BECAUSE YOU HAVE NOT KEPT BACK YOUR ONLY SON FROM HIM.
I MAKE A VOW BY MY OWN NAME THAT I WILL RICHLY BLESS YOU. BECAUSE YOU DID THIS, I PROMISE THAT I WILL GIVE YOU AS MANY DESCENDANTS AS THERE ARE STARS IN THE SKY OR GRAINS OF SAND ALONG THE SEASHORE. YOUR DESCENDANTS WILL CONQUER THEIR ENEMIES. ALL THE NATIONS WILL ASK ME TO BLESS THEM AS I HAVE BLESSED YOUR DESCENDANTS, ALL BECAUSE YOU OBEYED MY COMMAND.

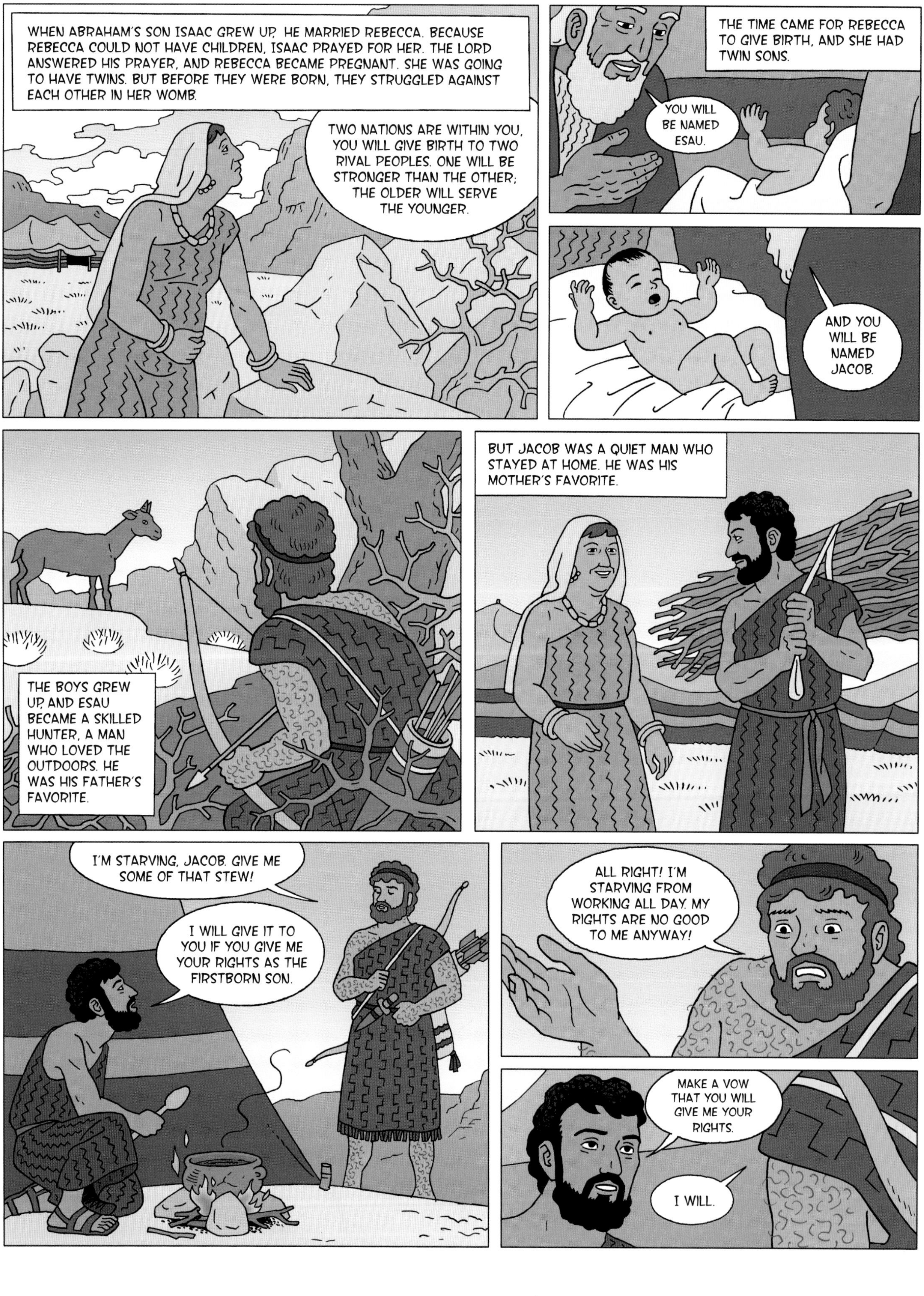
WHEN ABRAHAM'S SON ISAAC GREW UP, HE MARRIED REBECCA. BECAUSE REBECCA COULD NOT HAVE CHILDREN, ISAAC PRAYED FOR HER. THE LORD ANSWERED HIS PRAYER, AND REBECCA BECAME PREGNANT. SHE WAS GOING TO HAVE TWINS. BUT BEFORE THEY WERE BORN, THEY STRUGGLED AGAINST EACH OTHER IN HER WOMB.
TWO NATIONS ARE WITHIN YOU. YOU WILL GIVE BIRTH TO TWO RIVAL PEOPLES. ONE WILL BE STRONGER THAN THE OTHER; THE OLDER WILL SERVE THE YOUNGER.
THE TIME CAME FOR REBECCA TO GIVE BIRTH, AND SHE HAD TWIN SONS.
YOU WILL BE NAMED ESAU.
AND YOU WILL BE NAMED JACOB.
THE BOYS GREW UP, AND ESAU BECAME A SKILLED HUNTER, A MAN WHO LOVED THE OUTDOORS. HE WAS HIS FATHER'S FAVORITE.
BUT JACOB WAS A QUIET MAN WHO STAYED AT HOME. HE WAS HIS MOTHER'S FAVORITE.
I'M STARVING, JACOB. GIVE ME SOME OF THAT STEW!
I WILL GIVE IT TO YOU IF YOU GIVE ME YOUR RIGHTS AS THE FIRSTBORN SON.
ALL RIGHT! I'M STARVING FROM WORKING ALL DAY. MY RIGHTS ARE NO GOOD TO ME ANYWAY!
MAKE A VOW THAT YOU WILL GIVE ME YOUR RIGHTS.
I WILL.

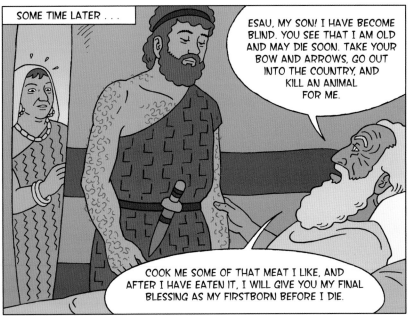

SOME TIME LATER . . .

ESAU, MY SON! I HAVE BECOME BLIND. YOU SEE THAT I AM OLD AND MAY DIE SOON. TAKE YOUR BOW AND ARROWS, GO OUT INTO THE COUNTRY, AND KILL AN ANIMAL FOR ME.

COOK ME SOME OF THAT MEAT I LIKE, AND AFTER I HAVE EATEN IT, I WILL GIVE YOU MY FINAL BLESSING AS MY FIRSTBORN BEFORE I DIE.

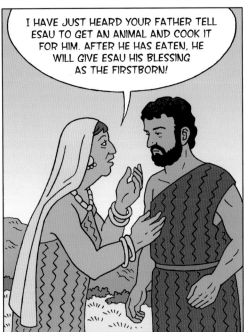

I HAVE JUST HEARD YOUR FATHER TELL ESAU TO GET AN ANIMAL AND COOK IT FOR HIM. AFTER HE HAS EATEN, HE WILL GIVE ESAU HIS BLESSING AS THE FIRSTBORN!

NOW, SON, LISTEN TO ME. PICK OUT TWO FAT YOUNG GOATS, SO I CAN COOK THEM AND MAKE SOME OF THAT FOOD YOUR FATHER LIKES. YOU CAN TAKE IT TO HIM TO EAT, AND HE WILL GIVE YOU HIS BLESSING BEFORE HE DIES.

BUT MOTHER, ESAU HAS HAIRY ARMS AND SKIN. WHAT IF OUR FATHER NOTICES THAT MY OWN SKIN IS SMOOTH? THEN I WILL BE CURSED INSTEAD OF BLESSED.

LET ANY CURSE AGAINST YOU FALL ON ME! JUST DO AS I SAY, AND GO GET THE GOATS FOR ME.

TAKE ESAU'S BEST CLOTHES AND PUT THE SKINS OF THE GOATS ON YOUR ARMS AND ON THE HAIRLESS PART OF YOUR NECK.

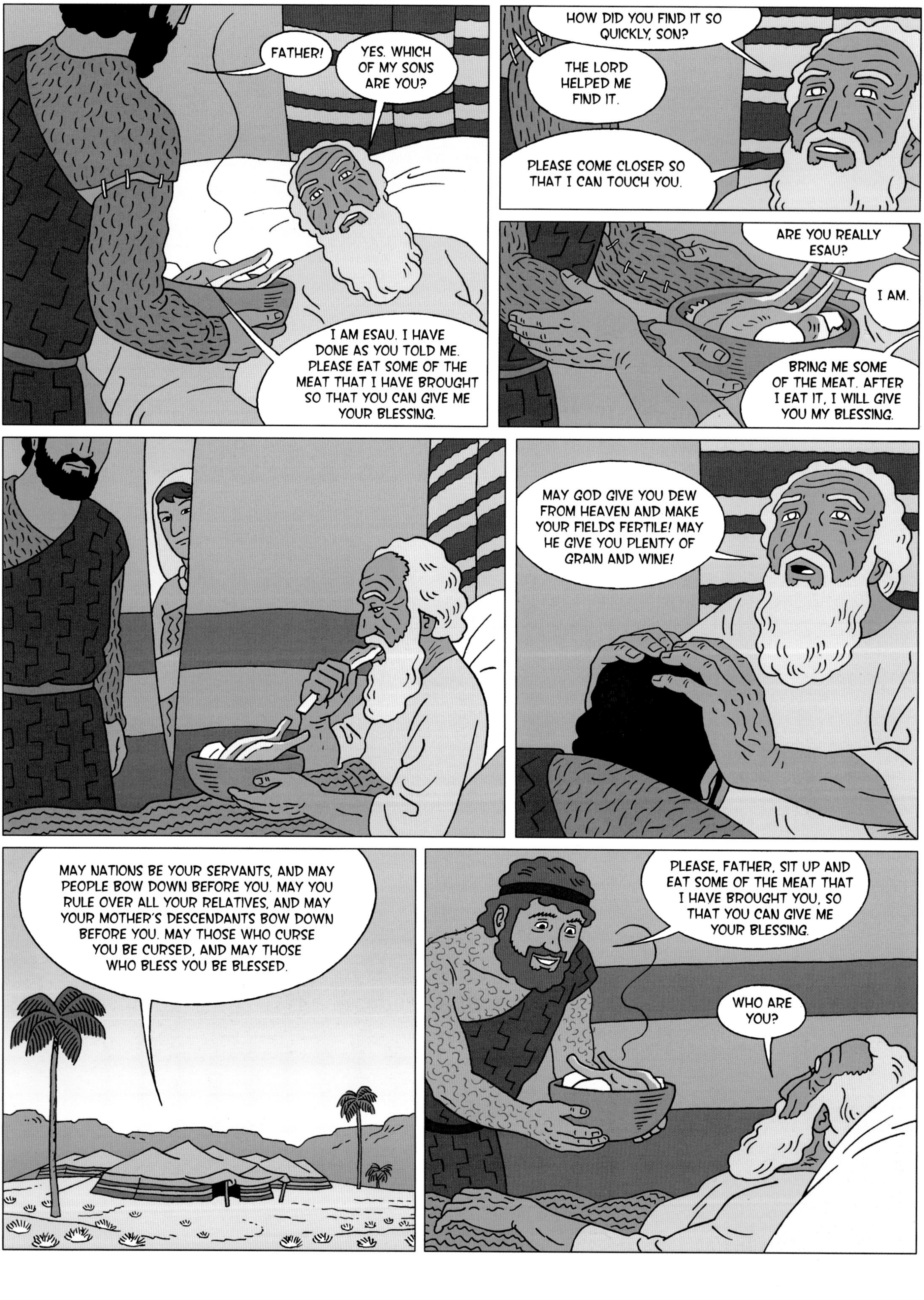
FATHER!
YES. WHICH OF MY SONS ARE YOU?
I AM ESAU. I HAVE DONE AS YOU TOLD ME. PLEASE EAT SOME OF THE MEAT THAT I HAVE BROUGHT SO THAT YOU CAN GIVE ME YOUR BLESSING.
HOW DID YOU FIND IT SO QUICKLY, SON?
THE LORD HELPED ME FIND IT.
PLEASE COME CLOSER SO THAT I CAN TOUCH YOU.
ARE YOU REALLY ESAU?
I AM.
BRING ME SOME OF THE MEAT. AFTER I EAT IT, I WILL GIVE YOU MY BLESSING.
MAY GOD GIVE YOU DEW FROM HEAVEN AND MAKE YOUR FIELDS FERTILE! MAY HE GIVE YOU PLENTY OF GRAIN AND WINE!
MAY NATIONS BE YOUR SERVANTS, AND MAY PEOPLE BOW DOWN BEFORE YOU. MAY YOU RULE OVER ALL YOUR RELATIVES, AND MAY YOUR MOTHER'S DESCENDANTS BOW DOWN BEFORE YOU. MAY THOSE WHO CURSE YOU BE CURSED, AND MAY THOSE WHO BLESS YOU BE BLESSED.
PLEASE, FATHER, SIT UP AND EAT SOME OF THE MEAT THAT I HAVE BROUGHT YOU, SO THAT YOU CAN GIVE ME YOUR BLESSING.
WHO ARE YOU?

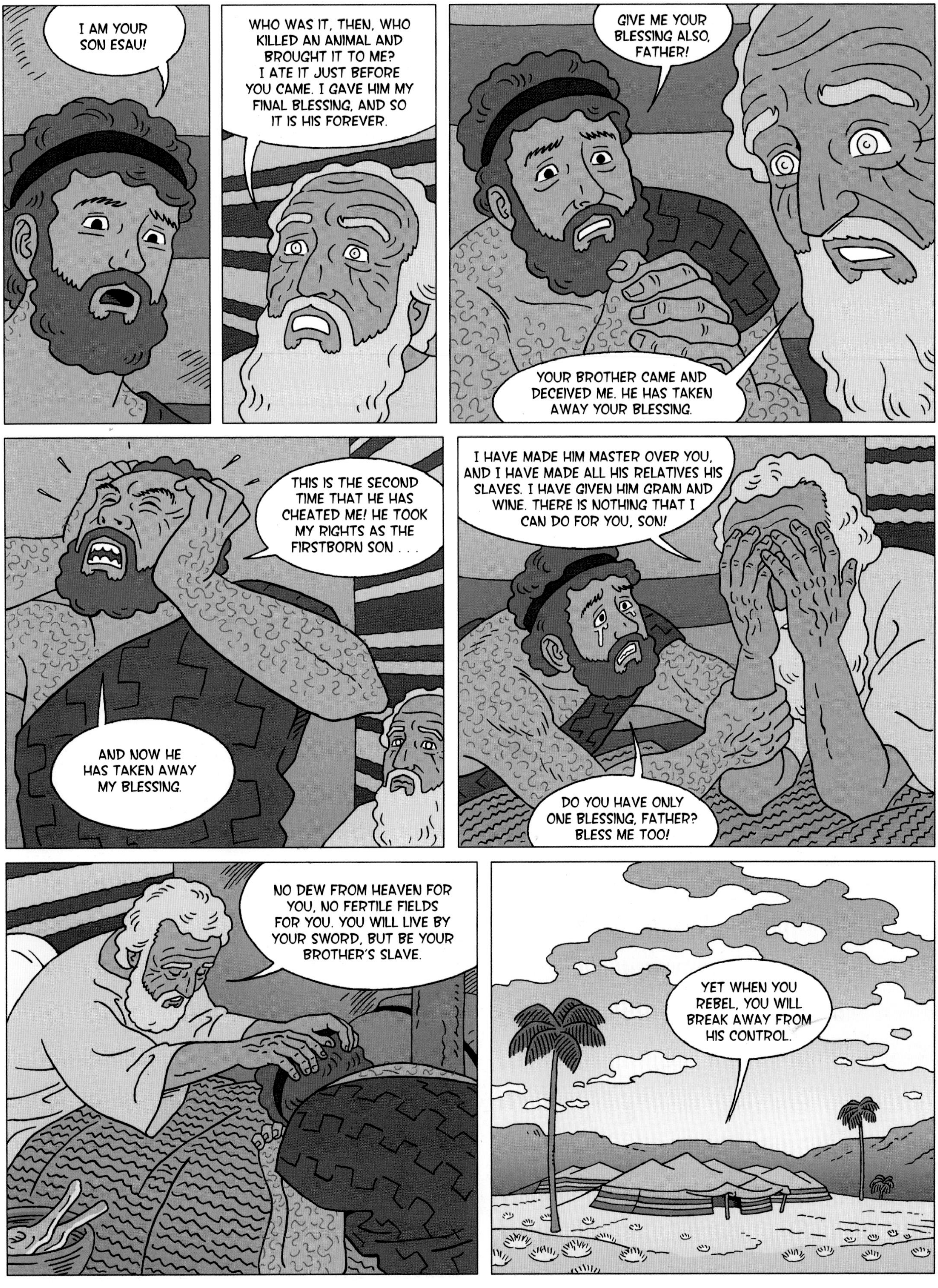
I AM YOUR SON ESAU!
WHO WAS IT, THEN, WHO KILLED AN ANIMAL AND BROUGHT IT TO ME? I ATE IT JUST BEFORE YOU CAME. I GAVE HIM MY FINAL BLESSING, AND SO IT IS HIS FOREVER.
GIVE ME YOUR BLESSING ALSO, FATHER!
YOUR BROTHER CAME AND DECEIVED ME. HE HAS TAKEN AWAY YOUR BLESSING.
THIS IS THE SECOND TIME THAT HE HAS CHEATED ME! HE TOOK MY RIGHTS AS THE FIRSTBORN SON . . .
AND NOW HE HAS TAKEN AWAY MY BLESSING.
I HAVE MADE HIM MASTER OVER YOU, AND I HAVE MADE ALL HIS RELATIVES HIS SLAVES. I HAVE GIVEN HIM GRAIN AND WINE. THERE IS NOTHING THAT I CAN DO FOR YOU, SON!
DO YOU HAVE ONLY ONE BLESSING, FATHER? BLESS ME TOO!
NO DEW FROM HEAVEN FOR YOU, NO FERTILE FIELDS FOR YOU. YOU WILL LIVE BY YOUR SWORD, BUT BE YOUR BROTHER'S SLAVE.
YET WHEN YOU REBEL, YOU WILL BREAK AWAY FROM HIS CONTROL.

JACOB HAD TWELVE SONS, BUT HE LOVED JOSEPH THE MOST. WHEN HIS OTHER SONS SAW THAT HE LOVED JOSEPH MORE THAN HE LOVED THEM, THEY HATED THEIR BROTHER SO MUCH THAT THEY WOULD NOT EVEN SPEAK TO HIM KINDLY.

BROTHERS, LISTEN TO THE DREAM I HAD.

WE WERE ALL IN THE FIELD TYING UP SHEAVES OF WHEAT. BUT THEN MY SHEAF STOOD UP STRAIGHT. YOURS FORMED A CIRCLE AROUND MINE AND BOWED DOWN TO IT.

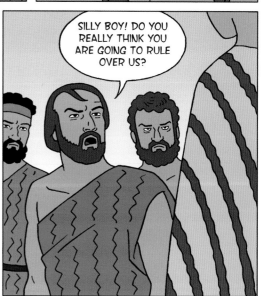

SILLY BOY! DO YOU REALLY THINK YOU ARE GOING TO RULE OVER US?

THEN, ONE DAY . . .

YOUR BROTHERS ARE IN THE FIELDS TAKING CARE OF THE FLOCK. GO SEE IF THEY ARE SAFE, AND THEN COME BACK AND TELL ME.

HERE COMES THAT DREAMER.

LET'S KILL HIM AND THROW HIS BODY INTO ONE OF THE DRY WELLS. WE CAN SAY THAT A WILD ANIMAL KILLED HIM. THEN WE WILL SEE WHAT BECOMES OF HIS DREAMS.

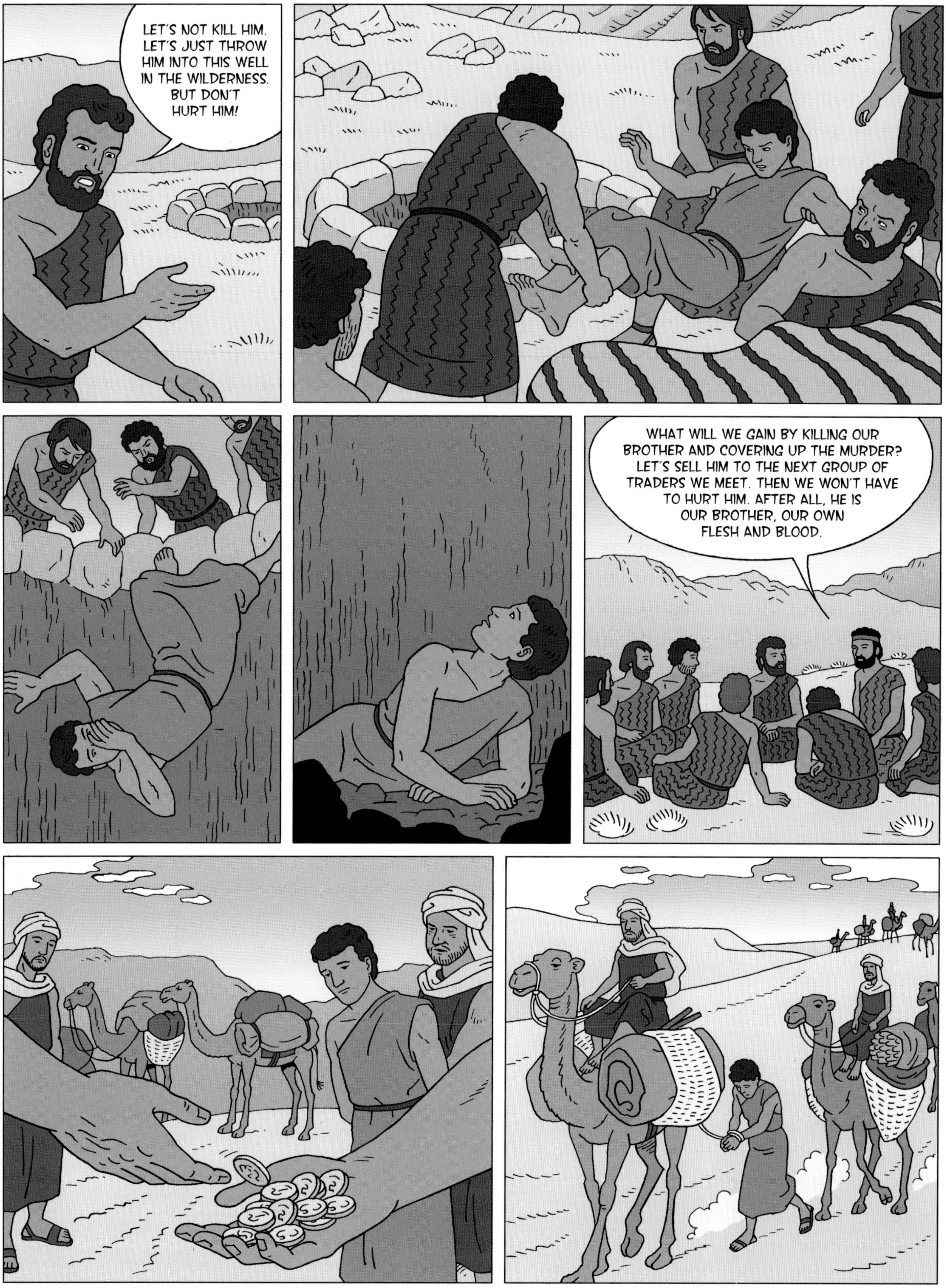
LET'S NOT KILL HIM. LET'S JUST THROW HIM INTO THIS WELL IN THE WILDERNESS. BUT DON'T HURT HIM!
WHAT WILL WE GAIN BY KILLING OUR BROTHER AND COVERING UP THE MURDER? LET'S SELL HIM TO THE NEXT GROUP OF TRADERS WE MEET. THEN WE WON'T HAVE TO HURT HIM. AFTER ALL, HE IS OUR BROTHER, OUR OWN FLESH AND BLOOD.

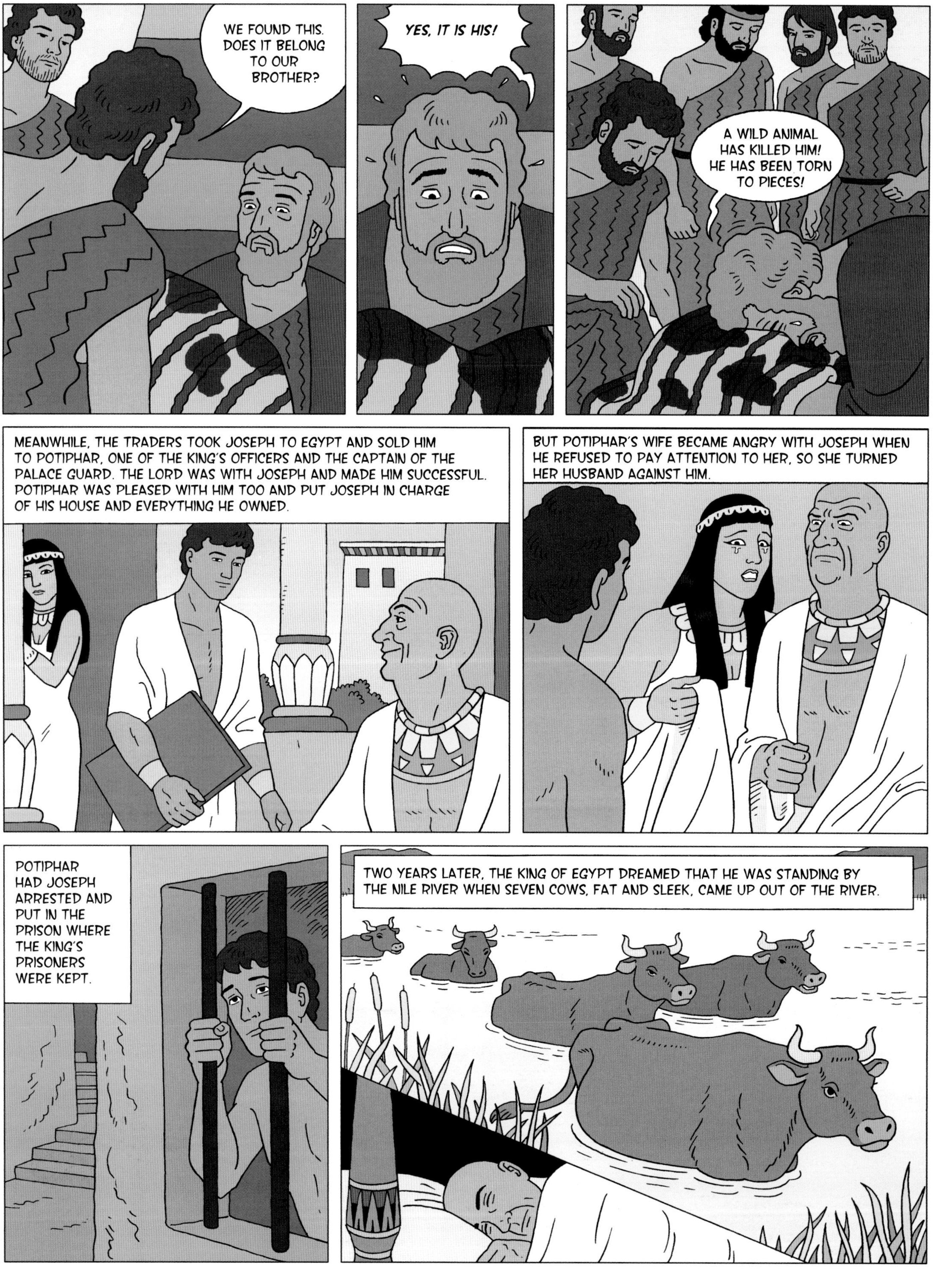
WE FOUND THIS. DOES IT BELONG TO OUR BROTHER?
YES, IT IS HIS!
A WILD ANIMAL HAS KILLED HIM! HE HAS BEEN TORN TO PIECES!
MEANWHILE, THE TRADERS TOOK JOSEPH TO EGYPT AND SOLD HIM TO POTIPHAR, ONE OF THE KING'S OFFICERS AND THE CAPTAIN OF THE PALACE GUARD. THE LORD WAS WITH JOSEPH AND MADE HIM SUCCESSFUL. POTIPHAR WAS PLEASED WITH HIM TOO AND PUT JOSEPH IN CHARGE OF HIS HOUSE AND EVERYTHING HE OWNED.
BUT POTIPHAR'S WIFE BECAME ANGRY WITH JOSEPH WHEN HE REFUSED TO PAY ATTENTION TO HER, SO SHE TURNED HER HUSBAND AGAINST HIM.
POTIPHAR HAD JOSEPH ARRESTED AND PUT IN THE PRISON WHERE THE KING'S PRISONERS WERE KEPT.
TWO YEARS LATER, THE KING OF EGYPT DREAMED THAT HE WAS STANDING BY THE NILE RIVER WHEN SEVEN COWS, FAT AND SLEEK, CAME UP OUT OF THE RIVER.

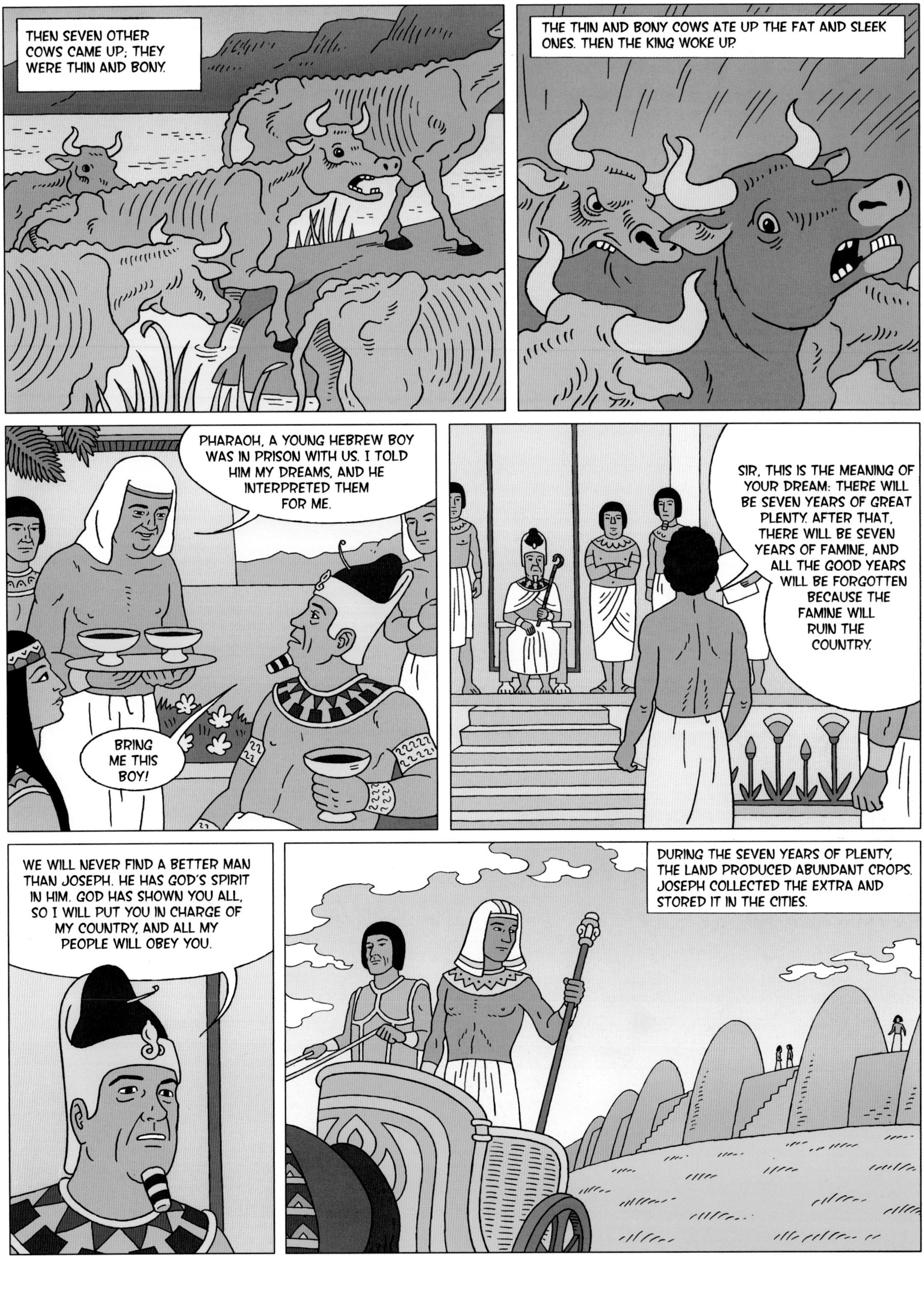
THEN SEVEN OTHER COWS CAME UP; THEY WERE THIN AND BONY.
THE THIN AND BONY COWS ATE UP THE FAT AND SLEEK ONES. THEN THE KING WOKE UP.
PHARAOH, A YOUNG HEBREW BOY WAS IN PRISON WITH US. I TOLD HIM MY DREAMS, AND HE INTERPRETED THEM FOR ME.
BRING ME THIS BOY!
SIR, THIS IS THE MEANING OF YOUR DREAM: THERE WILL BE SEVEN YEARS OF GREAT PLENTY. AFTER THAT, THERE WILL BE SEVEN YEARS OF FAMINE, AND ALL THE GOOD YEARS WILL BE FORGOTTEN BECAUSE THE FAMINE WILL RUIN THE COUNTRY.
WE WILL NEVER FIND A BETTER MAN THAN JOSEPH. HE HAS GOD'S SPIRIT IN HIM. GOD HAS SHOWN YOU ALL, SO I WILL PUT YOU IN CHARGE OF MY COUNTRY, AND ALL MY PEOPLE WILL OBEY YOU.
DURING THE SEVEN YEARS OF PLENTY, THE LAND PRODUCED ABUNDANT CROPS. JOSEPH COLLECTED THE EXTRA AND STORED IT IN THE CITIES.

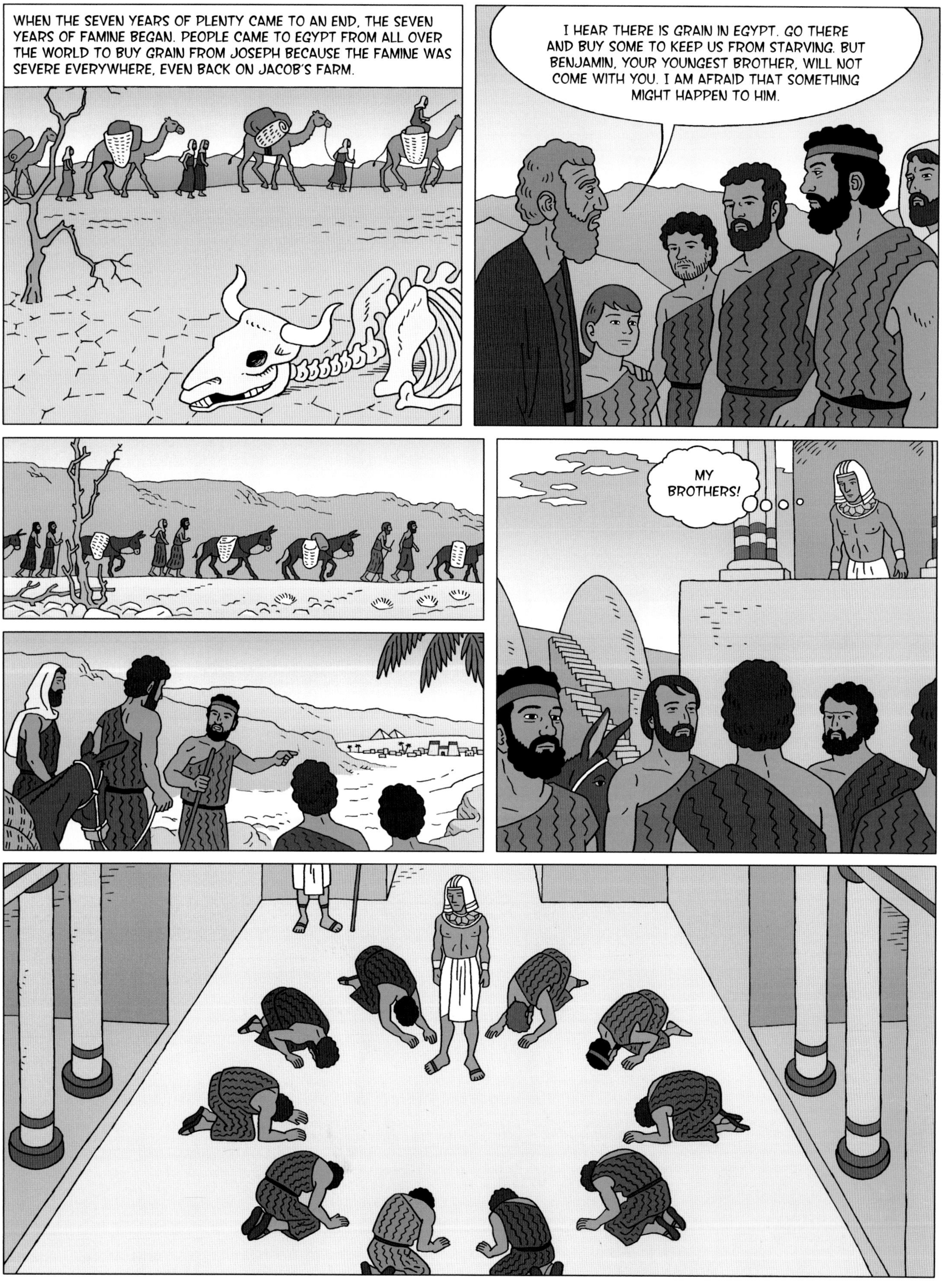
WHEN THE SEVEN YEARS OF PLENTY CAME TO AN END, THE SEVEN YEARS OF FAMINE BEGAN. PEOPLE CAME TO EGYPT FROM ALL OVER THE WORLD TO BUY GRAIN FROM JOSEPH BECAUSE THE FAMINE WAS SEVERE EVERYWHERE, EVEN BACK ON JACOB'S FARM.
I HEAR THERE IS GRAIN IN EGYPT. GO THERE AND BUY SOME TO KEEP US FROM STARVING. BUT BENJAMIN, YOUR YOUNGEST BROTHER, WILL NOT COME WITH YOU. I AM AFRAID THAT SOMETHING MIGHT HAPPEN TO HIM.
MY BROTHERS!

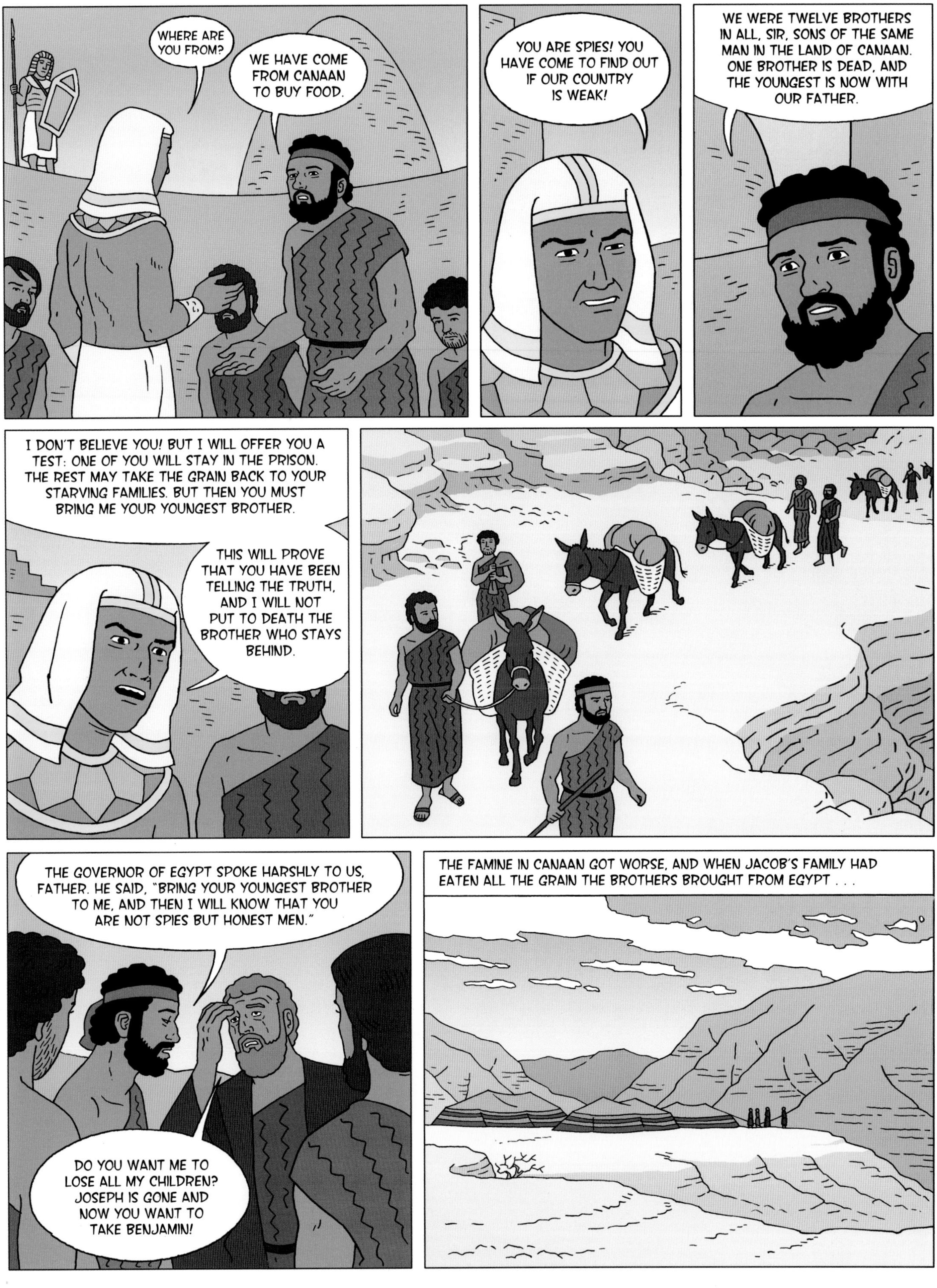
WHERE ARE YOU FROM?
WE HAVE COME FROM CANAAN TO BUY FOOD.
YOU ARE SPIES! YOU HAVE COME TO FIND OUT IF OUR COUNTRY IS WEAK!
WE WERE TWELVE BROTHERS IN ALL, SIR, SONS OF THE SAME MAN IN THE LAND OF CANAAN. ONE BROTHER IS DEAD, AND THE YOUNGEST IS NOW WITH OUR FATHER.
I DON'T BELIEVE YOU! BUT I WILL OFFER YOU A TEST: ONE OF YOU WILL STAY IN THE PRISON. THE REST MAY TAKE THE GRAIN BACK TO YOUR STARVING FAMILIES. BUT THEN YOU MUST BRING ME YOUR YOUNGEST BROTHER.
THIS WILL PROVE THAT YOU HAVE BEEN TELLING THE TRUTH, AND I WILL NOT PUT TO DEATH THE BROTHER WHO STAYS BEHIND.
THE GOVERNOR OF EGYPT SPOKE HARSHLY TO US, FATHER. HE SAID, "BRING YOUR YOUNGEST BROTHER TO ME, AND THEN I WILL KNOW THAT YOU ARE NOT SPIES BUT HONEST MEN."
DO YOU WANT ME TO LOSE ALL MY CHILDREN? JOSEPH IS GONE AND NOW YOU WANT TO TAKE BENJAMIN!
THE FAMINE IN CANAAN GOT WORSE, AND WHEN JACOB'S FAMILY HAD EATEN ALL THE GRAIN THE BROTHERS BROUGHT FROM EGYPT . . .

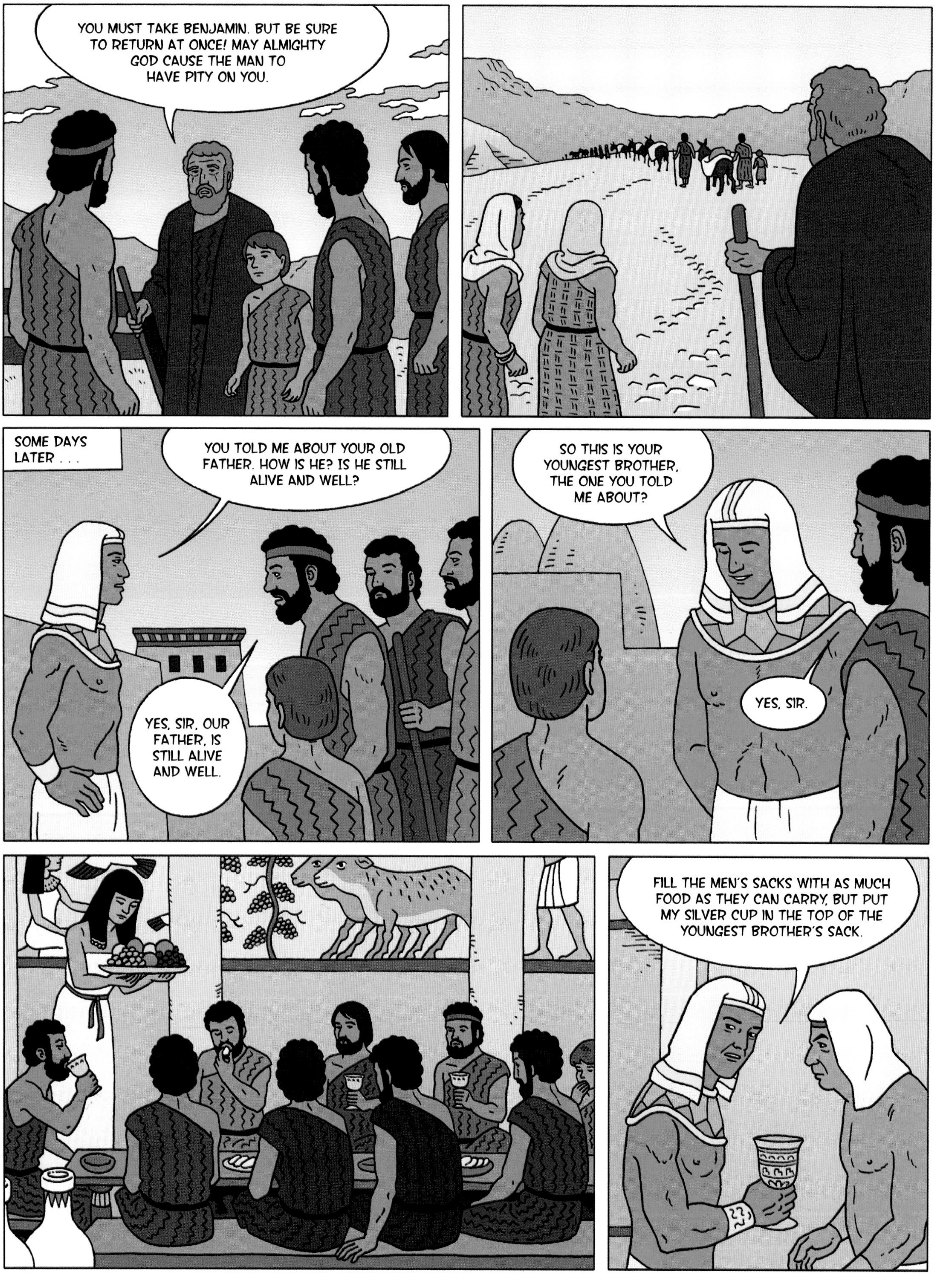
YOU MUST TAKE BENJAMIN. BUT BE SURE TO RETURN AT ONCE! MAY ALMIGHTY GOD CAUSE THE MAN TO HAVE PITY ON YOU.
SOME DAYS LATER . . .
YOU TOLD ME ABOUT YOUR OLD FATHER. HOW IS HE? IS HE STILL ALIVE AND WELL?
YES, SIR, OUR FATHER, IS STILL ALIVE AND WELL.
SO THIS IS YOUR YOUNGEST BROTHER, THE ONE YOU TOLD ME ABOUT?
YES, SIR.
FILL THE MEN'S SACKS WITH AS MUCH FOOD AS THEY CAN CARRY, BUT PUT MY SILVER CUP IN THE TOP OF THE YOUNGEST BROTHER'S SACK.

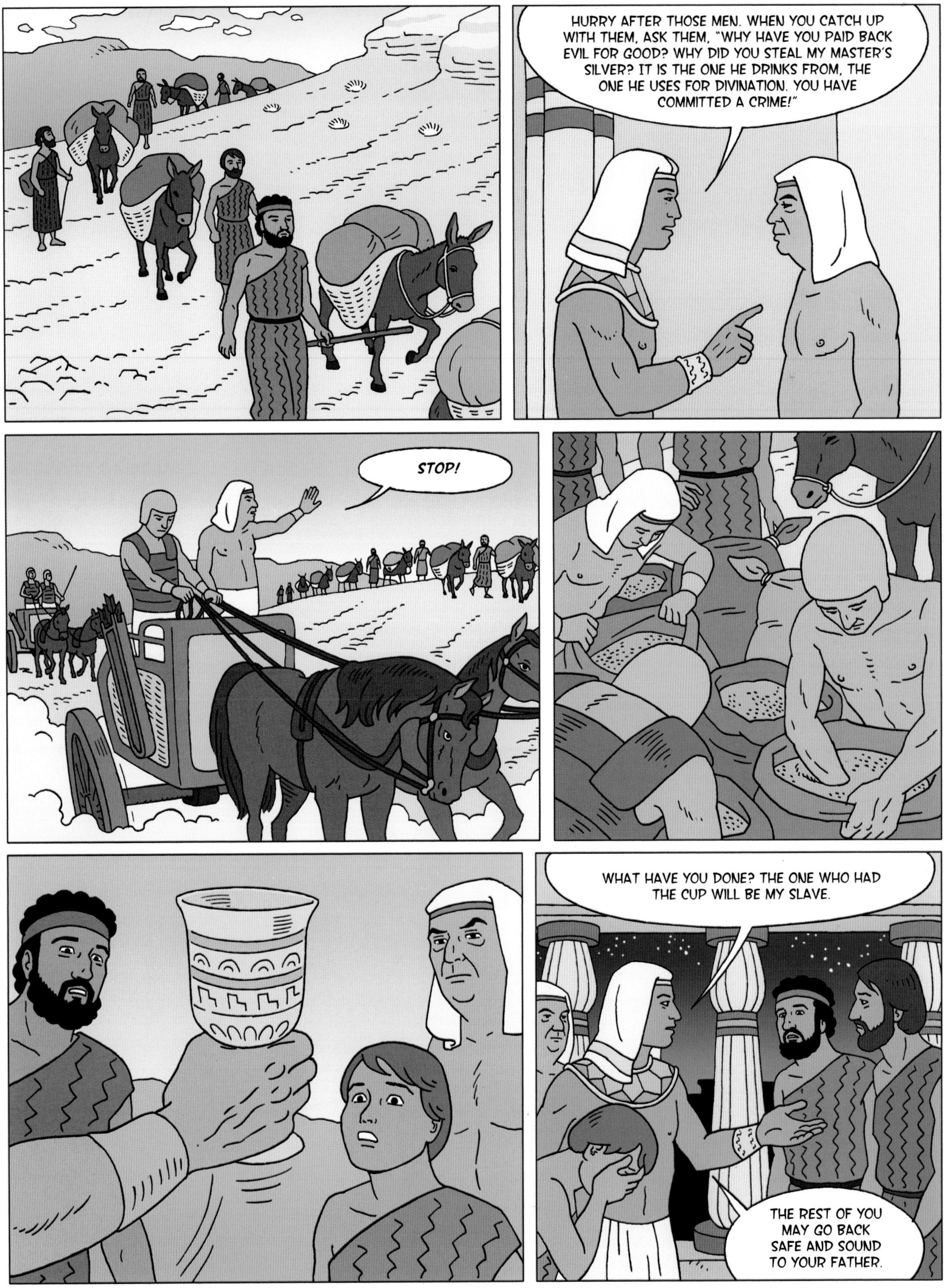
HURRY AFTER THOSE MEN. WHEN YOU CATCH UP WITH THEM, ASK THEM, "WHY HAVE YOU PAID BACK EVIL FOR GOOD? WHY DID YOU STEAL MY MASTER'S SILVER? IT IS THE ONE HE DRINKS FROM, THE ONE HE USES FOR DIVINATION. YOU HAVE COMMITTED A CRIME!"
STOP!
WHAT HAVE YOU DONE? THE ONE WHO HAD THE CUP WILL BE MY SLAVE.
THE REST OF YOU MAY GO BACK SAFE AND SOUND TO YOUR FATHER.

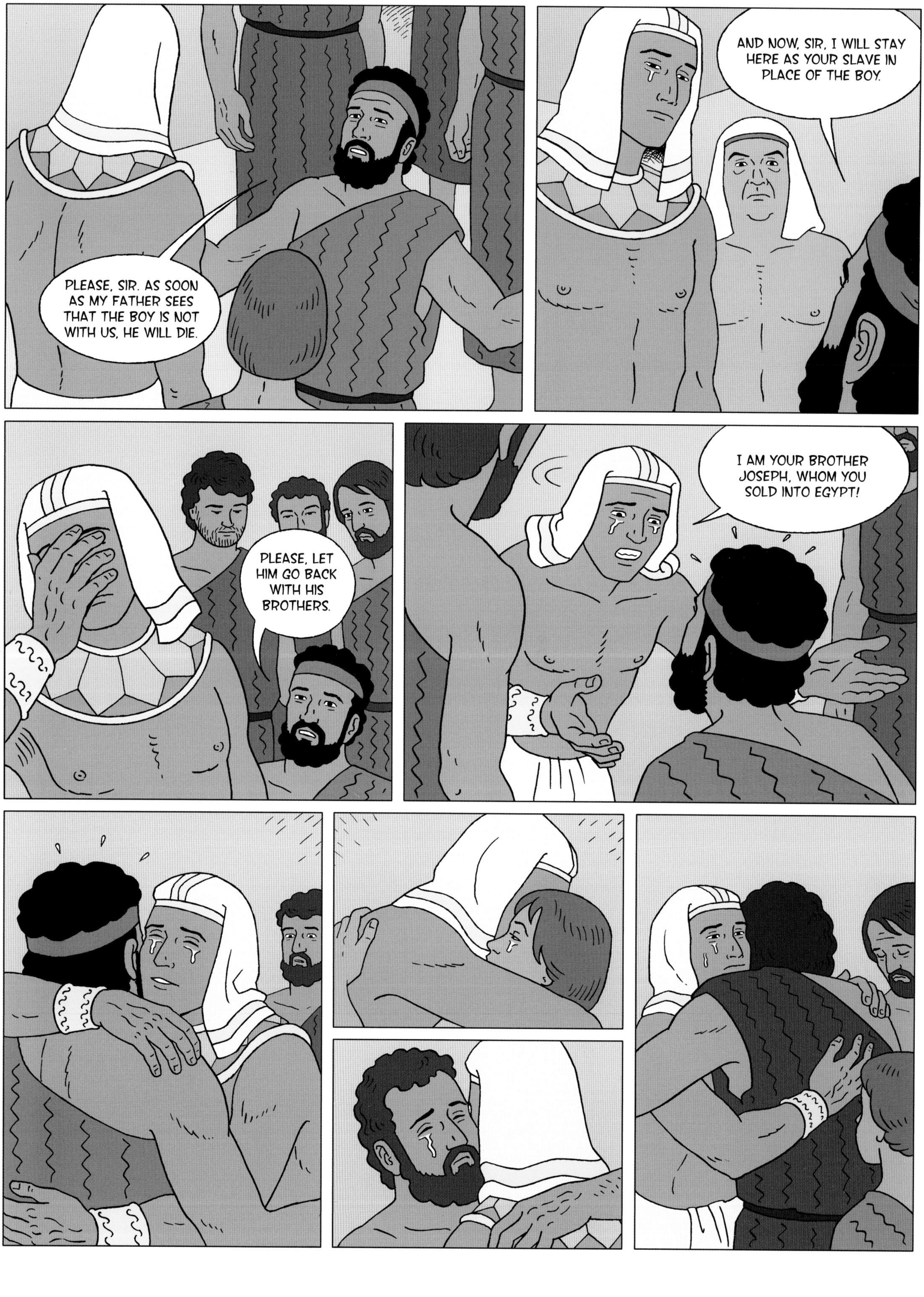
PLEASE, SIR. AS SOON AS MY FATHER SEES THAT THE BOY IS NOT WITH US, HE WILL DIE.
AND NOW, SIR, I WILL STAY HERE AS YOUR SLAVE IN PLACE OF THE BOY.
PLEASE, LET HIM GO BACK WITH HIS BROTHERS.
I AM YOUR BROTHER JOSEPH, WHOM YOU SOLD INTO EGYPT!

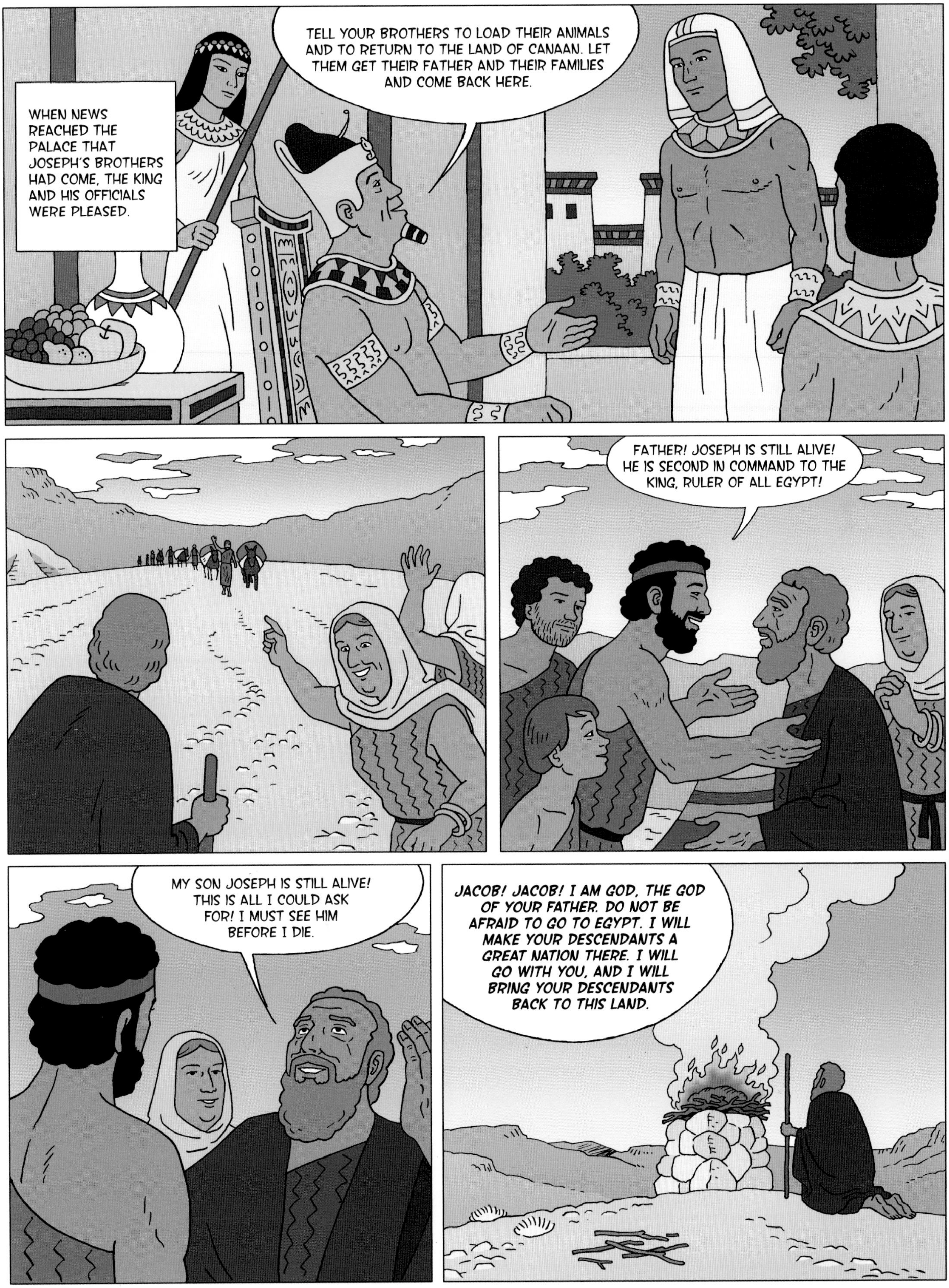
WHEN NEWS REACHED THE PALACE THAT JOSEPH'S BROTHERS HAD COME, THE KING AND HIS OFFICIALS WERE PLEASED.
TELL YOUR BROTHERS TO LOAD THEIR ANIMALS AND TO RETURN TO THE LAND OF CANAAN. LET THEM GET THEIR FATHER AND THEIR FAMILIES AND COME BACK HERE.
FATHER! JOSEPH IS STILL ALIVE! HE IS SECOND IN COMMAND TO THE KING, RULER OF ALL EGYPT!
MY SON JOSEPH IS STILL ALIVE! THIS IS ALL I COULD ASK FOR! I MUST SEE HIM BEFORE I DIE.
JACOB! JACOB! I AM GOD, THE GOD OF YOUR FATHER. DO NOT BE AFRAID TO GO TO EGYPT. I WILL MAKE YOUR DESCENDANTS A GREAT NATION THERE. I WILL GO WITH YOU, AND I WILL BRING YOUR DESCENDANTS BACK TO THIS LAND.

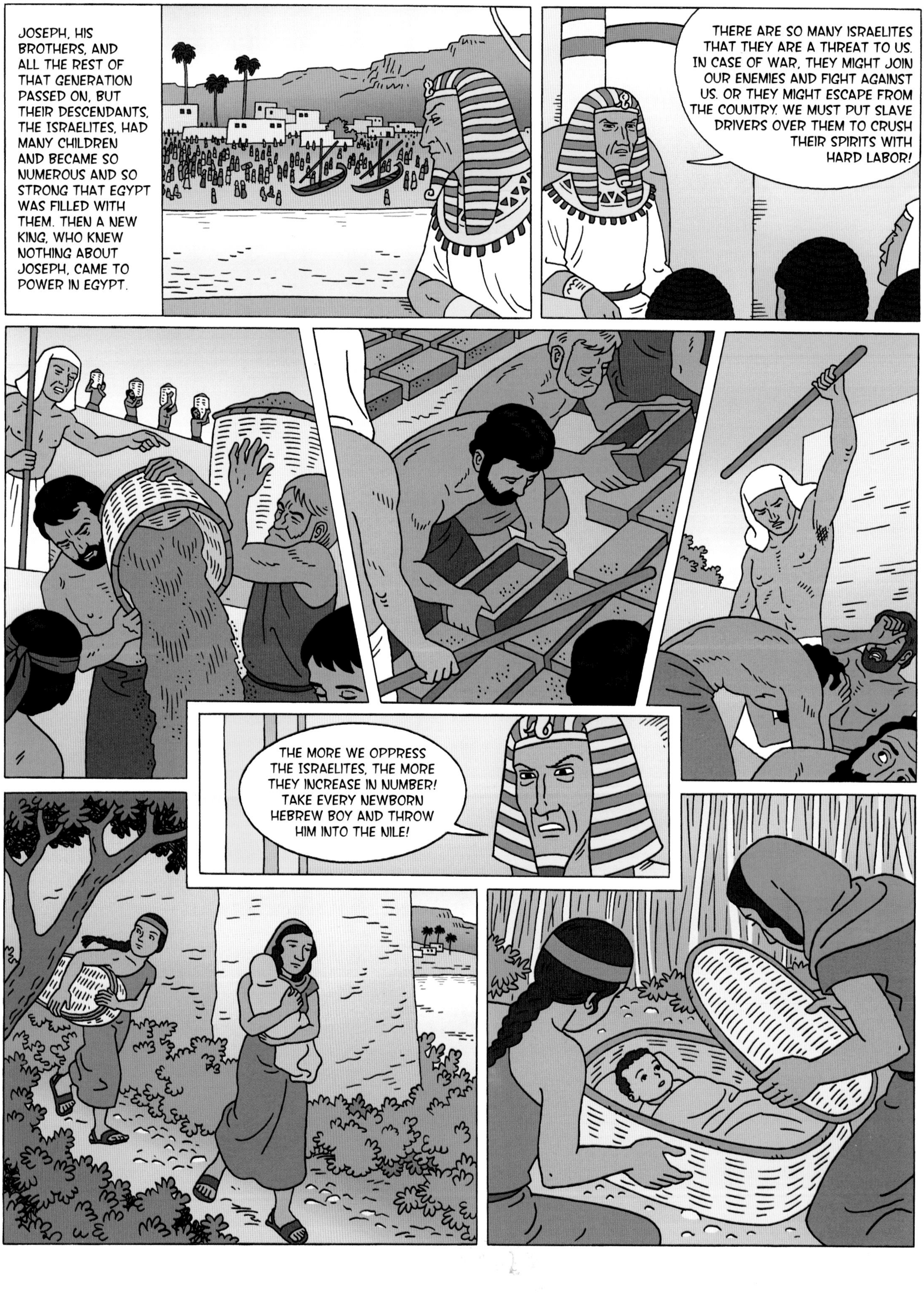
JOSEPH, HIS BROTHERS, AND ALL THE REST OF THAT GENERATION PASSED ON, BUT THEIR DESCENDANTS, THE ISRAELITES, HAD MANY CHILDREN AND BECAME SO NUMEROUS AND SO STRONG THAT EGYPT WAS FILLED WITH THEM. THEN A NEW KING, WHO KNEW NOTHING ABOUT JOSEPH, CAME TO POWER IN EGYPT.
THERE ARE SO MANY ISRAELITES THAT THEY ARE A THREAT TO US. IN CASE OF WAR, THEY MIGHT JOIN OUR ENEMIES AND FIGHT AGAINST US. OR THEY MIGHT ESCAPE FROM THE COUNTRY. WE MUST PUT SLAVE DRIVERS OVER THEM TO CRUSH THEIR SPIRITS WITH HARD LABOR!
THE MORE WE OPPRESS THE ISRAELITES, THE MORE THEY INCREASE IN NUMBER! TAKE EVERY NEWBORN HEBREW BOY AND THROW HIM INTO THE NILE!

OH!

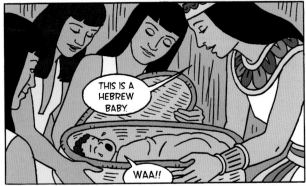

THIS IS A HEBREW BABY.

WAA!!

SHALL I FIND A HEBREW WOMAN TO NURSE THE BABY FOR YOU?

PLEASE DO.

TAKE THIS BABY AND NURSE HIM FOR ME, PLEASE. I WILL PAY YOU.

I ADOPTED HIM AS MY OWN SON. I PULLED HIM OUT OF THE WATER, AND I HAVE NAMED HIM MOSES.

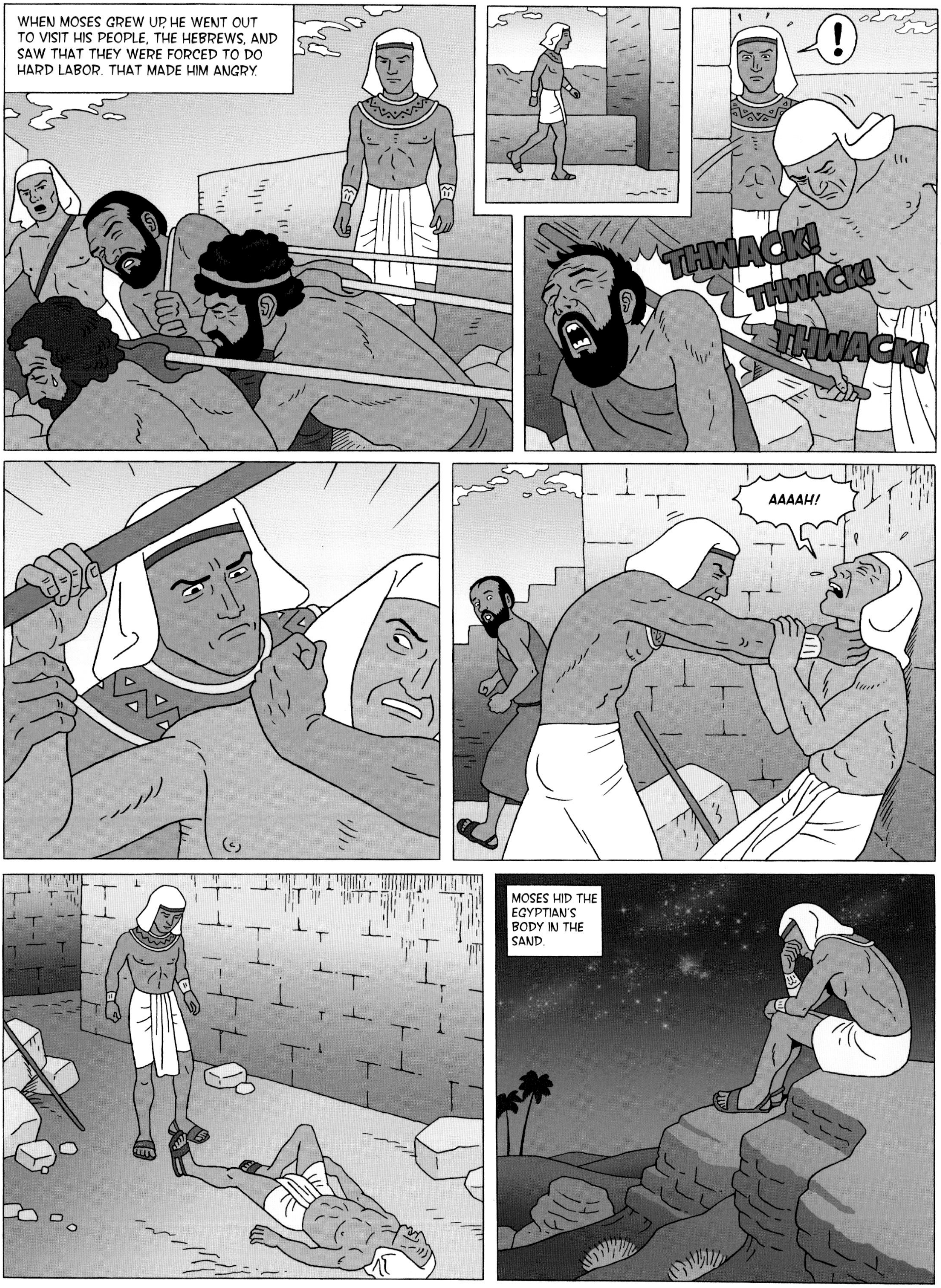
WHEN MOSES GREW UP, HE WENT OUT TO VISIT HIS PEOPLE, THE HEBREWS, AND SAW THAT THEY WERE FORCED TO DO HARD LABOR. THAT MADE HIM ANGRY.
!
THWACK!
THWACK!
THWACK!
AAAAH!
MOSES HID THE EGYPTIAN'S BODY IN THE SAND.

THE NEXT DAY . . .

DFT!

WHY ARE YOU HITTING A FELLOW HEBREW?

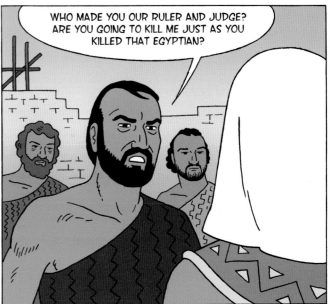

WHO MADE YOU OUR RULER AND JUDGE? ARE YOU GOING TO KILL ME JUST AS YOU KILLED THAT EGYPTIAN?

PEOPLE HAVE FOUND OUT WHAT I HAVE DONE. WHEN THE KING HEARS ABOUT WHAT HAPPENED, HE'LL KILL ME! I BETTER FLEE TO THE LAND OF MIDIAN.

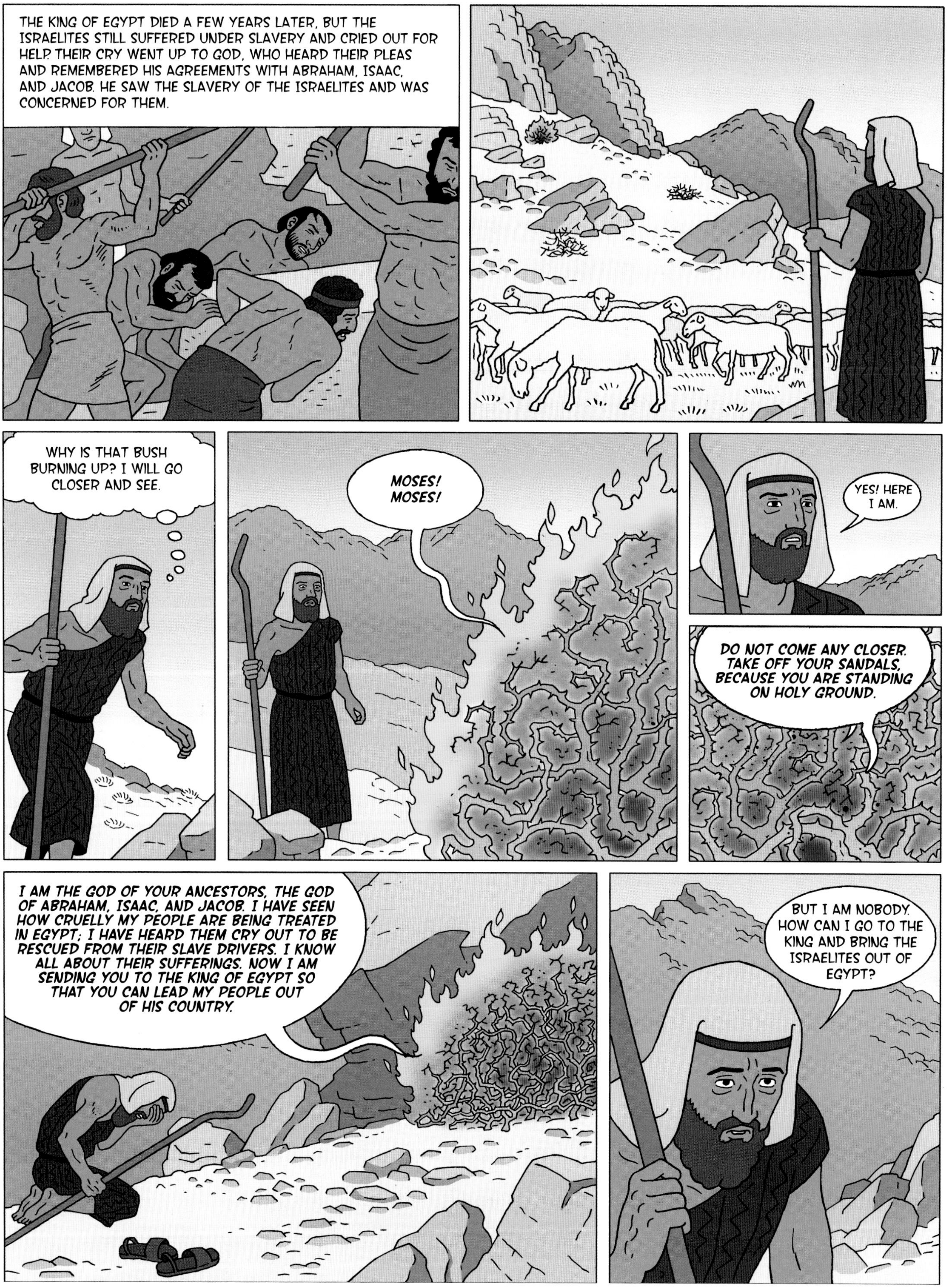

THE KING OF EGYPT DIED A FEW YEARS LATER, BUT THE ISRAELITES STILL SUFFERED UNDER SLAVERY AND CRIED OUT FOR HELP. THEIR CRY WENT UP TO GOD, WHO HEARD THEIR PLEAS AND REMEMBERED HIS AGREEMENTS WITH ABRAHAM, ISAAC, AND JACOB. HE SAW THE SLAVERY OF THE ISRAELITES AND WAS CONCERNED FOR THEM.
WHY IS THAT BUSH BURNING UP? I WILL GO CLOSER AND SEE.
MOSES! MOSES!
YES! HERE I AM.
DO NOT COME ANY CLOSER. TAKE OFF YOUR SANDALS, BECAUSE YOU ARE STANDING ON HOLY GROUND.
I AM THE GOD OF YOUR ANCESTORS, THE GOD OF ABRAHAM, ISAAC, AND JACOB. I HAVE SEEN HOW CRUELLY MY PEOPLE ARE BEING TREATED IN EGYPT; I HAVE HEARD THEM CRY OUT TO BE RESCUED FROM THEIR SLAVE DRIVERS. I KNOW ALL ABOUT THEIR SUFFERINGS. NOW I AM SENDING YOU TO THE KING OF EGYPT SO THAT YOU CAN LEAD MY PEOPLE OUT OF HIS COUNTRY.
BUT I AM NOBODY. HOW CAN I GO TO THE KING AND BRING THE ISRAELITES OUT OF EGYPT?

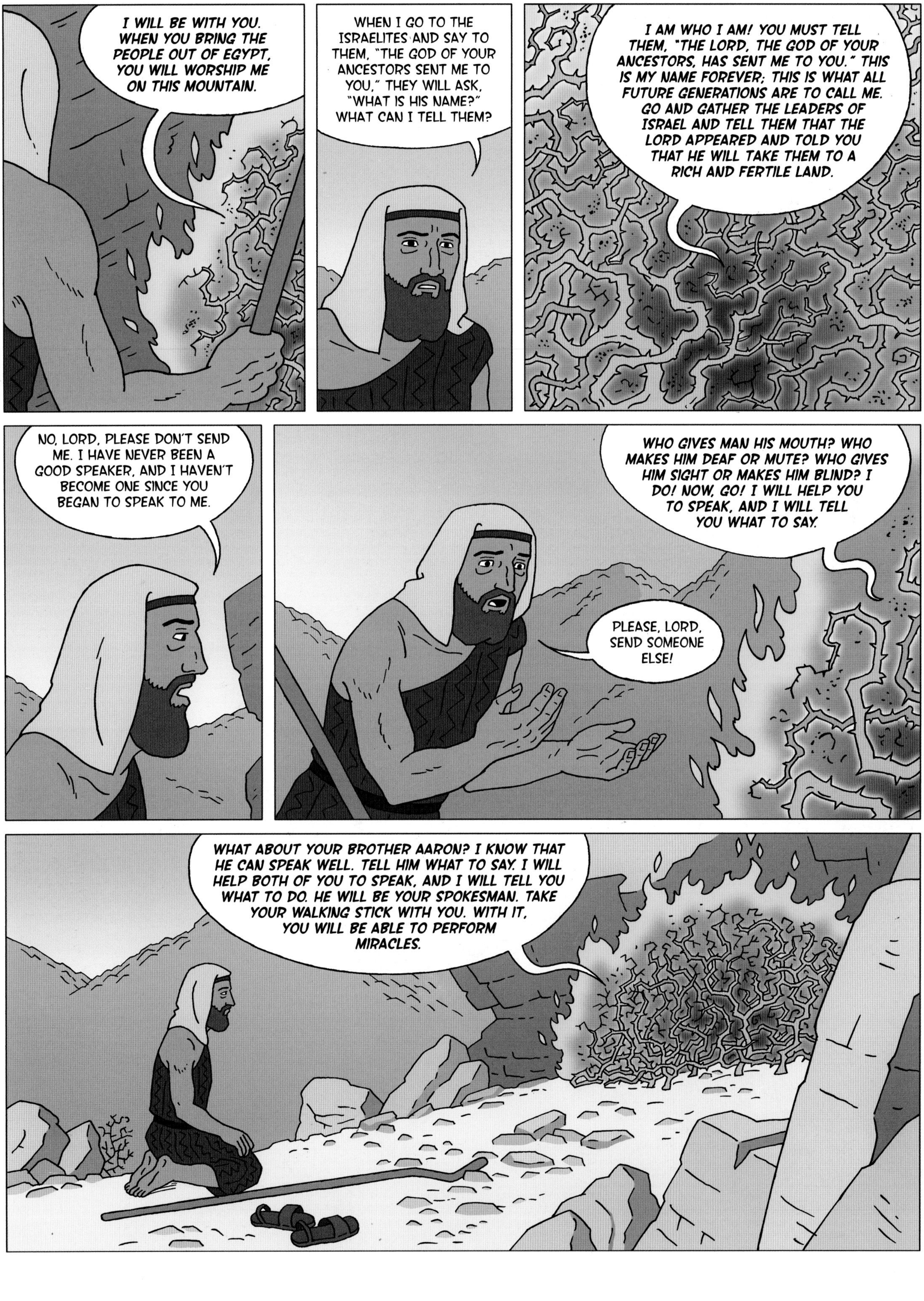
I WILL BE WITH YOU. WHEN YOU BRING THE PEOPLE OUT OF EGYPT, YOU WILL WORSHIP ME ON THIS MOUNTAIN.
WHEN I GO TO THE ISRAELITES AND SAY TO THEM, "THE GOD OF YOUR ANCESTORS SENT ME TO YOU," THEY WILL ASK, "WHAT IS HIS NAME?" WHAT CAN I TELL THEM?
I AM WHO I AM! YOU MUST TELL THEM, "THE LORD, THE GOD OF YOUR ANCESTORS, HAS SENT ME TO YOU." THIS IS MY NAME FOREVER; THIS IS WHAT ALL FUTURE GENERATIONS ARE TO CALL ME. GO AND GATHER THE LEADERS OF ISRAEL AND TELL THEM THAT THE LORD APPEARED AND TOLD YOU THAT HE WILL TAKE THEM TO A RICH AND FERTILE LAND.
NO, LORD, PLEASE DON'T SEND ME. I HAVE NEVER BEEN A GOOD SPEAKER, AND I HAVEN'T BECOME ONE SINCE YOU BEGAN TO SPEAK TO ME.
WHO GIVES MAN HIS MOUTH? WHO MAKES HIM DEAF OR MUTE? WHO GIVES HIM SIGHT OR MAKES HIM BLIND? I DO! NOW, GO! I WILL HELP YOU TO SPEAK, AND I WILL TELL YOU WHAT TO SAY.
PLEASE, LORD, SEND SOMEONE ELSE!
WHAT ABOUT YOUR BROTHER AARON? I KNOW THAT HE CAN SPEAK WELL. TELL HIM WHAT TO SAY. I WILL HELP BOTH OF YOU TO SPEAK, AND I WILL TELL YOU WHAT TO DO. HE WILL BE YOUR SPOKESMAN. TAKE YOUR WALKING STICK WITH YOU. WITH IT, YOU WILL BE ABLE TO PERFORM MIRACLES.

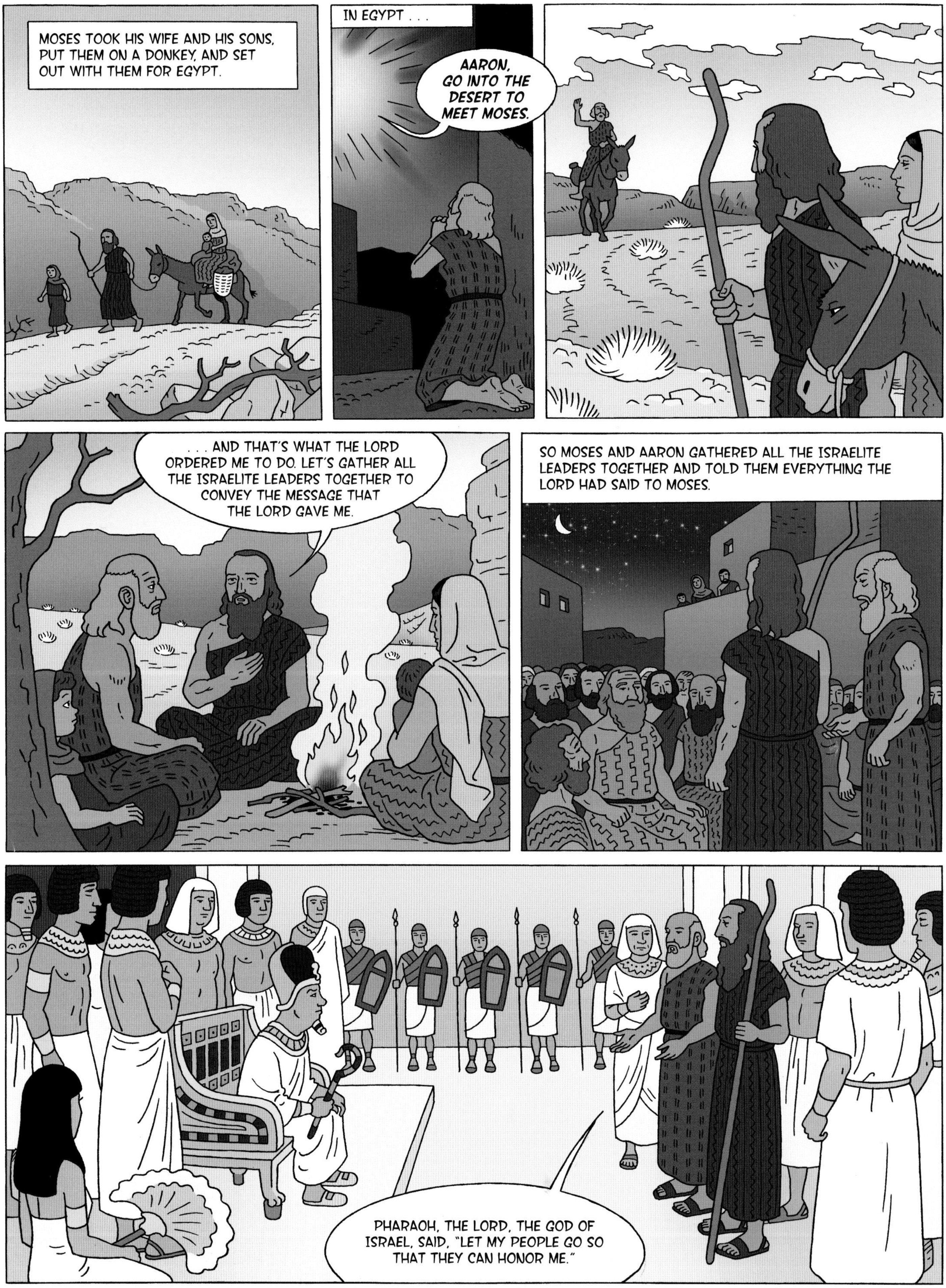
MOSES TOOK HIS WIFE AND HIS SONS, PUT THEM ON A DONKEY, AND SET OUT WITH THEM FOR EGYPT.
IN EGYPT . . .
AARON, GO INTO THE DESERT TO MEET MOSES.
. . . AND THAT'S WHAT THE LORD ORDERED ME TO DO. LET'S GATHER ALL THE ISRAELITE LEADERS TOGETHER TO CONVEY THE MESSAGE THAT THE LORD GAVE ME.
SO MOSES AND AARON GATHERED ALL THE ISRAELITE LEADERS TOGETHER AND TOLD THEM EVERYTHING THE LORD HAD SAID TO MOSES.
PHARAOH, THE LORD, THE GOD OF ISRAEL, SAID, "LET MY PEOPLE GO SO THAT THEY CAN HONOR ME."

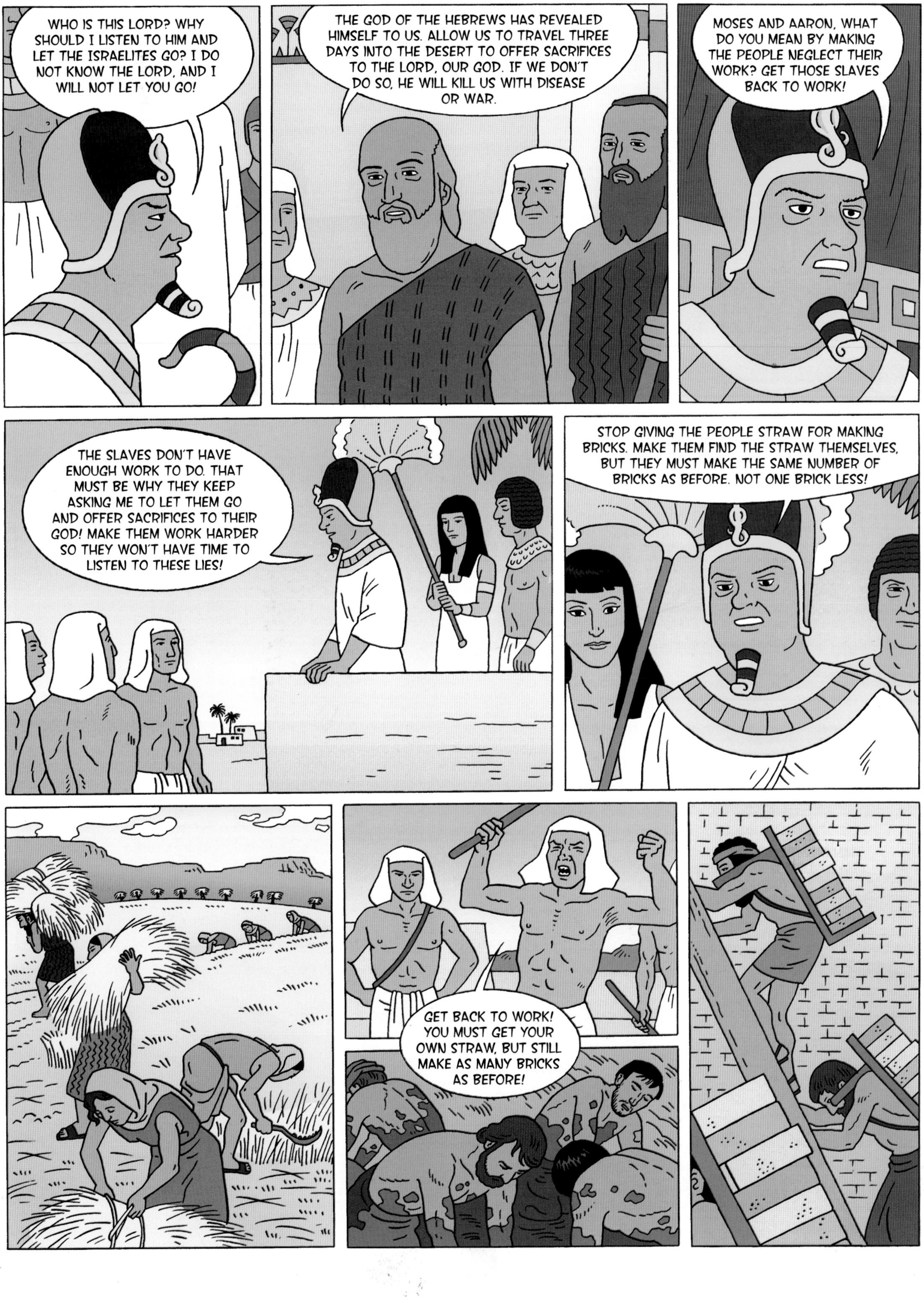
WHO IS THIS LORD? WHY SHOULD I LISTEN TO HIM AND LET THE ISRAELITES GO? I DO NOT KNOW THE LORD, AND I WILL NOT LET YOU GO!
THE GOD OF THE HEBREWS HAS REVEALED HIMSELF TO US. ALLOW US TO TRAVEL THREE DAYS INTO THE DESERT TO OFFER SACRIFICES TO THE LORD, OUR GOD. IF WE DON'T DO SO, HE WILL KILL US WITH DISEASE OR WAR.
MOSES AND AARON, WHAT DO YOU MEAN BY MAKING THE PEOPLE NEGLECT THEIR WORK? GET THOSE SLAVES BACK TO WORK!
THE SLAVES DON'T HAVE ENOUGH WORK TO DO. THAT MUST BE WHY THEY KEEP ASKING ME TO LET THEM GO AND OFFER SACRIFICES TO THEIR GOD! MAKE THEM WORK HARDER SO THEY WON'T HAVE TIME TO LISTEN TO THESE LIES!
STOP GIVING THE PEOPLE STRAW FOR MAKING BRICKS. MAKE THEM FIND THE STRAW THEMSELVES, BUT THEY MUST MAKE THE SAME NUMBER OF BRICKS AS BEFORE. NOT ONE BRICK LESS!
GET BACK TO WORK! YOU MUST GET YOUR OWN STRAW, BUT STILL MAKE AS MANY BRICKS AS BEFORE!

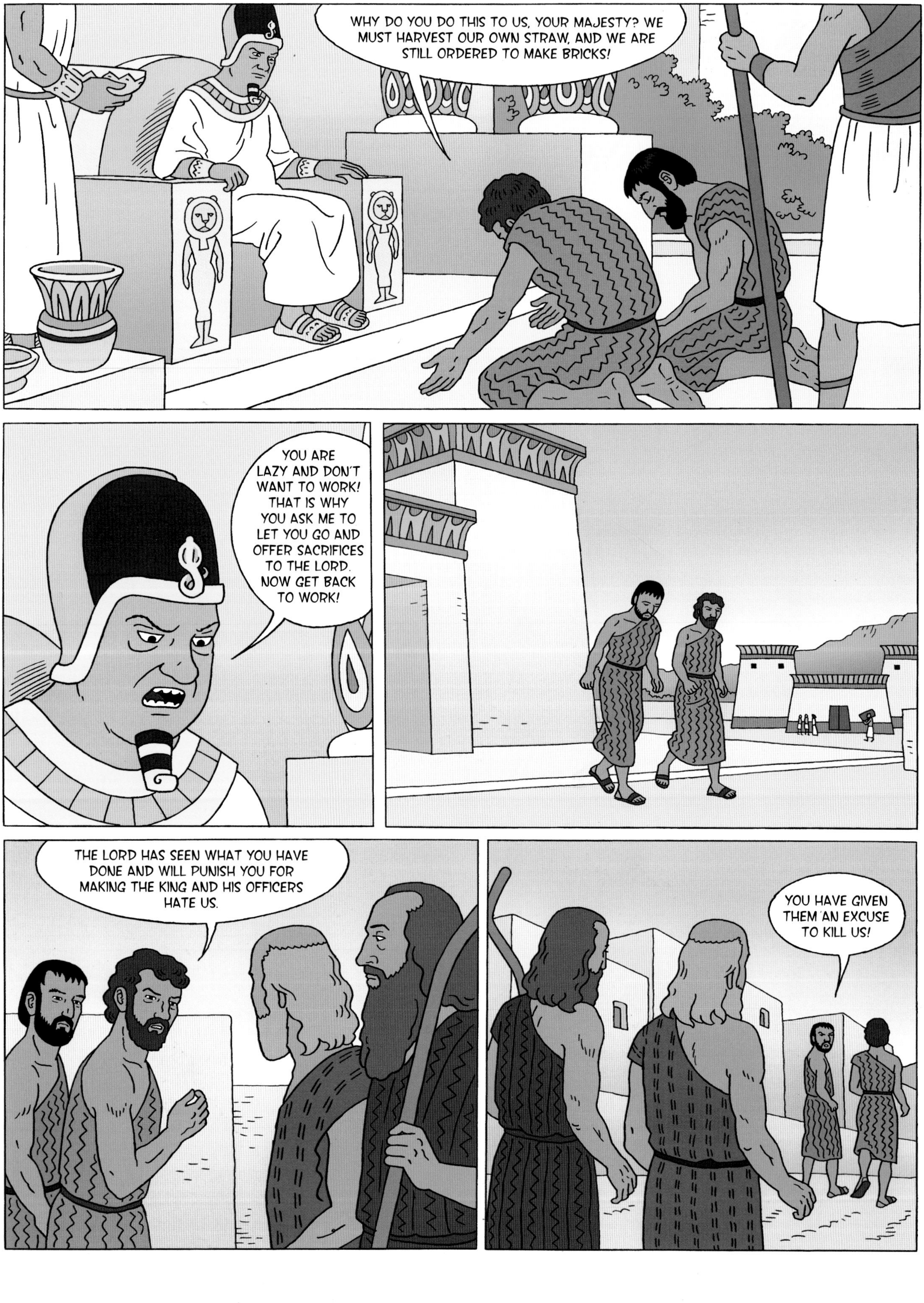
WHY DO YOU DO THIS TO US, YOUR MAJESTY? WE MUST HARVEST OUR OWN STRAW, AND WE ARE STILL ORDERED TO MAKE BRICKS!
YOU ARE LAZY AND DON'T WANT TO WORK! THAT IS WHY YOU ASK ME TO LET YOU GO AND OFFER SACRIFICES TO THE LORD. NOW GET BACK TO WORK!
THE LORD HAS SEEN WHAT YOU HAVE DONE AND WILL PUNISH YOU FOR MAKING THE KING AND HIS OFFICERS HATE US.
YOU HAVE GIVEN THEM AN EXCUSE TO KILL US!

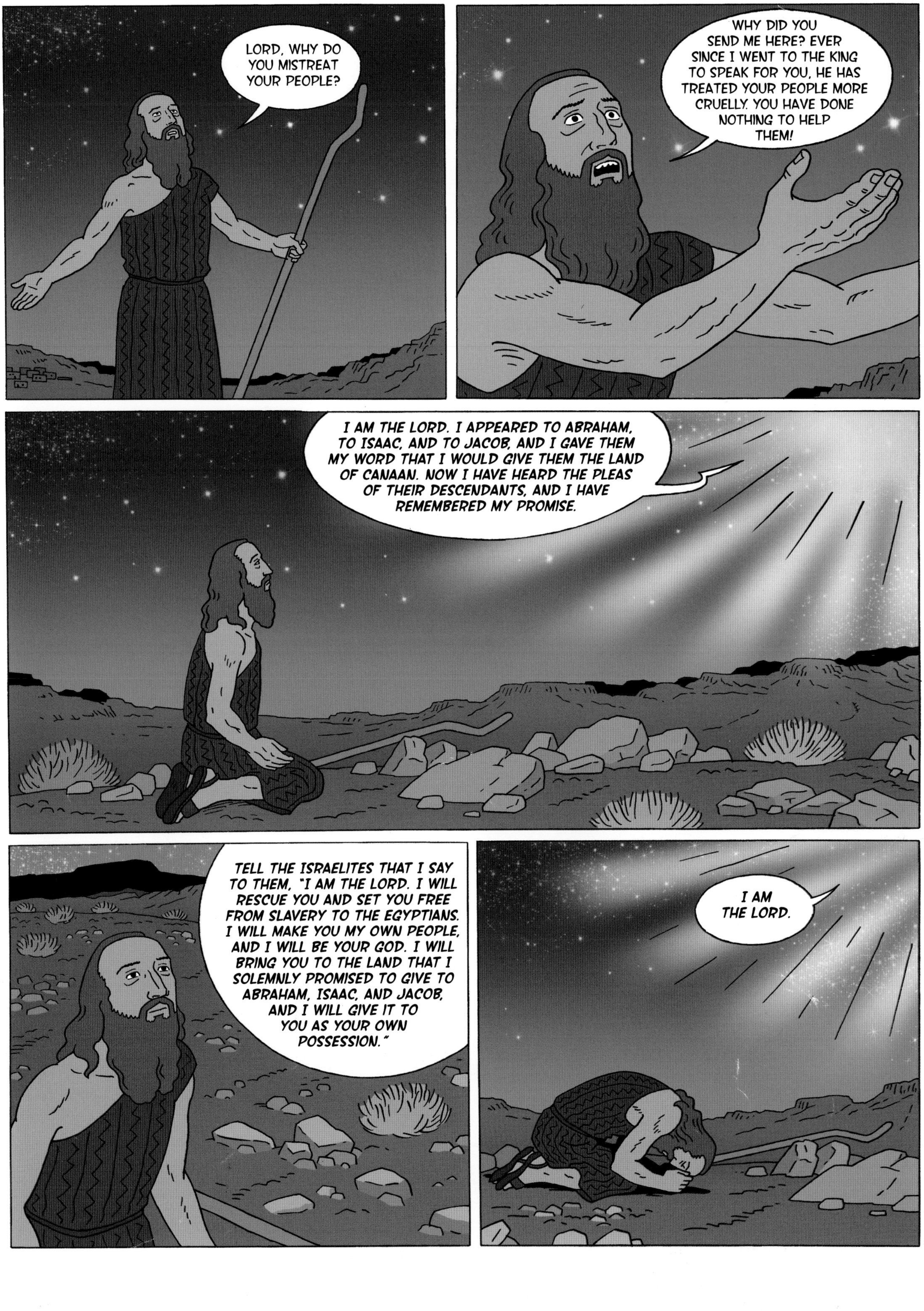
LORD, WHY DO YOU MISTREAT YOUR PEOPLE?
WHY DID YOU SEND ME HERE? EVER SINCE I WENT TO THE KING TO SPEAK FOR YOU, HE HAS TREATED YOUR PEOPLE MORE CRUELLY. YOU HAVE DONE NOTHING TO HELP THEM!
I AM THE LORD. I APPEARED TO ABRAHAM, TO ISAAC, AND TO JACOB, AND I GAVE THEM MY WORD THAT I WOULD GIVE THEM THE LAND OF CANAAN. NOW I HAVE HEARD THE PLEAS OF THEIR DESCENDANTS, AND I HAVE REMEMBERED MY PROMISE.
TELL THE ISRAELITES THAT I SAY TO THEM, "I AM THE LORD. I WILL RESCUE YOU AND SET YOU FREE FROM SLAVERY TO THE EGYPTIANS. I WILL MAKE YOU MY OWN PEOPLE, AND I WILL BE YOUR GOD. I WILL BRING YOU TO THE LAND THAT I SOLEMNLY PROMISED TO GIVE TO ABRAHAM, ISAAC, AND JACOB, AND I WILL GIVE IT TO YOU AS YOUR OWN POSSESSION."
I AM THE LORD.

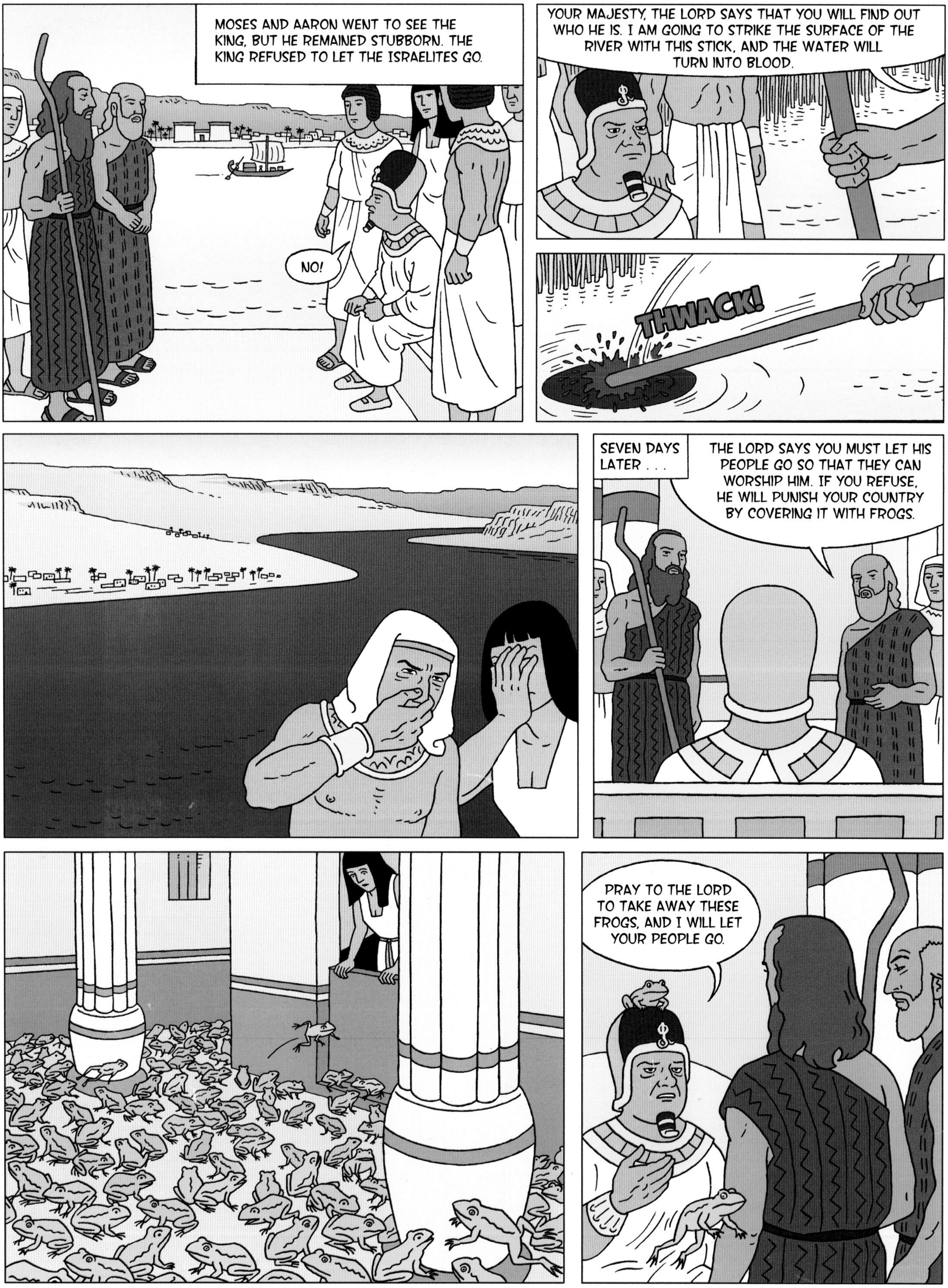
MOSES AND AARON WENT TO SEE THE KING, BUT HE REMAINED STUBBORN. THE KING REFUSED TO LET THE ISRAELITES GO.
NO!
YOUR MAJESTY, THE LORD SAYS THAT YOU WILL FIND OUT WHO HE IS. I AM GOING TO STRIKE THE SURFACE OF THE RIVER WITH THIS STICK, AND THE WATER WILL TURN INTO BLOOD.
THWACK!
SEVEN DAYS LATER . . .
THE LORD SAYS YOU MUST LET HIS PEOPLE GO SO THAT THEY CAN WORSHIP HIM. IF YOU REFUSE, HE WILL PUNISH YOUR COUNTRY BY COVERING IT WITH FROGS.
PRAY TO THE LORD TO TAKE AWAY THESE FROGS, AND I WILL LET YOUR PEOPLE GO.

I CHANGED MY MIND. I WON'T LET YOUR PEOPLE GO AFTER ALL.

SO GNATS COVERED THE PEOPLE AND THE ANIMALS.

WILL YOU LET OUR PEOPLE GO?

NO!

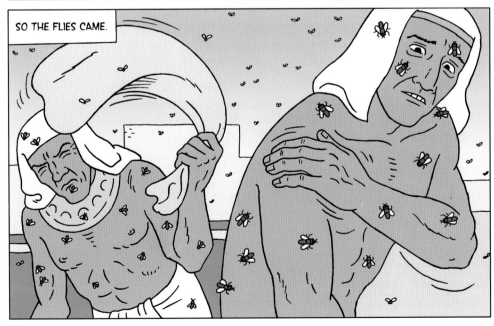

SO THE FLIES CAME.

WILL YOU LET OUR PEOPLE GO?

NO!

WITH EACH REFUSAL OF THE KING, A NEW PLAGUE CAME.

THE ANIMALS DIED!

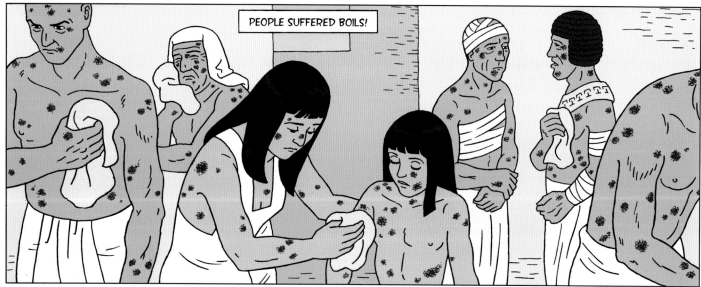

PEOPLE SUFFERED BOILS!

HAIL LASHED THE LAND!

LOCUSTS DESTROYED CROPS!

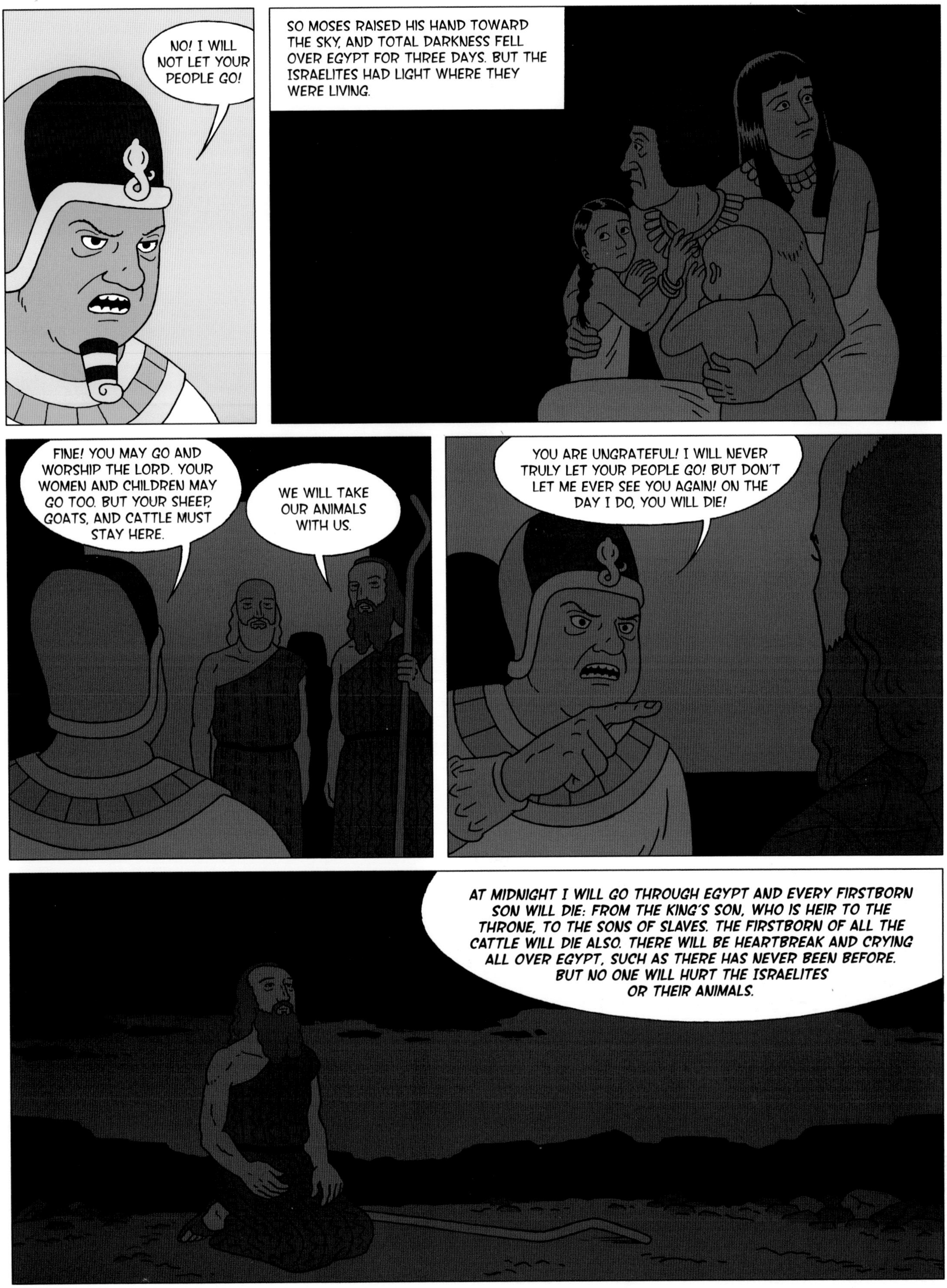
NO! I WILL NOT LET YOUR PEOPLE GO!
SO MOSES RAISED HIS HAND TOWARD THE SKY, AND TOTAL DARKNESS FELL OVER EGYPT FOR THREE DAYS. BUT THE ISRAELITES HAD LIGHT WHERE THEY WERE LIVING.
FINE! YOU MAY GO AND WORSHIP THE LORD. YOUR WOMEN AND CHILDREN MAY GO TOO. BUT YOUR SHEEP, GOATS, AND CATTLE MUST STAY HERE.
WE WILL TAKE OUR ANIMALS WITH US.
YOU ARE UNGRATEFUL! I WILL NEVER TRULY LET YOUR PEOPLE GO! BUT DON'T LET ME EVER SEE YOU AGAIN! ON THE DAY I DO, YOU WILL DIE!
AT MIDNIGHT I WILL GO THROUGH EGYPT AND EVERY FIRSTBORN SON WILL DIE: FROM THE KING'S SON, WHO IS HEIR TO THE THRONE, TO THE SONS OF SLAVES. THE FIRSTBORN OF ALL THE CATTLE WILL DIE ALSO. THERE WILL BE HEARTBREAK AND CRYING ALL OVER EGYPT, SUCH AS THERE HAS NEVER BEEN BEFORE. BUT NO ONE WILL HURT THE ISRAELITES OR THEIR ANIMALS.

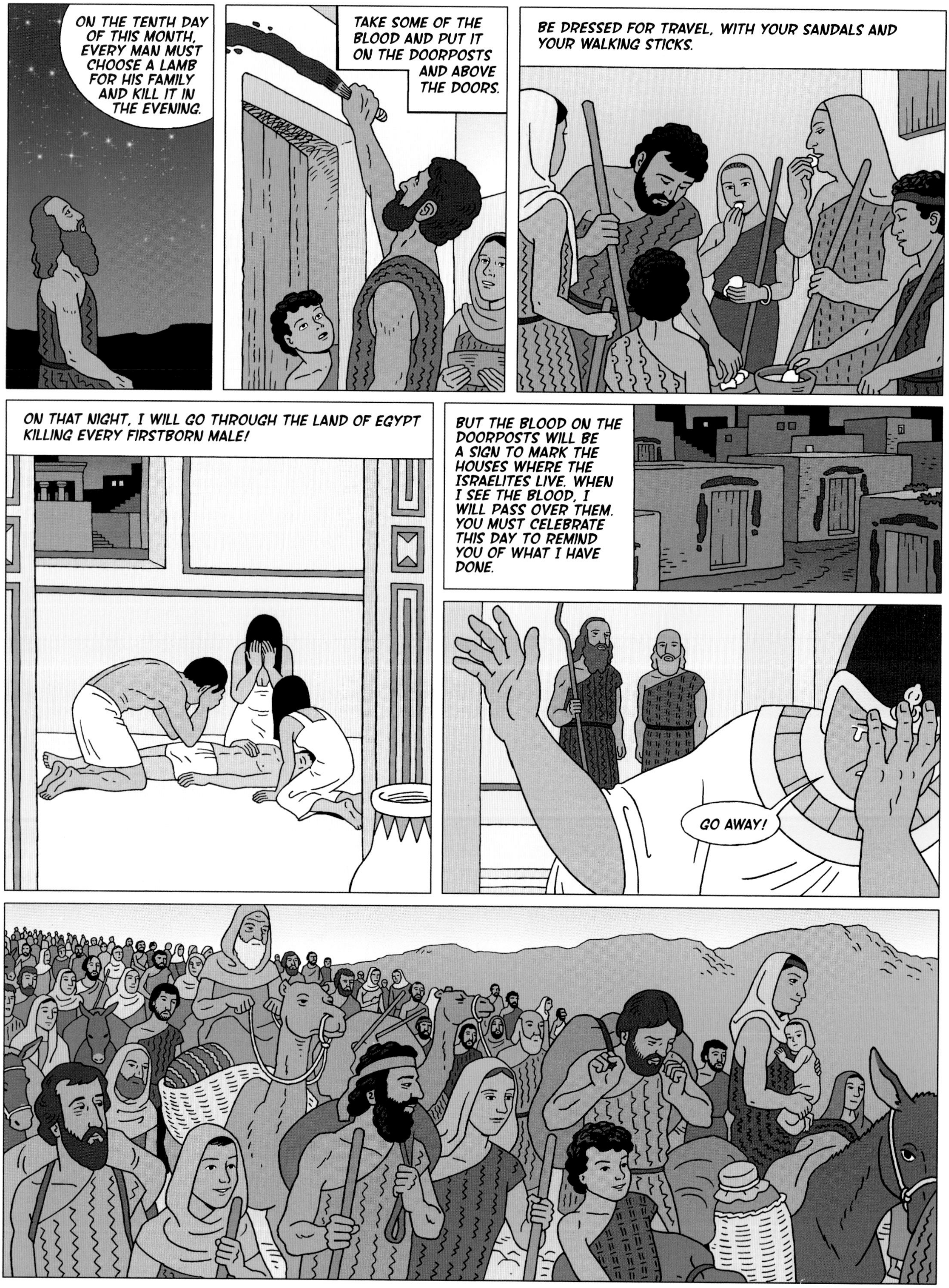
ON THE TENTH DAY OF THIS MONTH, EVERY MAN MUST CHOOSE A LAMB FOR HIS FAMILY AND KILL IT IN THE EVENING.
TAKE SOME OF THE BLOOD AND PUT IT ON THE DOORPOSTS AND ABOVE THE DOORS.
BE DRESSED FOR TRAVEL, WITH YOUR SANDALS AND YOUR WALKING STICKS.
ON THAT NIGHT, I WILL GO THROUGH THE LAND OF EGYPT KILLING EVERY FIRSTBORN MALE!
BUT THE BLOOD ON THE DOORPOSTS WILL BE A SIGN TO MARK THE HOUSES WHERE THE ISRAELITES LIVE. WHEN I SEE THE BLOOD, I WILL PASS OVER THEM. YOU MUST CELEBRATE THIS DAY TO REMIND YOU OF WHAT I HAVE DONE.
GO AWAY!

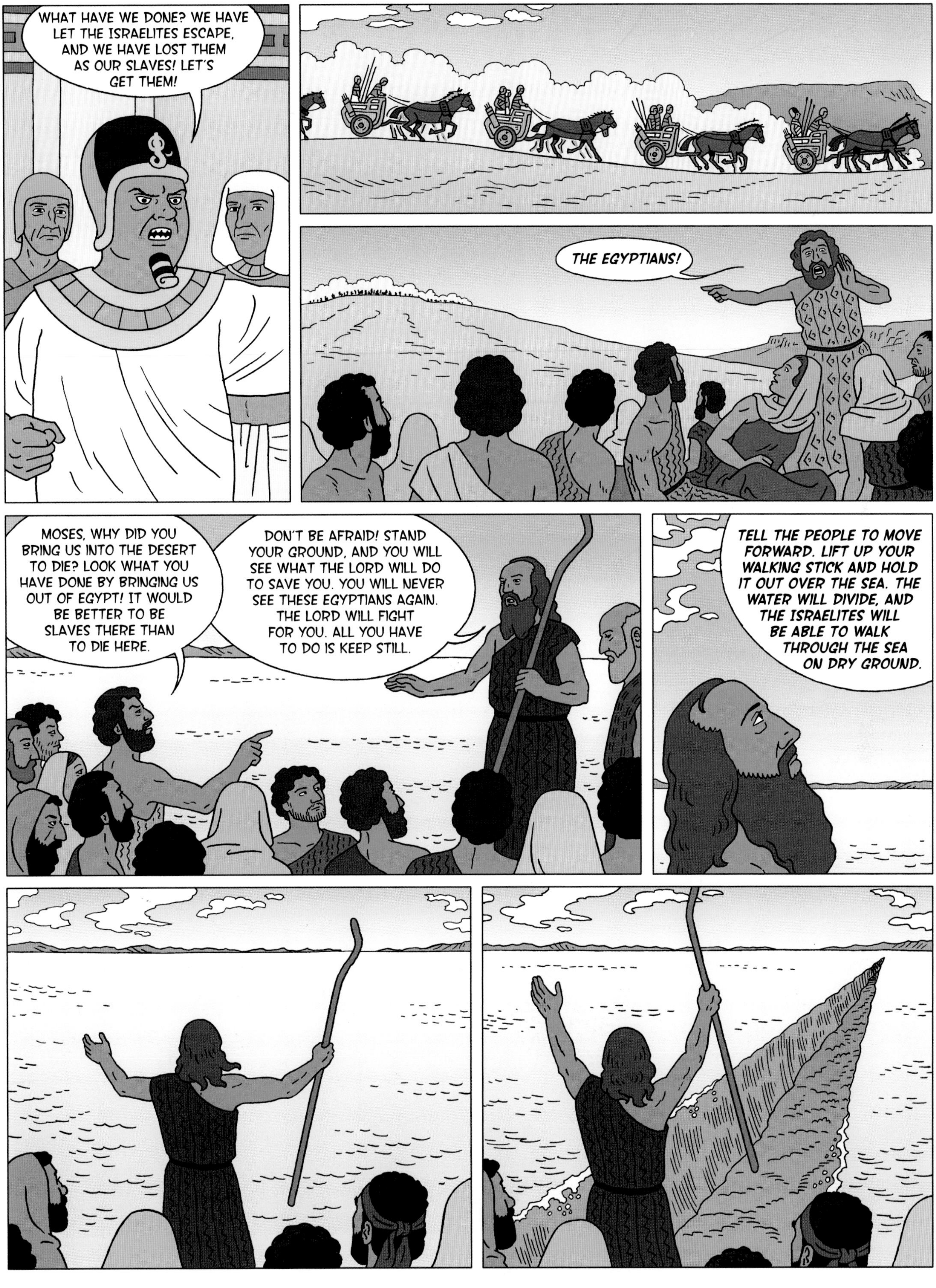
WHAT HAVE WE DONE? WE HAVE LET THE ISRAELITES ESCAPE, AND WE HAVE LOST THEM AS OUR SLAVES! LET'S GET THEM!
THE EGYPTIANS!
MOSES, WHY DID YOU BRING US INTO THE DESERT TO DIE? LOOK WHAT YOU HAVE DONE BY BRINGING US OUT OF EGYPT! IT WOULD BE BETTER TO BE SLAVES THERE THAN TO DIE HERE.
DON'T BE AFRAID! STAND YOUR GROUND, AND YOU WILL SEE WHAT THE LORD WILL DO TO SAVE YOU. YOU WILL NEVER SEE THESE EGYPTIANS AGAIN. THE LORD WILL FIGHT FOR YOU. ALL YOU HAVE TO DO IS KEEP STILL.
TELL THE PEOPLE TO MOVE FORWARD. LIFT UP YOUR WALKING STICK AND HOLD IT OUT OVER THE SEA. THE WATER WILL DIVIDE, AND THE ISRAELITES WILL BE ABLE TO WALK THROUGH THE SEA ON DRY GROUND.

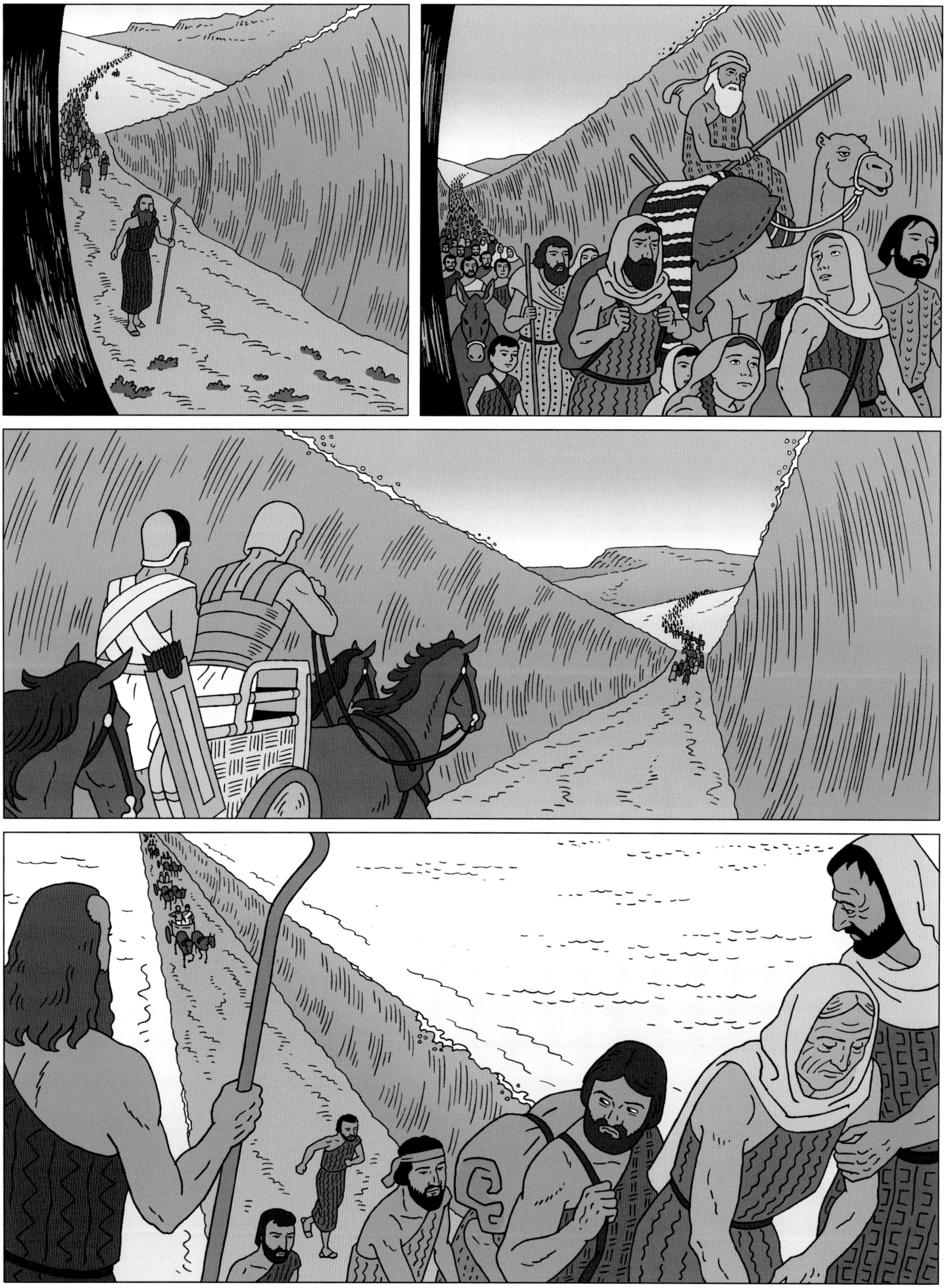

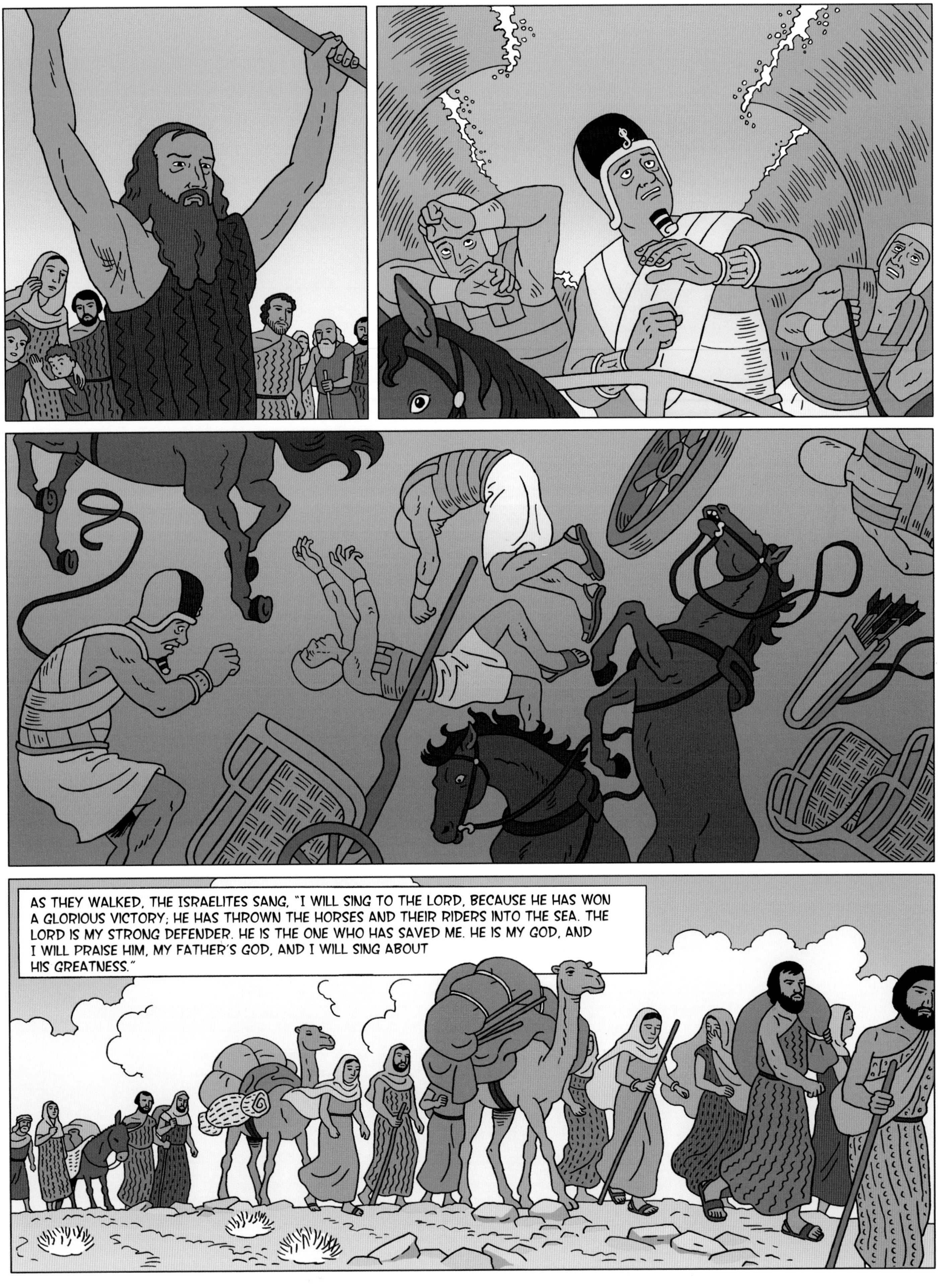
AS THEY WALKED, THE ISRAELITES SANG, "I WILL SING TO THE LORD, BECAUSE HE HAS WON A GLORIOUS VICTORY; HE HAS THROWN THE HORSES AND THEIR RIDERS INTO THE SEA. THE LORD IS MY STRONG DEFENDER. HE IS THE ONE WHO HAS SAVED ME. HE IS MY GOD, AND I WILL PRAISE HIM, MY FATHER'S GOD, AND I WILL SING ABOUT HIS GREATNESS."

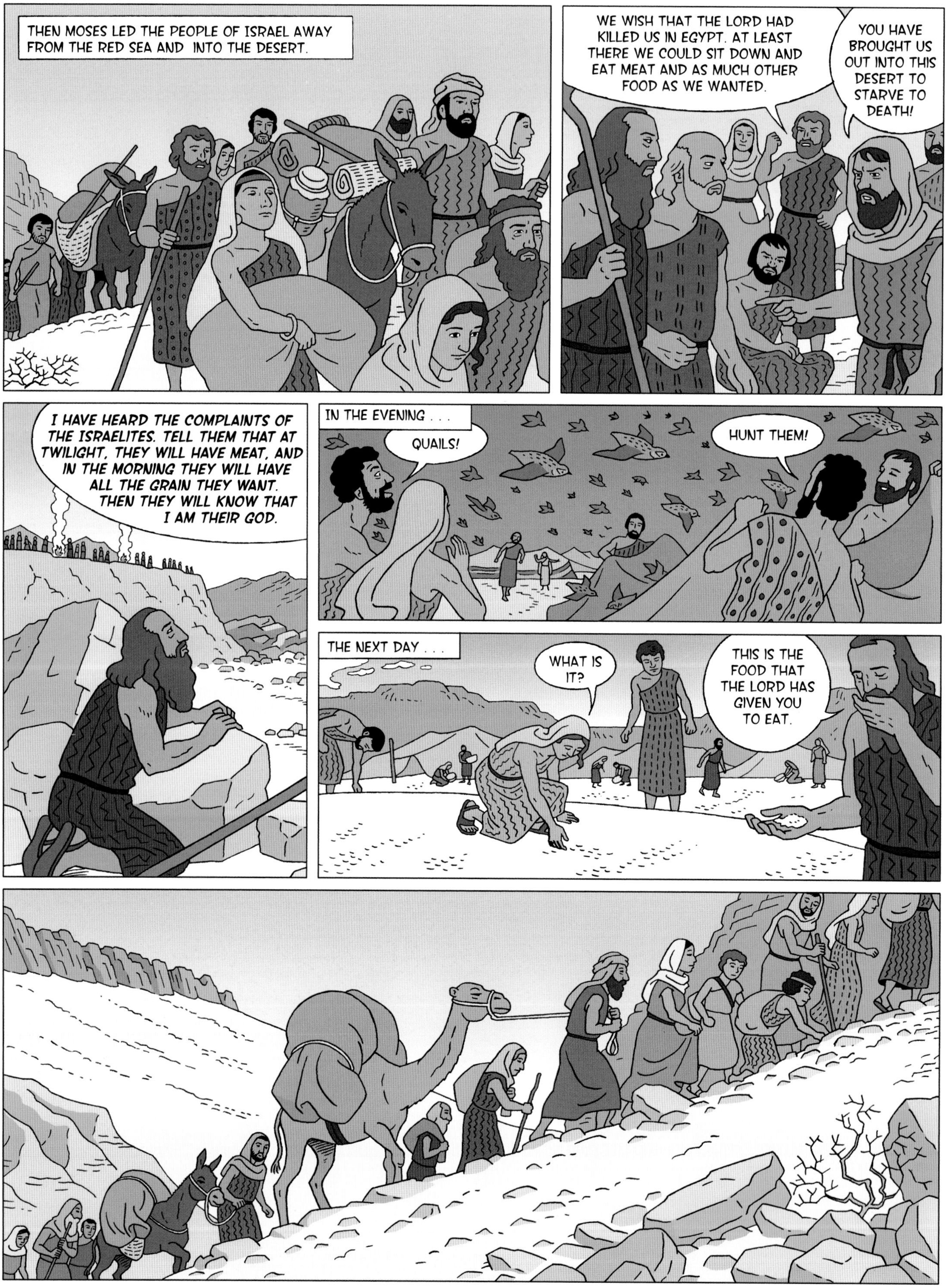

THEN MOSES LED THE PEOPLE OF ISRAEL AWAY FROM THE RED SEA AND INTO THE DESERT.
WE WISH THAT THE LORD HAD KILLED US IN EGYPT. AT LEAST THERE WE COULD SIT DOWN AND EAT MEAT AND AS MUCH OTHER FOOD AS WE WANTED.
YOU HAVE BROUGHT US OUT INTO THIS DESERT TO STARVE TO DEATH!
I HAVE HEARD THE COMPLAINTS OF THE ISRAELITES. TELL THEM THAT AT TWILIGHT, THEY WILL HAVE MEAT, AND IN THE MORNING THEY WILL HAVE ALL THE GRAIN THEY WANT. THEN THEY WILL KNOW THAT I AM THEIR GOD.
IN THE EVENING . . .
QUAILS!
HUNT THEM!
THE NEXT DAY . . .
WHAT IS IT?
THIS IS THE FOOD THAT THE LORD HAS GIVEN YOU TO EAT.

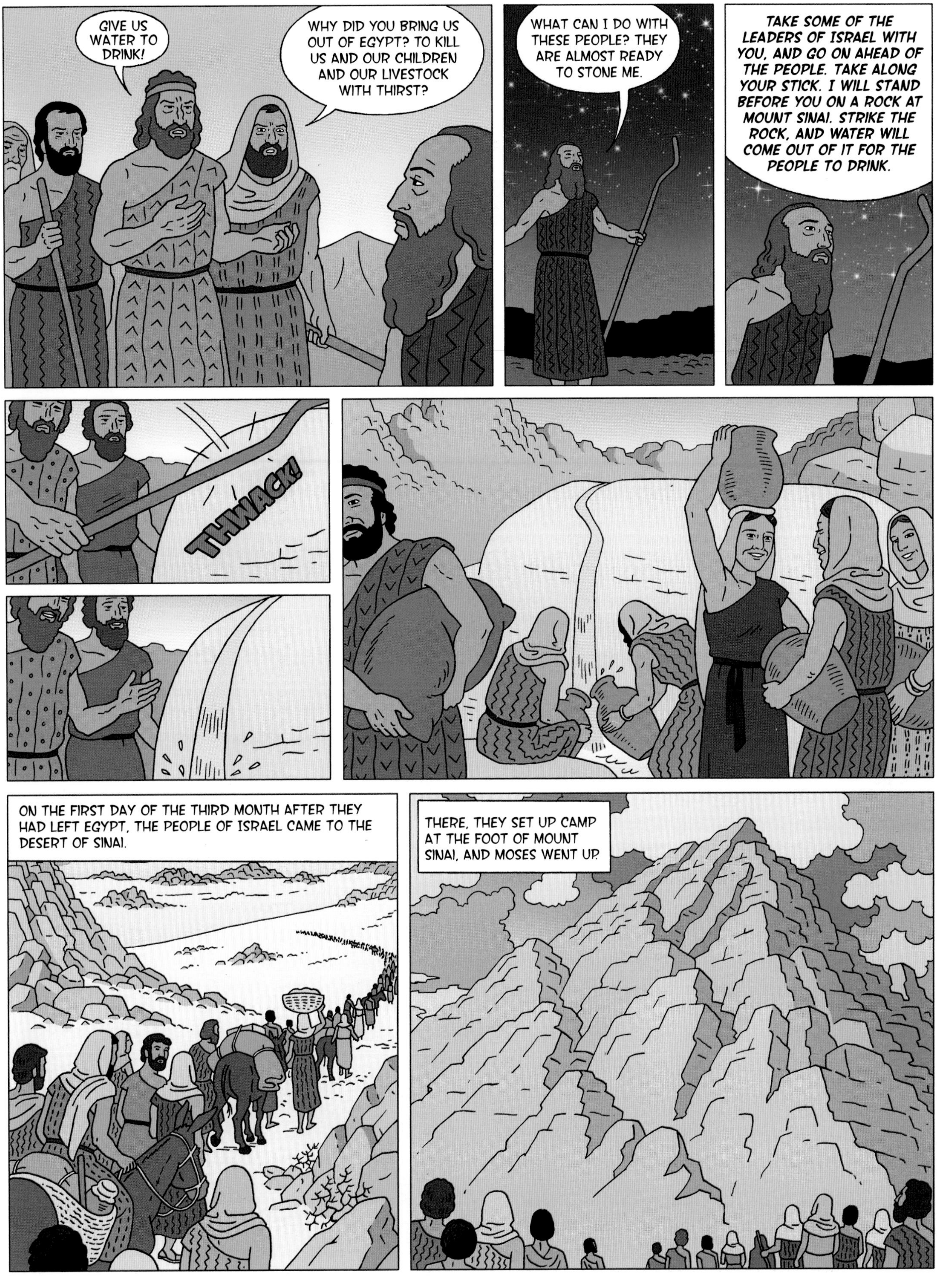
GIVE US WATER TO DRINK!
WHY DID YOU BRING US OUT OF EGYPT? TO KILL US AND OUR CHILDREN AND OUR LIVESTOCK WITH THIRST?
WHAT CAN I DO WITH THESE PEOPLE? THEY ARE ALMOST READY TO STONE ME.
TAKE SOME OF THE LEADERS OF ISRAEL WITH YOU, AND GO ON AHEAD OF THE PEOPLE. TAKE ALONG YOUR STICK. I WILL STAND BEFORE YOU ON A ROCK AT MOUNT SINAI. STRIKE THE ROCK, AND WATER WILL COME OUT OF IT FOR THE PEOPLE TO DRINK.
THWACK!
ON THE FIRST DAY OF THE THIRD MONTH AFTER THEY HAD LEFT EGYPT, THE PEOPLE OF ISRAEL CAME TO THE DESERT OF SINAI.
THERE, THEY SET UP CAMP AT THE FOOT OF MOUNT SINAI, AND MOSES WENT UP.

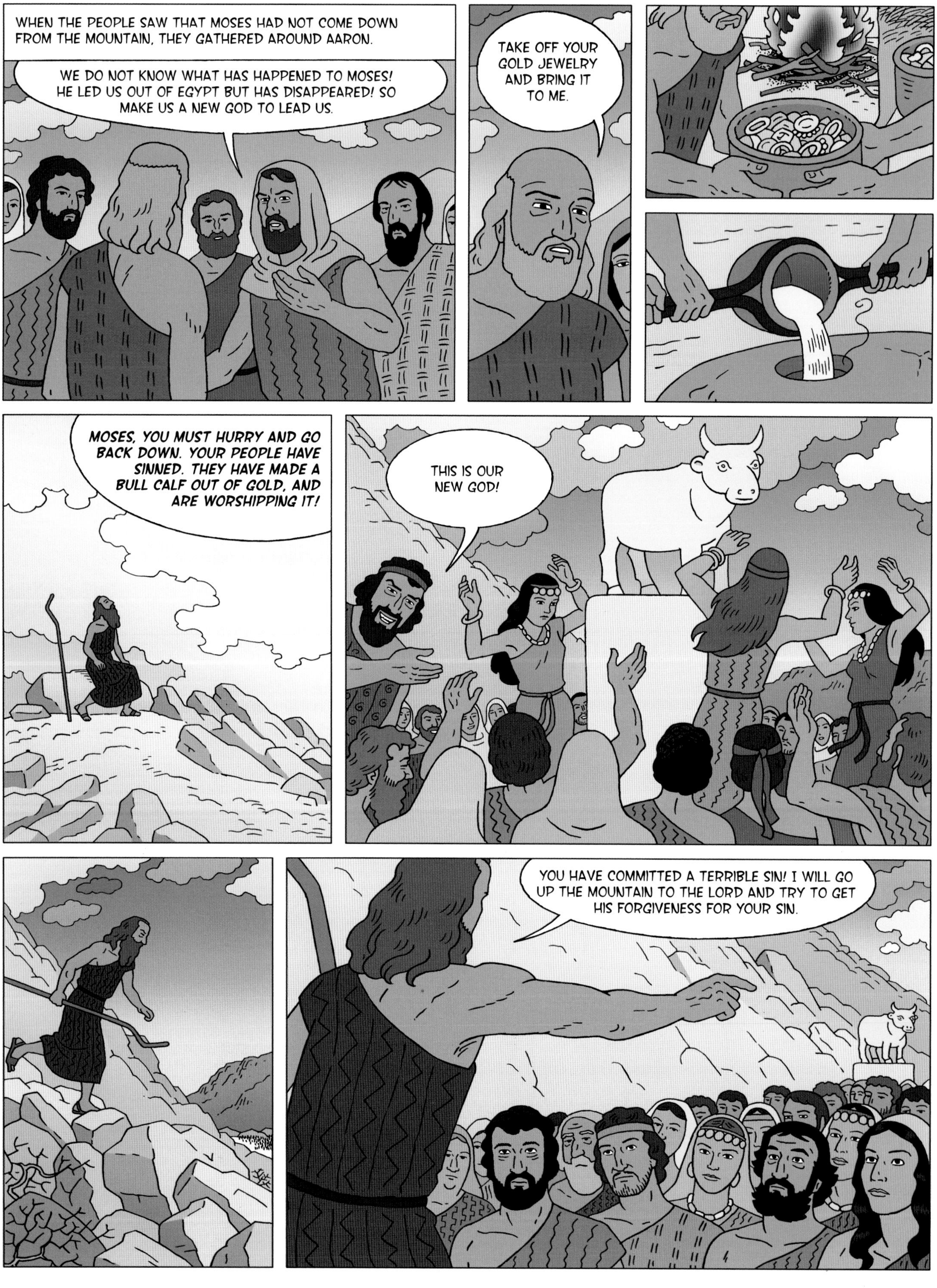
WHEN THE PEOPLE SAW THAT MOSES HAD NOT COME DOWN FROM THE MOUNTAIN, THEY GATHERED AROUND AARON.
WE DO NOT KNOW WHAT HAS HAPPENED TO MOSES! HE LED US OUT OF EGYPT BUT HAS DISAPPEARED! SO MAKE US A NEW GOD TO LEAD US.
TAKE OFF YOUR GOLD JEWELRY AND BRING IT TO ME.
MOSES, YOU MUST HURRY AND GO BACK DOWN. YOUR PEOPLE HAVE SINNED. THEY HAVE MADE A BULL CALF OUT OF GOLD, AND ARE WORSHIPPING IT!
THIS IS OUR NEW GOD!
YOU HAVE COMMITTED A TERRIBLE SIN! I WILL GO UP THE MOUNTAIN TO THE LORD AND TRY TO GET HIS FORGIVENESS FOR YOUR SIN.

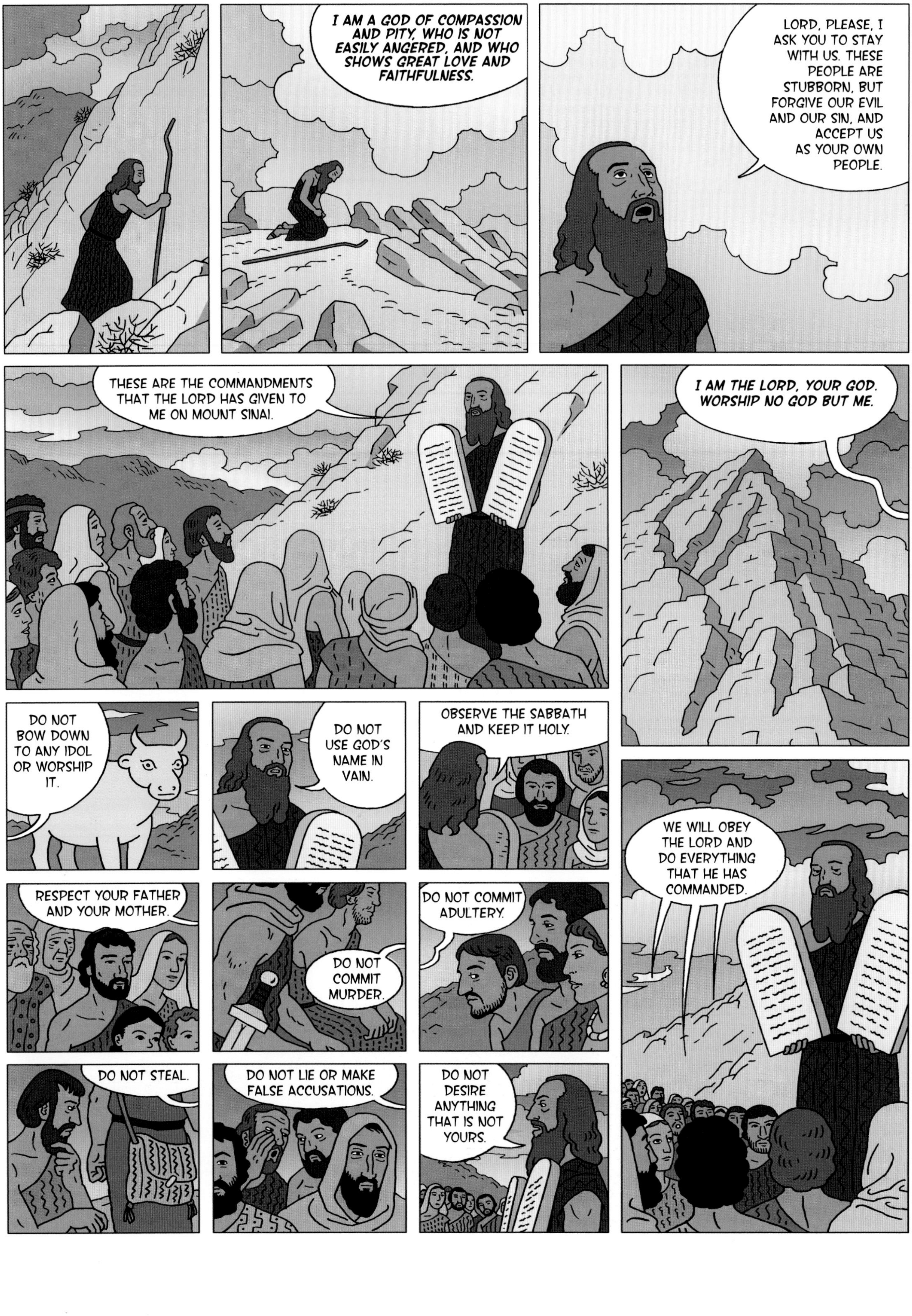
I AM A GOD OF COMPASSION AND PITY, WHO IS NOT EASILY ANGERED, AND WHO SHOWS GREAT LOVE AND FAITHFULNESS.
LORD, PLEASE, I ASK YOU TO STAY WITH US. THESE PEOPLE ARE STUBBORN, BUT FORGIVE OUR EVIL AND OUR SIN, AND ACCEPT US AS YOUR OWN PEOPLE.
THESE ARE THE COMMANDMENTS THAT THE LORD HAS GIVEN TO ME ON MOUNT SINAI.
I AM THE LORD, YOUR GOD. WORSHIP NO GOD BUT ME.
DO NOT BOW DOWN TO ANY IDOL OR WORSHIP IT.
DO NOT USE GOD'S NAME IN VAIN.
OBSERVE THE SABBATH AND KEEP IT HOLY.
RESPECT YOUR FATHER AND YOUR MOTHER.
DO NOT COMMIT MURDER.
DO NOT COMMIT ADULTERY.
DO NOT STEAL.
DO NOT LIE OR MAKE FALSE ACCUSATIONS.
DO NOT DESIRE ANYTHING THAT IS NOT YOURS.
WE WILL OBEY THE LORD AND DO EVERYTHING THAT HE HAS COMMANDED.

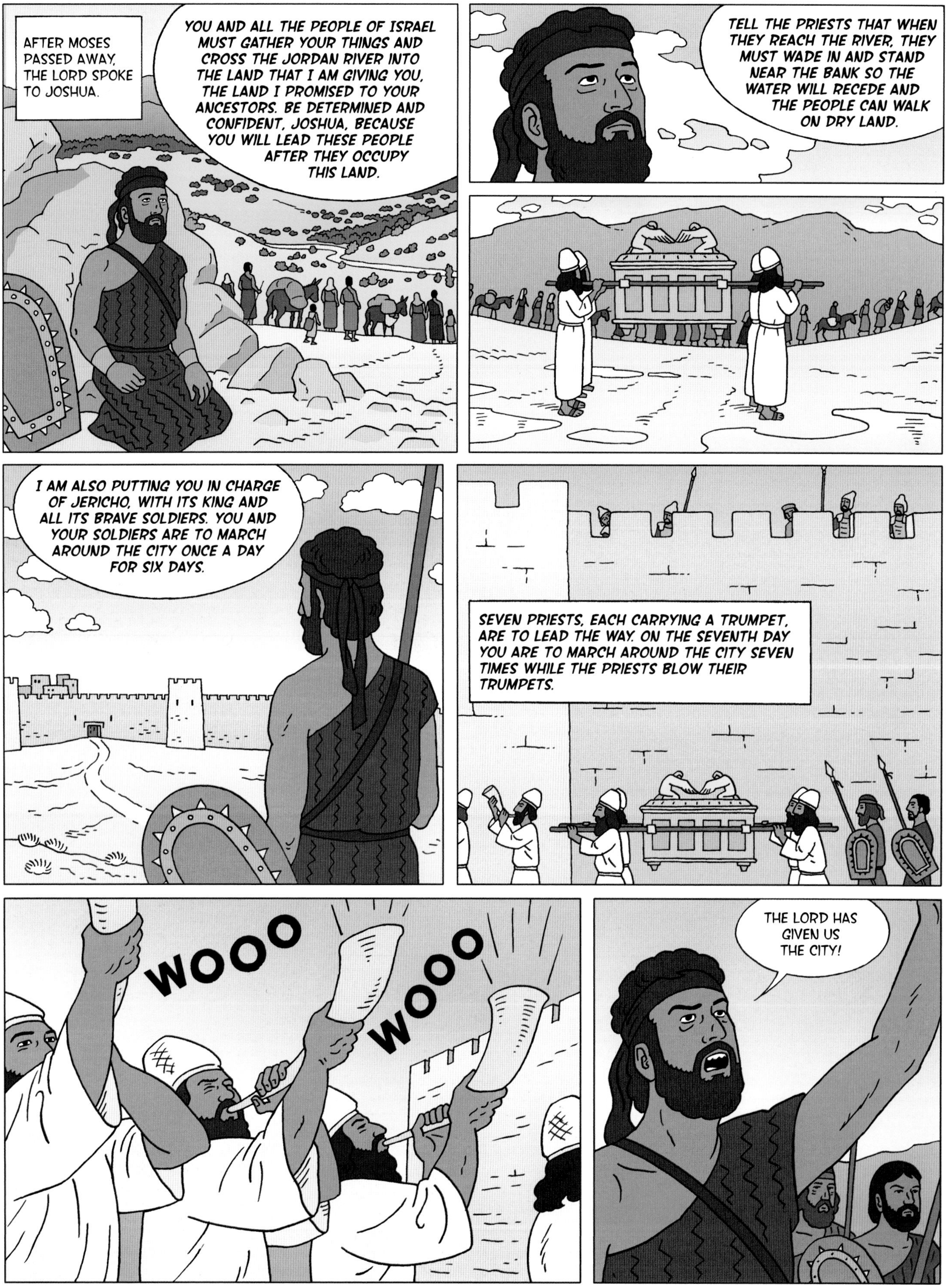
AFTER MOSES PASSED AWAY, THE LORD SPOKE TO JOSHUA.
YOU AND ALL THE PEOPLE OF ISRAEL MUST GATHER YOUR THINGS AND CROSS THE JORDAN RIVER INTO THE LAND THAT I AM GIVING YOU, THE LAND I PROMISED TO YOUR ANCESTORS. BE DETERMINED AND CONFIDENT, JOSHUA, BECAUSE YOU WILL LEAD THESE PEOPLE AFTER THEY OCCUPY THIS LAND.
TELL THE PRIESTS THAT WHEN THEY REACH THE RIVER, THEY MUST WADE IN AND STAND NEAR THE BANK SO THE WATER WILL RECEDE AND THE PEOPLE CAN WALK ON DRY LAND.
I AM ALSO PUTTING YOU IN CHARGE OF JERICHO, WITH ITS KING AND ALL ITS BRAVE SOLDIERS. YOU AND YOUR SOLDIERS ARE TO MARCH AROUND THE CITY ONCE A DAY FOR SIX DAYS.
SEVEN PRIESTS, EACH CARRYING A TRUMPET, ARE TO LEAD THE WAY. ON THE SEVENTH DAY YOU ARE TO MARCH AROUND THE CITY SEVEN TIMES WHILE THE PRIESTS BLOW THEIR TRUMPETS.
WOOO
WOOO
THE LORD HAS GIVEN US THE CITY!

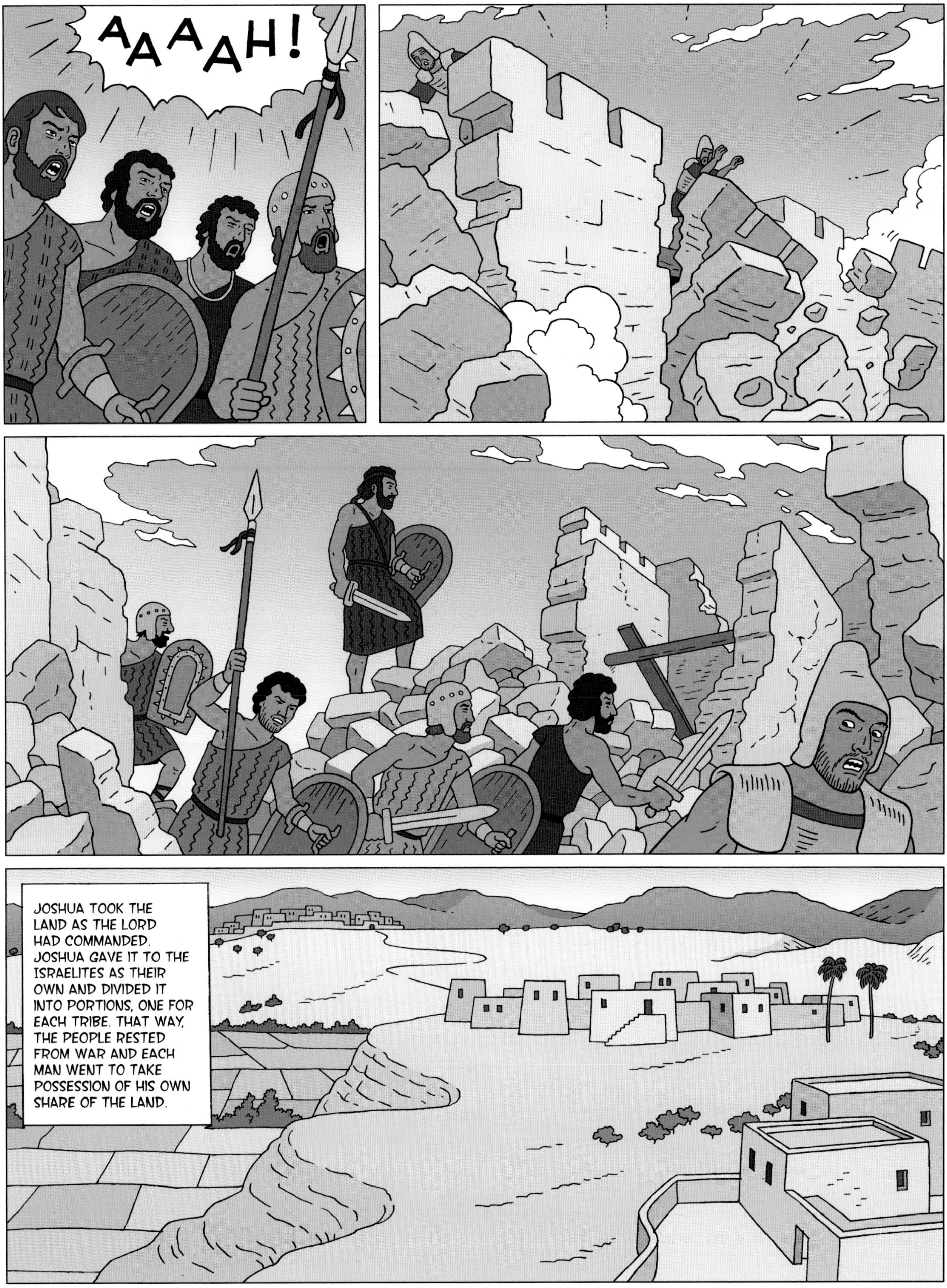
AAAAH!
JOSHUA TOOK THE LAND AS THE LORD HAD COMMANDED. JOSHUA GAVE IT TO THE ISRAELITES AS THEIR OWN AND DIVIDED IT INTO PORTIONS, ONE FOR EACH TRIBE. THAT WAY, THE PEOPLE RESTED FROM WAR AND EACH MAN WENT TO TAKE POSSESSION OF HIS OWN SHARE OF THE LAND.

BUT THE ISRAELITES SINNED AGAINST THE LORD AGAIN, SO HE LET THE PHILISTINES RULE THEM FOR FORTY YEARS.

YOU HAVE NEVER BEEN ABLE TO HAVE CHILDREN, BUT YOU WILL SOON BE PREGNANT AND HAVE A SON. YOU WILL NAME HIM SAMSON. YOU MUST NEVER CUT HIS HAIR. FROM THE DAY OF HIS BIRTH, HE WILL BE DEDICATED TO GOD. HE WILL BEGIN THE WORK OF RESCUING ISRAEL FROM THE PHILISTINES.

WHEN SAMSON GOT OLDER, HE FACED THE PHILISTINES. HE CAUGHT THREE HUNDRED FOXES, TIED THEIR TAILS TOGETHER, AND PUT TORCHES IN THE KNOTS. THEN HE SET FIRE TO THE TORCHES AND TURNED THE FOXES LOOSE IN THE PHILISTINES' FIELDS. THEY BURNED UP NOT ONLY THE WHEAT THAT HAD BEEN HARVESTED BUT ALSO THE WHEAT THAT WAS STILL IN THE FIELDS.

THEN HE FOUND A JAWBONE FROM A DONKEY THAT HAD RECENTLY DIED. HE PICKED IT UP, AND KILLED A THOUSAND PHILISTINE MEN WITH IT.

DELILAH, SAMSON IS IN LOVE WITH YOU. TRICK HIM INTO TELLING YOU WHY HE IS SO STRONG. THEN WE CAN OVERPOWER HIM AND MAKE HIM HELPLESS.

WHAT MAKES YOU SO STRONG?

MY HAIR HAS NEVER BEEN CUT. I HAVE BEEN DEDICATED TO GOD FROM THE TIME I WAS BORN. IF MY HAIR WERE CUT, I WOULD LOSE ALL MY STRENGTH.

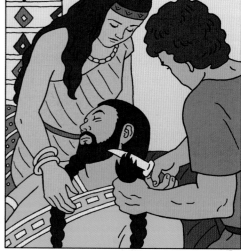

DELILAH LULLED SAMSON TO SLEEP AND THEN SUMMONED A MAN TO CUT OFF HIS SEVEN LOCKS OF HAIR.

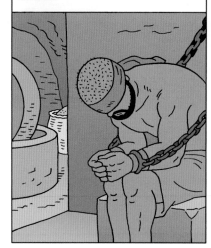

THAT WAS HOW SAMSON LOST HIS STRENGTH. THE PHILISTINES CAPTURED AND BLINDED HIM. THEN THEY CHAINED HIM UP WITH BRONZE CHAINS.

BUT HIS HAIR STARTED GROWING BACK AGAIN.

LET ME TOUCH THE COLUMNS THAT HOLD UP THE BUILDING. I WANT TO LEAN ON THEM.

SOVEREIGN LORD, PLEASE REMEMBER ME. PLEASE, GOD, GIVE ME MY STRENGTH JUST THIS ONE TIME MORE, SO THAT WITH THIS ONE BLOW I CAN PUNISH THE PHILISTINES FOR WHAT THEY HAVE DONE TO ME.

LET ME DIE WITH THESE PHILISTINES!

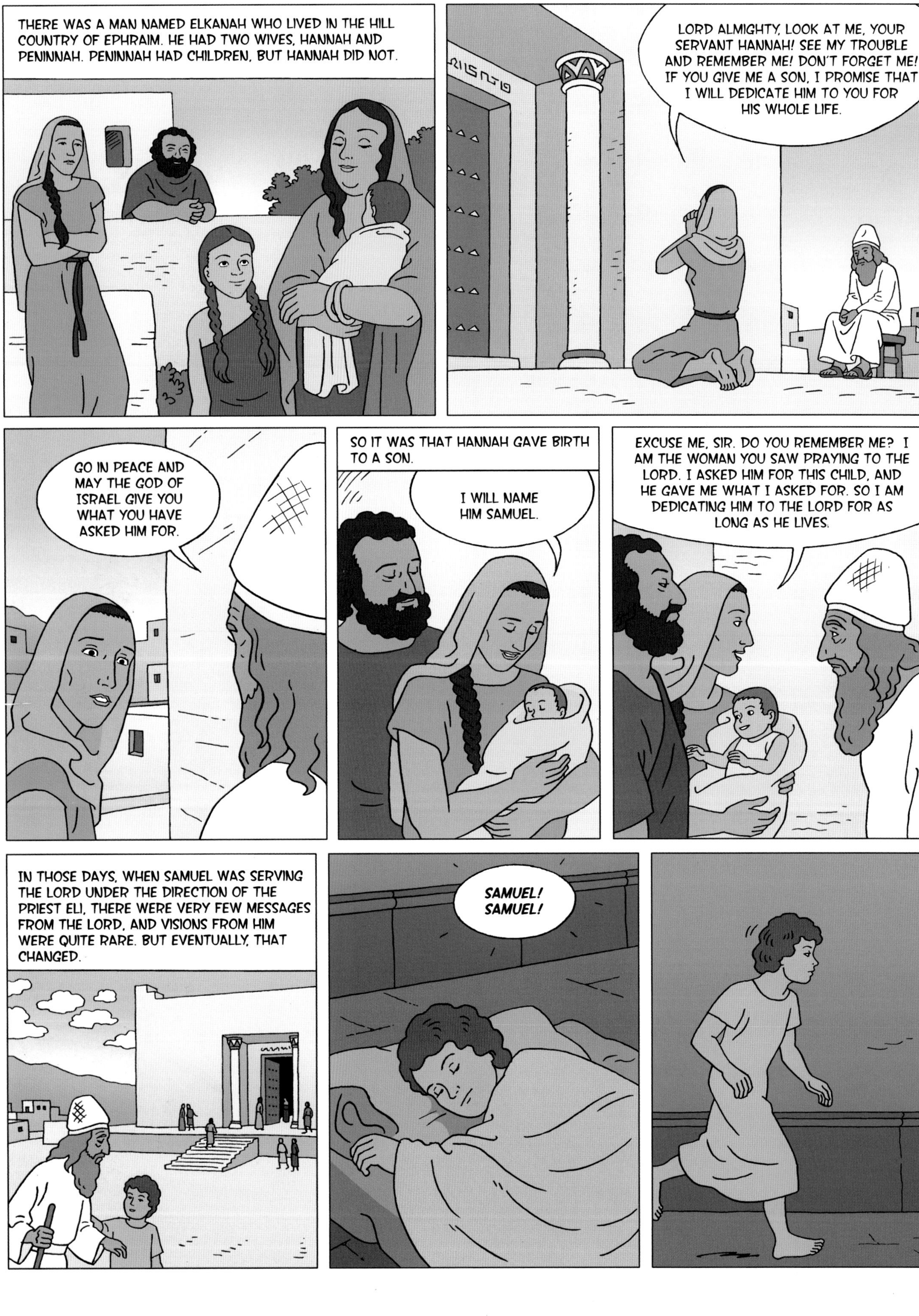
THERE WAS A MAN NAMED ELKANAH WHO LIVED IN THE HILL COUNTRY OF EPHRAIM. HE HAD TWO WIVES, HANNAH AND PENINNAH. PENINNAH HAD CHILDREN, BUT HANNAH DID NOT.
LORD ALMIGHTY, LOOK AT ME, YOUR SERVANT HANNAH! SEE MY TROUBLE AND REMEMBER ME! DON'T FORGET ME! IF YOU GIVE ME A SON, I PROMISE THAT I WILL DEDICATE HIM TO YOU FOR HIS WHOLE LIFE.
GO IN PEACE AND MAY THE GOD OF ISRAEL GIVE YOU WHAT YOU HAVE ASKED HIM FOR.
SO IT WAS THAT HANNAH GAVE BIRTH TO A SON.
I WILL NAME HIM SAMUEL.
EXCUSE ME, SIR. DO YOU REMEMBER ME? I AM THE WOMAN YOU SAW PRAYING TO THE LORD. I ASKED HIM FOR THIS CHILD, AND HE GAVE ME WHAT I ASKED FOR. SO I AM DEDICATING HIM TO THE LORD FOR AS LONG AS HE LIVES.
IN THOSE DAYS, WHEN SAMUEL WAS SERVING THE LORD UNDER THE DIRECTION OF THE PRIEST ELI, THERE WERE VERY FEW MESSAGES FROM THE LORD, AND VISIONS FROM HIM WERE QUITE RARE. BUT EVENTUALLY, THAT CHANGED.
SAMUEL! SAMUEL!

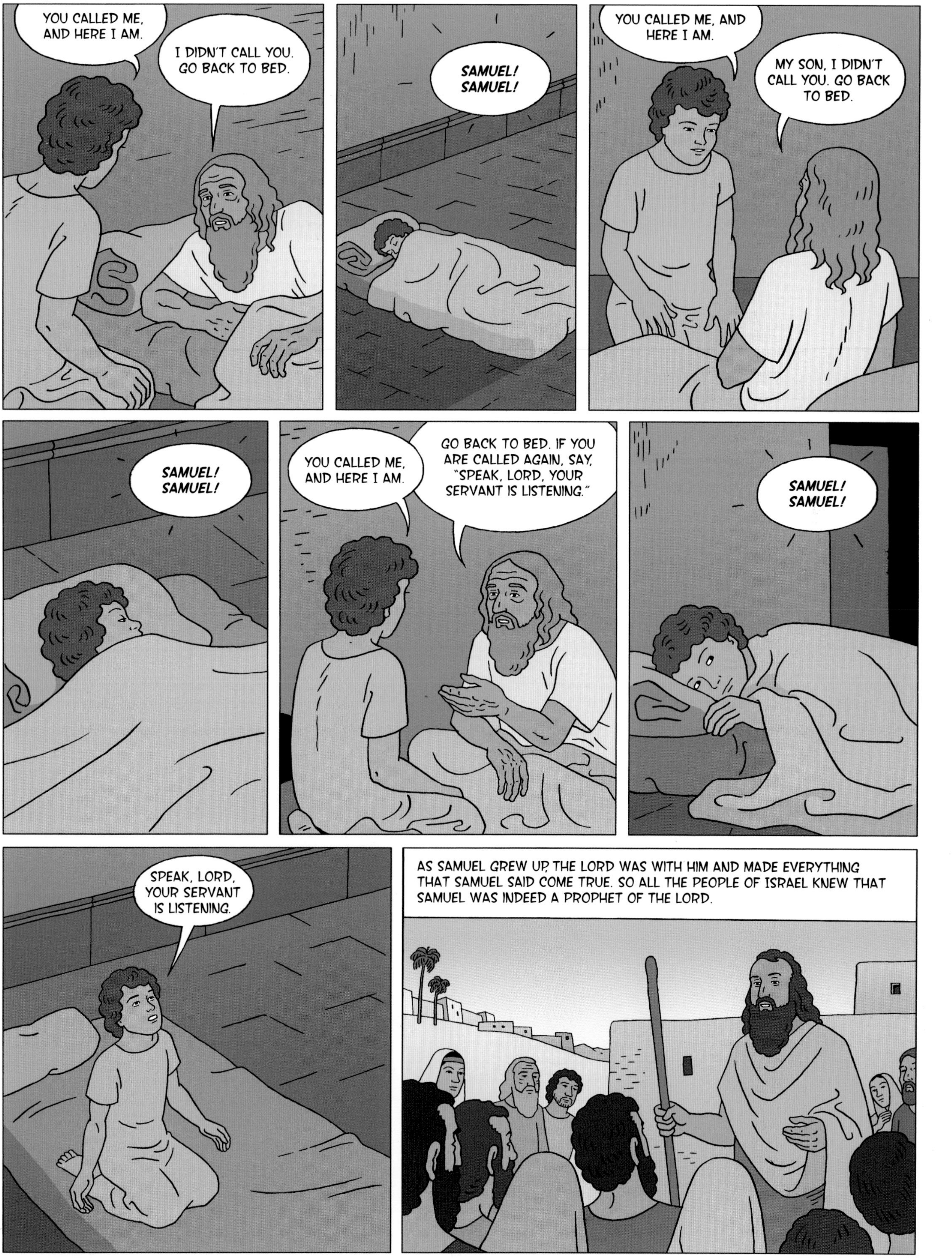
YOU CALLED ME, AND HERE I AM.
I DIDN'T CALL YOU. GO BACK TO BED.
SAMUEL! SAMUEL!
YOU CALLED ME, AND HERE I AM.
MY SON, I DIDN'T CALL YOU. GO BACK TO BED.
SAMUEL! SAMUEL!
YOU CALLED ME, AND HERE I AM.
GO BACK TO BED. IF YOU ARE CALLED AGAIN, SAY, "SPEAK, LORD, YOUR SERVANT IS LISTENING."
SAMUEL! SAMUEL!
SPEAK, LORD, YOUR SERVANT IS LISTENING.
AS SAMUEL GREW UP, THE LORD WAS WITH HIM AND MADE EVERYTHING THAT SAMUEL SAID COME TRUE. SO ALL THE PEOPLE OF ISRAEL KNEW THAT SAMUEL WAS INDEED A PROPHET OF THE LORD.

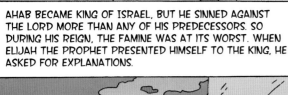

AHAB BECAME KING OF ISRAEL, BUT HE SINNED AGAINST THE LORD MORE THAN ANY OF HIS PREDECESSORS. SO DURING HIS REIGN, THE FAMINE WAS AT ITS WORST. WHEN ELIJAH THE PROPHET PRESENTED HIMSELF TO THE KING, HE ASKED FOR EXPLANATIONS.

THERE YOU ARE, THE WORST TROUBLEMAKER IN ISRAEL!

I'M NOT THE TROUBLEMAKER! YOU ARE! YOU ARE DISOBEYING THE LORD'S COMMANDS AND WORSHIPPING THE IDOLS OF BAAL.

TELL ALL THE PEOPLE OF ISRAEL TO MEET ME AT MOUNT CARMEL. BRING ALONG THE PROPHETS OF BAAL.

HOW MUCH LONGER WILL IT TAKE YOU TO MAKE UP YOUR MINDS? IF THE LORD IS GOD, WORSHIP HIM; BUT IF BAAL IS GOD, WORSHIP HIM!

BRING TWO BULLS; LET THE PROPHETS OF BAAL TAKE ONE, KILL IT, CUT IT IN PIECES, AND PUT IT ON THE WOOD, BUT DON'T LIGHT THE FIRE. I WILL DO THE SAME WITH THE OTHER BULL. THEN LET THE PROPHETS OF BAAL PRAY TO THEIR GOD, AND I WILL PRAY TO THE LORD. THE ONE WHO ANSWERS BY SENDING FIRE IS THE TRUE GOD.

ANSWER US, BAAL!

ANSWER US, BAAL!

ANSWER US, BAAL!

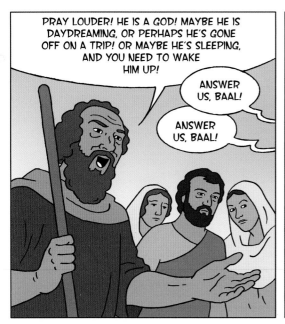

PRAY LOUDER! HE IS A GOD! MAYBE HE IS DAYDREAMING, OR PERHAPS HE'S GONE OFF ON A TRIP! OR MAYBE HE'S SLEEPING, AND YOU NEED TO WAKE HIM UP!

ANSWER US, BAAL!

ANSWER US, BAAL!

O LORD, THE GOD OF ABRAHAM, ISAAC, AND JACOB, PROVE NOW THAT YOU ARE THE GOD OF ISRAEL AND THAT I AM YOUR SERVANT AND HAVE DONE ALL THIS AT YOUR COMMAND.

ANSWER ME, LORD, SO PEOPLE WILL KNOW THAT YOU ARE GOD AND THAT YOU ARE BRINGING THEM BACK TO YOU.

THE LORD IS GOD!

THE LORD IS GOD!

JEREMIAH, GO DOWN TO THE POTTER'S HOUSE, WHERE I WILL GIVE YOU MY MESSAGE.

JEREMIAH WENT THERE AND SAW THE POTTER WORKING AT HIS WHEEL. WHENEVER A PIECE TURNED OUT IMPERFECTLY, THE POTTER TOOK THE CLAY AND MADE IT INTO SOMETHING ELSE.

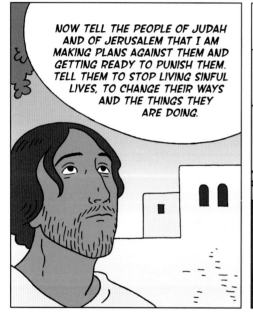

NOW TELL THE PEOPLE OF JUDAH AND OF JERUSALEM THAT I AM MAKING PLANS AGAINST THEM AND GETTING READY TO PUNISH THEM. TELL THEM TO STOP LIVING SINFUL LIVES, TO CHANGE THEIR WAYS AND THE THINGS THEY ARE DOING.

BUT THE PEOPLE OF JERUSALEM ANSWERED . . .

NO! WHY SHOULD WE?

HA, HA, HA!

WE WILL ALL BE JUST AS STUBBORN AND EVIL AS WE WANT TO BE!

THE LORD TOLD JEREMIAH TO GO BUY A CLAY JAR. HE ALSO TOLD JEREMIAH TO TAKE SOME OF THE PEOPLE'S ELDERS AND SOME OF THE OLDER PRIESTS WITH HIM.

CRACK!

THE LORD ALMIGHTY HAS SAID, "I WILL BREAK THESE PEOPLE AND THIS CITY, AND IT WILL BE LIKE THIS BROKEN CLAY JAR THAT CANNOT BE PUT TOGETHER AGAIN, BECAUSE ON THEIR ROOFS INCENSE HAS BEEN BURNED TO THE STARS AND WINE HAS BEEN POURED OUT AS AN OFFERING TO OTHER GODS.

SO THE LORD BROUGHT THE KING OF BABYLONIA TO ATTACK THEM.

THE KING KILLED THE YOUNG MEN OF JUDAH, EVEN IN THE TEMPLE.

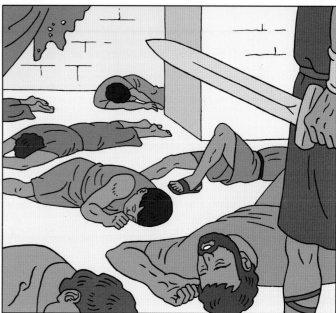

THEY LOOTED THE TEMPLE TREASURY AND TOOK EVERYTHING BACK TO BABYLON. THEY BROKE DOWN THE CITY WALLS AND TOOK ALL THE SURVIVORS AS SLAVES.

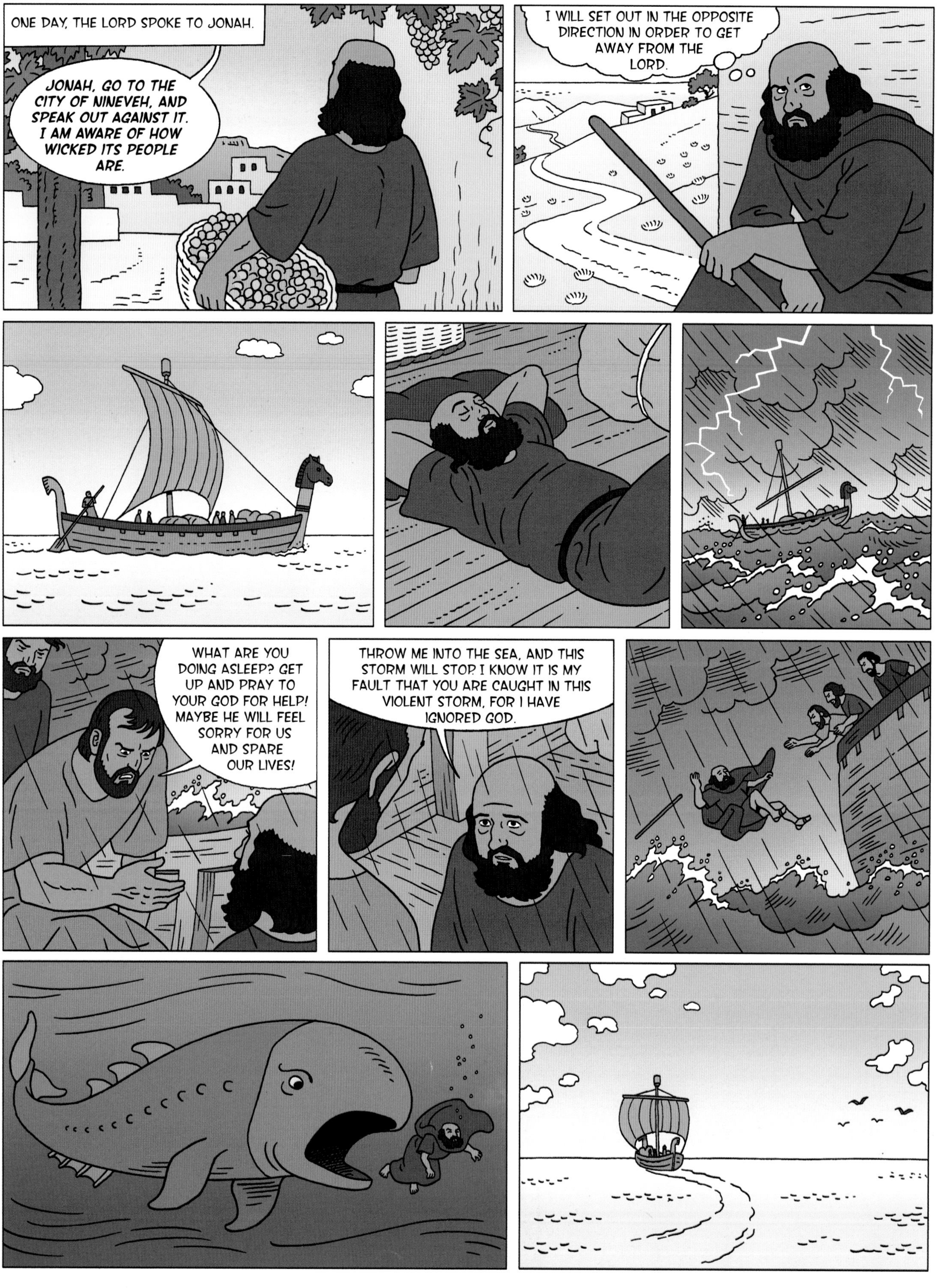
ONE DAY, THE LORD SPOKE TO JONAH.
JONAH, GO TO THE CITY OF NINEVEH, AND SPEAK OUT AGAINST IT. I AM AWARE OF HOW WICKED ITS PEOPLE ARE.
I WILL SET OUT IN THE OPPOSITE DIRECTION IN ORDER TO GET AWAY FROM THE LORD.
WHAT ARE YOU DOING ASLEEP? GET UP AND PRAY TO YOUR GOD FOR HELP! MAYBE HE WILL FEEL SORRY FOR US AND SPARE OUR LIVES!
THROW ME INTO THE SEA, AND THIS STORM WILL STOP. I KNOW IT IS MY FAULT THAT YOU ARE CAUGHT IN THIS VIOLENT STORM, FOR I HAVE IGNORED GOD.

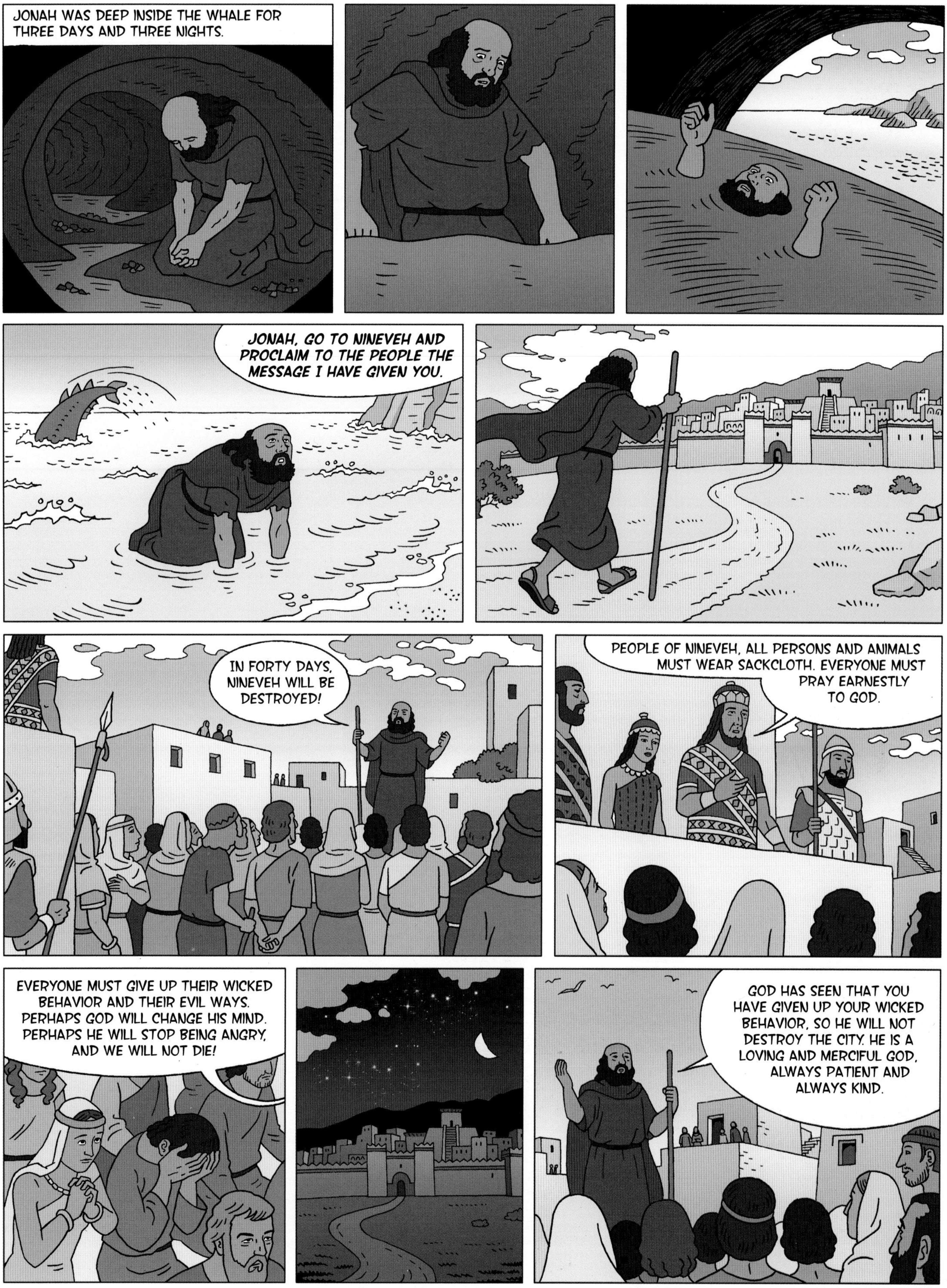
JONAH WAS DEEP INSIDE THE WHALE FOR THREE DAYS AND THREE NIGHTS.
JONAH, GO TO NINEVEH AND PROCLAIM TO THE PEOPLE THE MESSAGE I HAVE GIVEN YOU.
IN FORTY DAYS, NINEVEH WILL BE DESTROYED!
PEOPLE OF NINEVEH, ALL PERSONS AND ANIMALS MUST WEAR SACKCLOTH. EVERYONE MUST PRAY EARNESTLY TO GOD.
EVERYONE MUST GIVE UP THEIR WICKED BEHAVIOR AND THEIR EVIL WAYS. PERHAPS GOD WILL CHANGE HIS MIND. PERHAPS HE WILL STOP BEING ANGRY, AND WE WILL NOT DIE!
GOD HAS SEEN THAT YOU HAVE GIVEN UP YOUR WICKED BEHAVIOR, SO HE WILL NOT DESTROY THE CITY. HE IS A LOVING AND MERCIFUL GOD, ALWAYS PATIENT AND ALWAYS KIND.

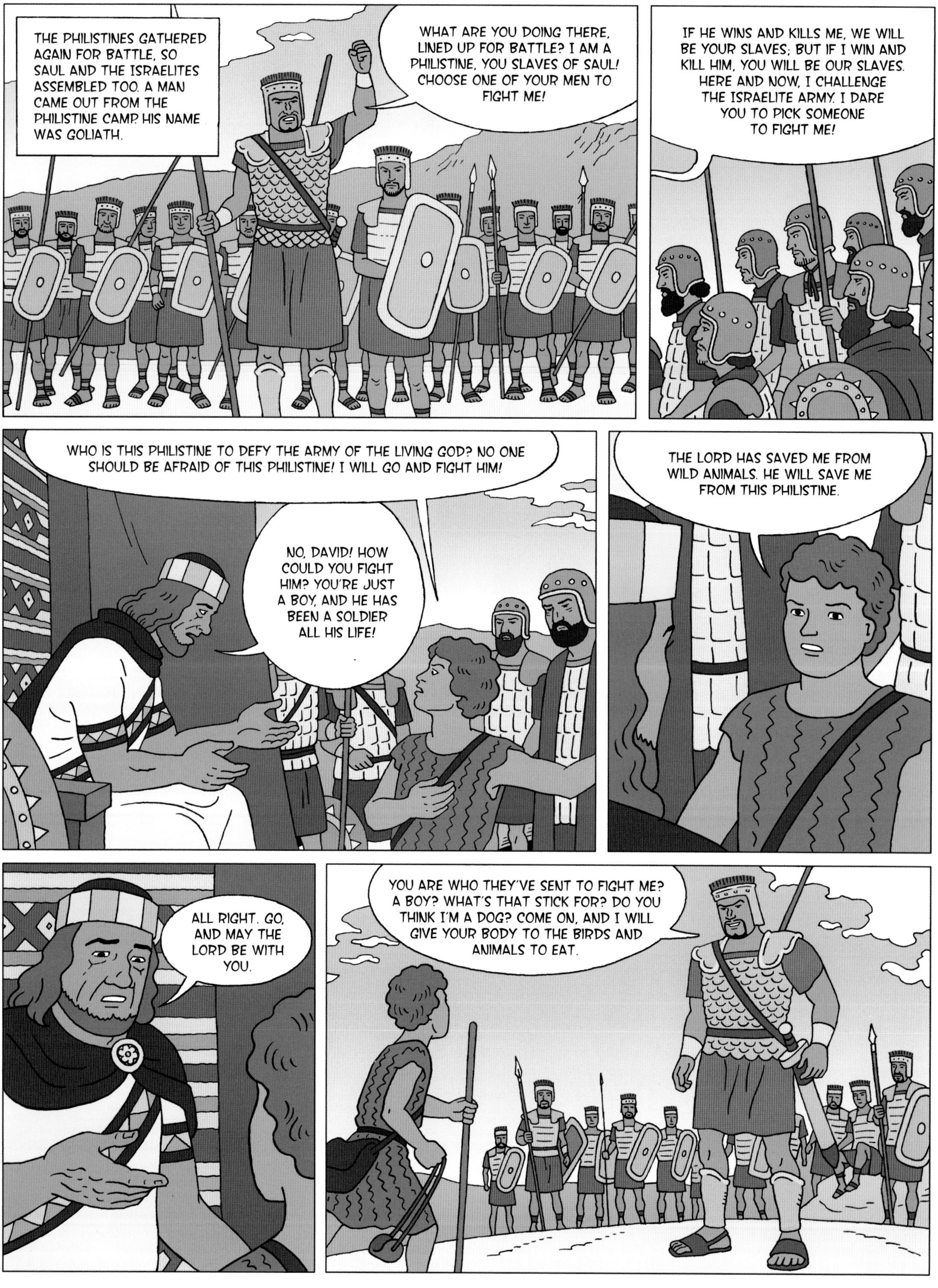
THE PHILISTINES GATHERED AGAIN FOR BATTLE, SO SAUL AND THE ISRAELITES ASSEMBLED TOO. A MAN CAME OUT FROM THE PHILISTINE CAMP. HIS NAME WAS GOLIATH.
WHAT ARE YOU DOING THERE, LINED UP FOR BATTLE? I AM A PHILISTINE, YOU SLAVES OF SAUL! CHOOSE ONE OF YOUR MEN TO FIGHT ME!
IF HE WINS AND KILLS ME, WE WILL BE YOUR SLAVES; BUT IF I WIN AND KILL HIM, YOU WILL BE OUR SLAVES. HERE AND NOW, I CHALLENGE THE ISRAELITE ARMY. I DARE YOU TO PICK SOMEONE TO FIGHT ME!
WHO IS THIS PHILISTINE TO DEFY THE ARMY OF THE LIVING GOD? NO ONE SHOULD BE AFRAID OF THIS PHILISTINE! I WILL GO AND FIGHT HIM!
NO, DAVID! HOW COULD YOU FIGHT HIM? YOU'RE JUST A BOY, AND HE HAS BEEN A SOLDIER ALL HIS LIFE!
THE LORD HAS SAVED ME FROM WILD ANIMALS. HE WILL SAVE ME FROM THIS PHILISTINE.
ALL RIGHT. GO, AND MAY THE LORD BE WITH YOU.
YOU ARE WHO THEY'VE SENT TO FIGHT ME? A BOY? WHAT'S THAT STICK FOR? DO YOU THINK I'M A DOG? COME ON, AND I WILL GIVE YOUR BODY TO THE BIRDS AND ANIMALS TO EAT.

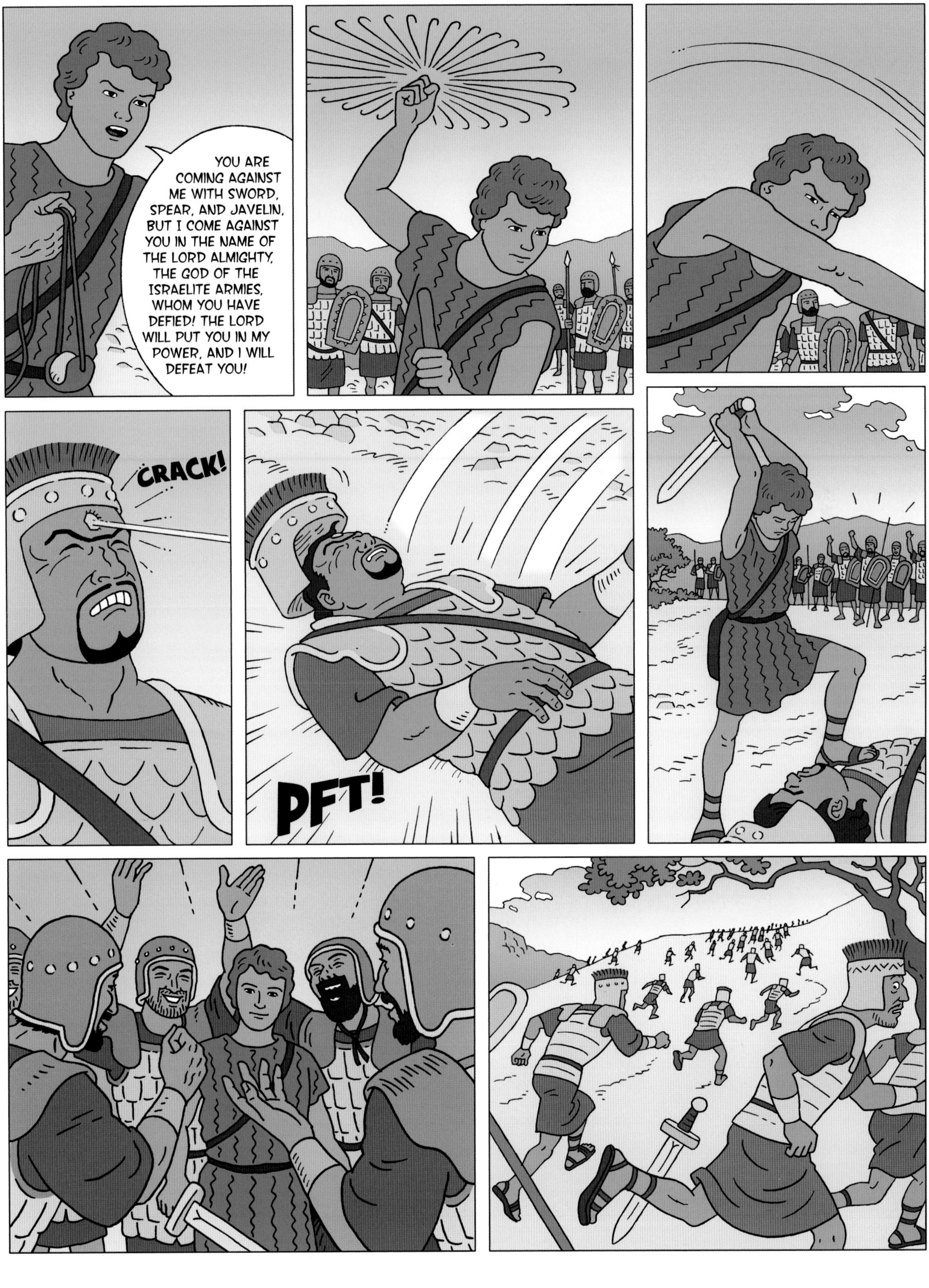
YOU ARE COMING AGAINST ME WITH SWORD, SPEAR, AND JAVELIN, BUT I COME AGAINST YOU IN THE NAME OF THE LORD ALMIGHTY, THE GOD OF THE ISRAELITE ARMIES, WHOM YOU HAVE DEFIED! THE LORD WILL PUT YOU IN MY POWER, AND I WILL DEFEAT YOU!
CRACK!
PFT!

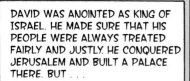

DAVID WAS ANOINTED AS KING OF ISRAEL. HE MADE SURE THAT HIS PEOPLE WERE ALWAYS TREATED FAIRLY AND JUSTLY. HE CONQUERED JERUSALEM AND BUILT A PALACE THERE. BUT . . .

WHO IS THE WOMAN WHO IS TAKING A BATH?

SHE IS BATHSHEBA, THE WIFE OF URIAH.

BRING THAT WOMAN TO ME; I WANT TO SPEAK WITH HER.

JOAB, PUT URIAH ON THE FRONT LINE, WHERE THE FIGHTING IS HEAVIEST. THEN RETREAT AND LET HIM BE KILLED.

OUR ENEMIES WERE STRONGER THAN WE WERE AND CAME OUT OF THE CITY TO FIGHT US IN THE OPEN. SOME OF YOUR MAJESTY'S OFFICERS WERE KILLED, INCLUDING URIAH.

TELL BATHSHEBA THAT HER HUSBAND HAS BEEN KILLED. WHEN THE TIME OF MOURNING IS OVER, TELL HER TO MEET ME AT THE PALACE, SO SHE CAN BECOME MY WIFE.

SOME MONTHS LATER . . .

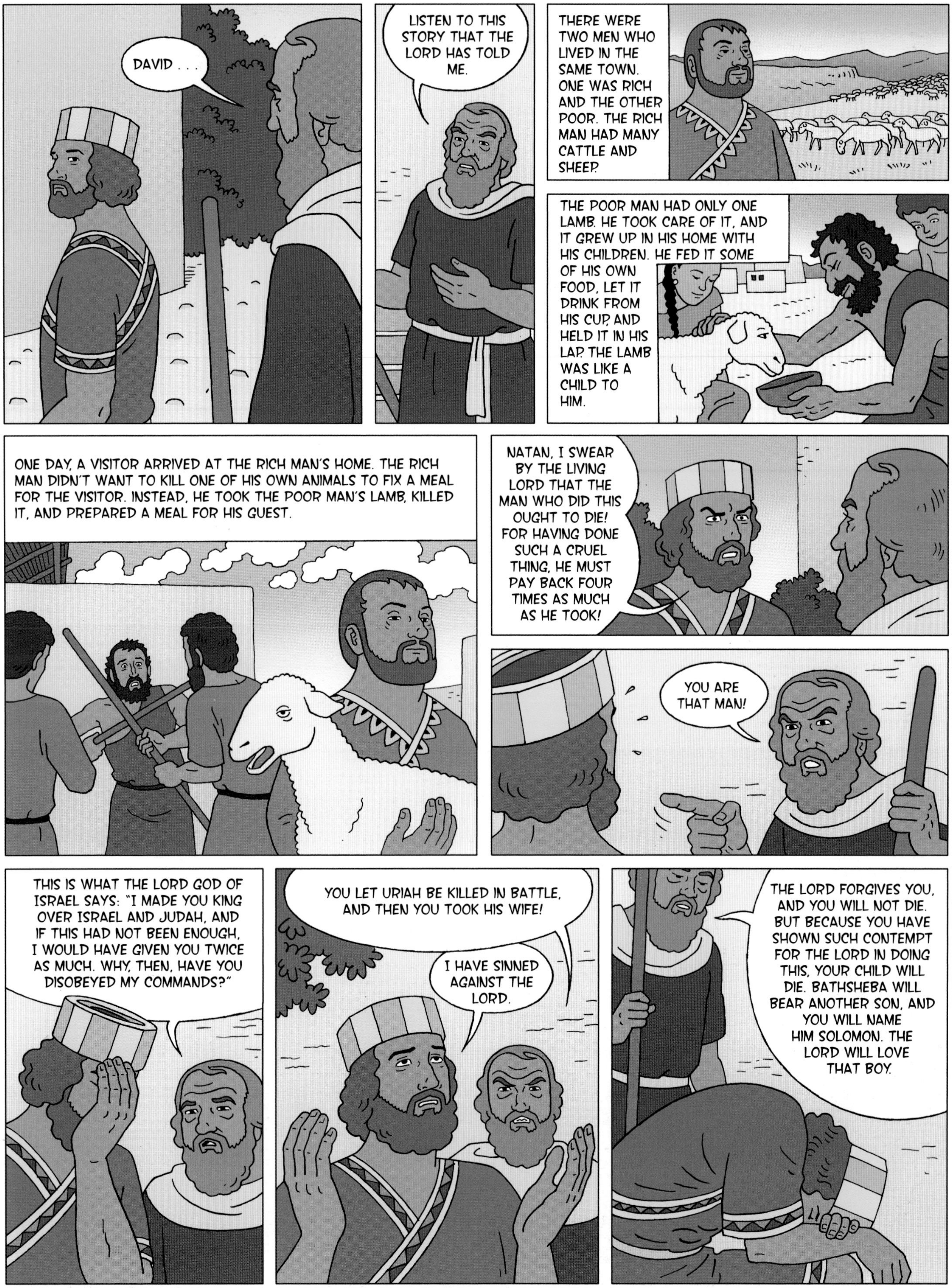
DAVID . . .
LISTEN TO THIS STORY THAT THE LORD HAS TOLD ME.
THERE WERE TWO MEN WHO LIVED IN THE SAME TOWN. ONE WAS RICH AND THE OTHER POOR. THE RICH MAN HAD MANY CATTLE AND SHEEP.
THE POOR MAN HAD ONLY ONE LAMB. HE TOOK CARE OF IT, AND IT GREW UP IN HIS HOME WITH HIS CHILDREN. HE FED IT SOME OF HIS OWN FOOD, LET IT DRINK FROM HIS CUP, AND HELD IT IN HIS LAP. THE LAMB WAS LIKE A CHILD TO HIM.
ONE DAY, A VISITOR ARRIVED AT THE RICH MAN'S HOME. THE RICH MAN DIDN'T WANT TO KILL ONE OF HIS OWN ANIMALS TO FIX A MEAL FOR THE VISITOR. INSTEAD, HE TOOK THE POOR MAN'S LAMB, KILLED IT, AND PREPARED A MEAL FOR HIS GUEST.
NATAN, I SWEAR BY THE LIVING LORD THAT THE MAN WHO DID THIS OUGHT TO DIE! FOR HAVING DONE SUCH A CRUEL THING, HE MUST PAY BACK FOUR TIMES AS MUCH AS HE TOOK!
YOU ARE THAT MAN!
THIS IS WHAT THE LORD GOD OF ISRAEL SAYS: "I MADE YOU KING OVER ISRAEL AND JUDAH, AND IF THIS HAD NOT BEEN ENOUGH, I WOULD HAVE GIVEN YOU TWICE AS MUCH. WHY, THEN, HAVE YOU DISOBEYED MY COMMANDS?"
YOU LET URIAH BE KILLED IN BATTLE, AND THEN YOU TOOK HIS WIFE!
I HAVE SINNED AGAINST THE LORD.
THE LORD FORGIVES YOU, AND YOU WILL NOT DIE. BUT BECAUSE YOU HAVE SHOWN SUCH CONTEMPT FOR THE LORD IN DOING THIS, YOUR CHILD WILL DIE. BATHSHEBA WILL BEAR ANOTHER SON, AND YOU WILL NAME HIM SOLOMON. THE LORD WILL LOVE THAT BOY.

WHEN SOLOMON GREW UP, DAVID NAMED HIM THE KING OF ISRAEL. THE PEOPLE OF ISRAEL WERE ALL FILLED WITH DEEP RESPECT FOR SOLOMON, BECAUSE THEY KNEW THAT GOD HAD GIVEN HIM THE WISDOM TO SETTLE DISPUTES FAIRLY.

YOUR MAJESTY, THIS WOMAN AND I LIVE IN THE SAME HOUSE, AND I GAVE BIRTH TO A BABY BOY AT HOME WHILE SHE WAS THERE. TWO DAYS AFTER MY CHILD WAS BORN, SHE ALSO GAVE BIRTH TO A BABY BOY.

THEN ONE NIGHT HER BABY DIED. SHE GOT UP DURING THE NIGHT, TOOK MY SON FROM MY SIDE WHILE I WAS ASLEEP, AND CARRIED HIM TO HER BED. THEN SHE PUT HER DEAD CHILD IN MY BED.

THE NEXT MORNING, WHEN I WOKE UP AND WAS GOING TO NURSE MY BABY, I SAW THAT HE WAS DEAD. I LOOKED AT HIM MORE CLOSELY AND SAW THAT HE WAS NOT MY CHILD.

NO! THE LIVING CHILD IS MINE, AND THE DEAD ONE IS YOURS!

NO! THE DEAD CHILD IS YOURS, AND THE LIVING ONE IS MINE!

BRING ME A SWORD.

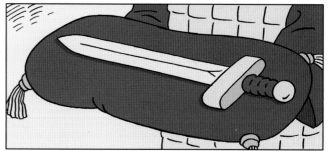

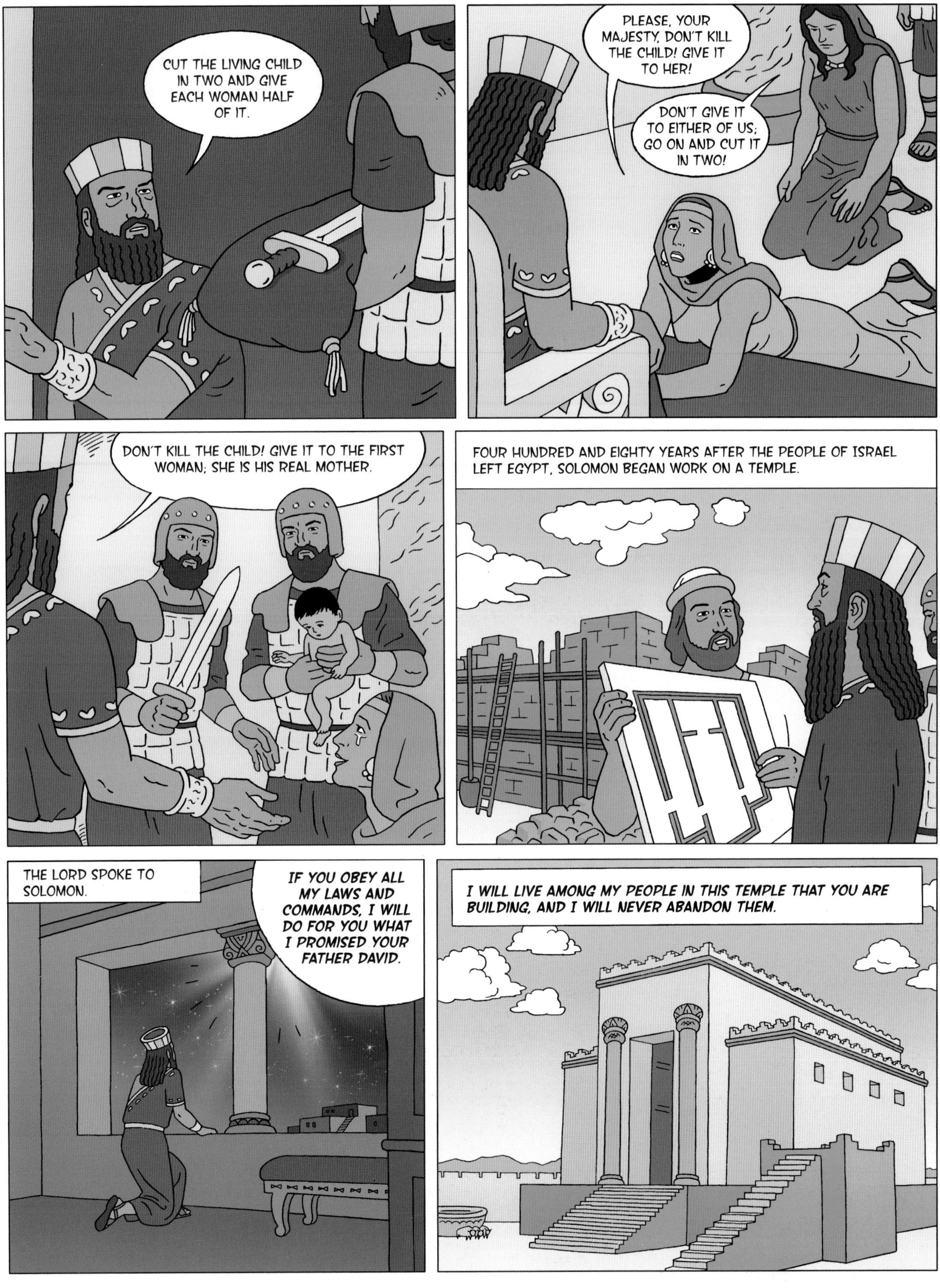
CUT THE LIVING CHILD IN TWO AND GIVE EACH WOMAN HALF OF IT.
PLEASE, YOUR MAJESTY, DON'T KILL THE CHILD! GIVE IT TO HER!
DON'T GIVE IT TO EITHER OF US; GO ON AND CUT IT IN TWO!
DON'T KILL THE CHILD! GIVE IT TO THE FIRST WOMAN; SHE IS HIS REAL MOTHER.
FOUR HUNDRED AND EIGHTY YEARS AFTER THE PEOPLE OF ISRAEL LEFT EGYPT, SOLOMON BEGAN WORK ON A TEMPLE.
THE LORD SPOKE TO SOLOMON.
IF YOU OBEY ALL MY LAWS AND COMMANDS, I WILL DO FOR YOU WHAT I PROMISED YOUR FATHER DAVID.
I WILL LIVE AMONG MY PEOPLE IN THIS TEMPLE THAT YOU ARE BUILDING, AND I WILL NEVER ABANDON THEM.

THERE WAS A MAN NAMED JOB WHO LIVED IN THE LAND OF UZ. HE WORSHIPPED GOD AND WAS FAITHFUL TO HIM. HE WAS A GOOD MAN. HE HAD SEVEN SONS AND THREE DAUGHTERS AND WAS THE RICHEST MAN IN THE LAND.

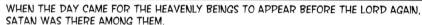

WHEN THE DAY CAME FOR THE HEAVENLY BEINGS TO APPEAR BEFORE THE LORD AGAIN, SATAN WAS THERE AMONG THEM.

YOU, SATAN, HAVE BEEN ROAMING AROUND THE EARTH. DID YOU NOTICE MY SERVANT JOB? THERE IS NO ONE ON EARTH AS FAITHFUL AND GOOD AS HE IS. HE WORSHIPS ME AND IS CAREFUL NOT TO DO ANYTHING EVIL.

OF COURSE HE IS! YOU BLESS EVERYTHING JOB DOES! WOULD HE WORSHIP YOU IF HE GOT NOTHING OUT OF IT? SUPPOSE YOU TAKE AWAY EVERYTHING HE HAS. I BET HE WILL CURSE YOU TO YOUR FACE!

SATAN ARRANGED FOR ALL OF JOB'S OXEN TO BE STOLEN. LIGHTNING STRUCK THE SHEEP AND THE SHEPHERDS. A STORM BLEW HIS ELDEST SON'S HOUSE DOWN AND KILLED ALL HIS CHILDREN. BUT IN SPITE OF EVERYTHING THAT HAPPENED, JOB DID NOT SIN BY BLAMING GOD.

THE LORD GAVE, AND NOW HE HAS TAKEN AWAY. MAY HIS NAME BE PRAISED!

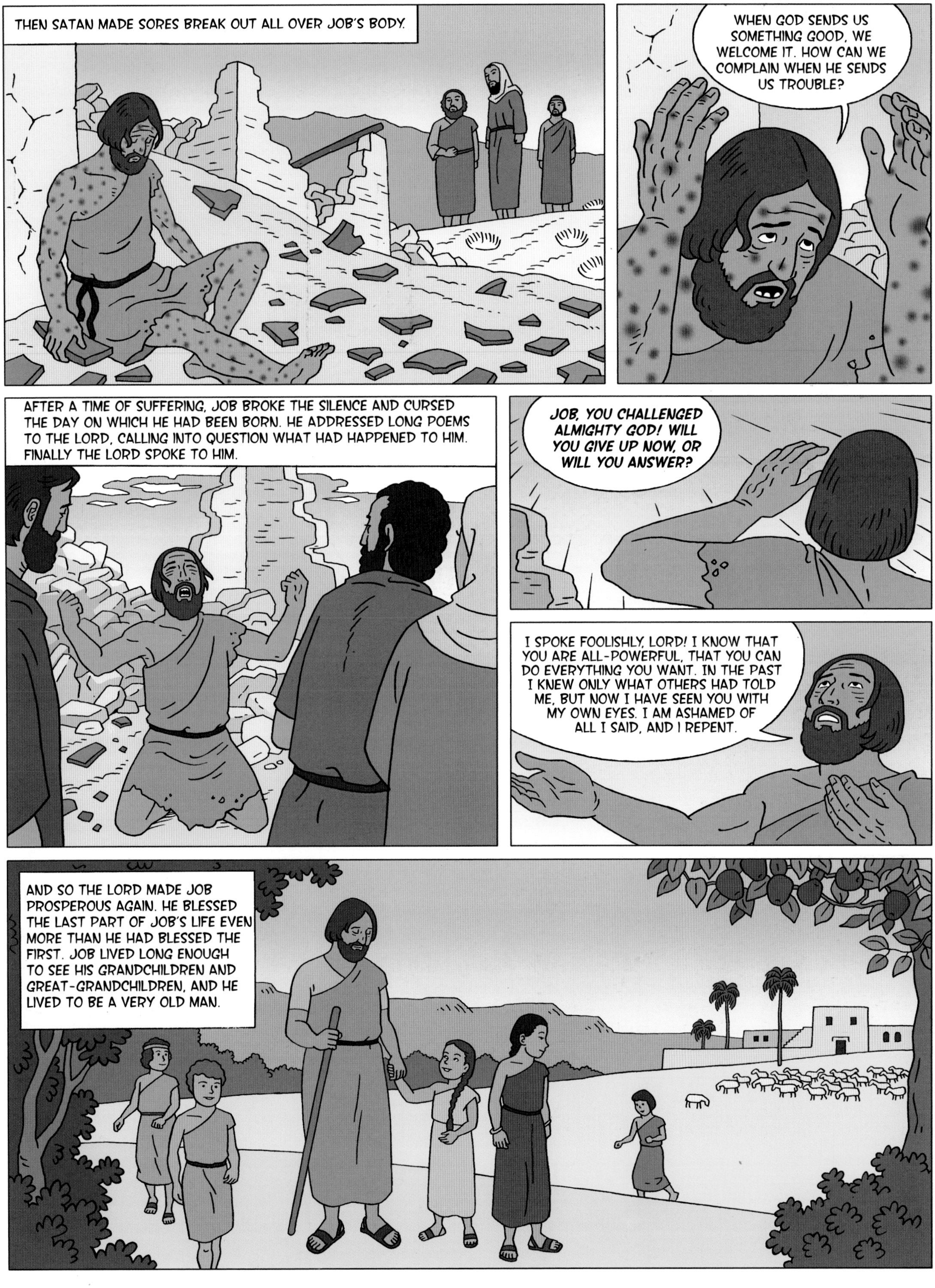
THEN SATAN MADE SORES BREAK OUT ALL OVER JOB'S BODY.
WHEN GOD SENDS US SOMETHING GOOD, WE WELCOME IT. HOW CAN WE COMPLAIN WHEN HE SENDS US TROUBLE?
AFTER A TIME OF SUFFERING, JOB BROKE THE SILENCE AND CURSED THE DAY ON WHICH HE HAD BEEN BORN. HE ADDRESSED LONG POEMS TO THE LORD, CALLING INTO QUESTION WHAT HAD HAPPENED TO HIM. FINALLY THE LORD SPOKE TO HIM.
JOB, YOU CHALLENGED ALMIGHTY GOD! WILL YOU GIVE UP NOW, OR WILL YOU ANSWER?
I SPOKE FOOLISHLY, LORD! I KNOW THAT YOU ARE ALL-POWERFUL, THAT YOU CAN DO EVERYTHING YOU WANT. IN THE PAST I KNEW ONLY WHAT OTHERS HAD TOLD ME, BUT NOW I HAVE SEEN YOU WITH MY OWN EYES. I AM ASHAMED OF ALL I SAID, AND I REPENT.
AND SO THE LORD MADE JOB PROSPEROUS AGAIN. HE BLESSED THE LAST PART OF JOB'S LIFE EVEN MORE THAN HE HAD BLESSED THE FIRST. JOB LIVED LONG ENOUGH TO SEE HIS GRANDCHILDREN AND GREAT-GRANDCHILDREN, AND HE LIVED TO BE A VERY OLD MAN.

THE PROPHET ISAIAH SAID, "I SAW THE LORD, AND AROUND HIM WERE STANDING CREATURES OF LIGHT."

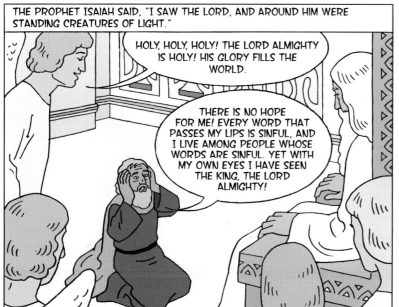

HOLY, HOLY, HOLY! THE LORD ALMIGHTY IS HOLY! HIS GLORY FILLS THE WORLD.

THERE IS NO HOPE FOR ME! EVERY WORD THAT PASSES MY LIPS IS SINFUL, AND I LIVE AMONG PEOPLE WHOSE WORDS ARE SINFUL. YET WITH MY OWN EYES I HAVE SEEN THE KING, THE LORD ALMIGHTY!

THEN ONE OF THE CREATURES FLEW DOWN TO HIM, CARRYING A BURNING COAL THAT HE HAD TAKEN FROM THE ALTAR WITH A PAIR OF TONGS. HE TOUCHED ISAIAH'S LIPS WITH THE BURNING COAL.

THIS HAS TOUCHED YOUR LIPS, AND NOW YOUR GUILT IS GONE, AND YOUR SINS ARE FORGIVEN.

WHOM SHALL I SEND? WHO WILL BE OUR MESSENGER?

I WILL GO! SEND ME!

GIVE THE PEOPLE THIS MESSAGE: "NO MATTER HOW MUCH YOU LISTEN, YOU WILL NOT UNDERSTAND. NO MATTER HOW MUCH YOU LOOK, YOU WILL NOT KNOW WHAT IS HAPPENING.

HOW LONG WILL IT BE LIKE THIS, LORD?

UNTIL THE CITIES ARE RUINED AND EMPTY.

EVEN IF ONE PERSON OUT OF TEN REMAINS IN THE LAND, HE TOO WILL BE DESTROYED. HE WILL BE LIKE THE STUMP OF AN OAK TREE THAT HAS BEEN CUT DOWN.

BUT A YOUNG WOMAN WILL HAVE A SON AND WILL NAME HIM IMMANUEL, WHICH MEANS "GOD IS WITH US."

THE PEOPLE WHO WALKED IN DARKNESS HAVE SEEN A GREAT LIGHT. THEY LIVED IN A LAND OF SHADOWS, BUT NOW LIGHT IS SHINING ON THEM.

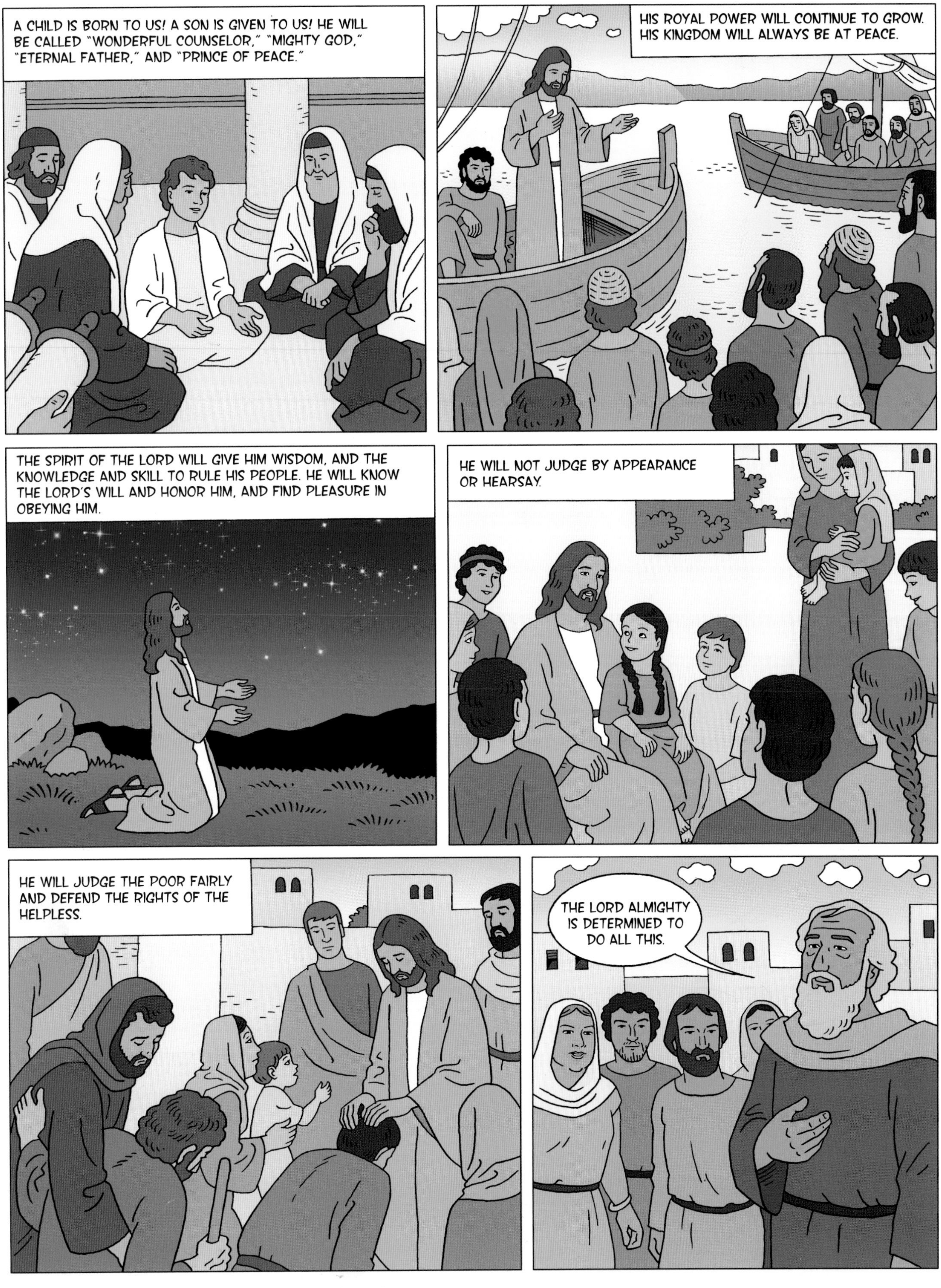
A CHILD IS BORN TO US! A SON IS GIVEN TO US! HE WILL BE CALLED "WONDERFUL COUNSELOR," "MIGHTY GOD," "ETERNAL FATHER," AND "PRINCE OF PEACE."
HIS ROYAL POWER WILL CONTINUE TO GROW. HIS KINGDOM WILL ALWAYS BE AT PEACE.
THE SPIRIT OF THE LORD WILL GIVE HIM WISDOM, AND THE KNOWLEDGE AND SKILL TO RULE HIS PEOPLE. HE WILL KNOW THE LORD'S WILL AND HONOR HIM, AND FIND PLEASURE IN OBEYING HIM.
HE WILL NOT JUDGE BY APPEARANCE OR HEARSAY.
HE WILL JUDGE THE POOR FAIRLY AND DEFEND THE RIGHTS OF THE HELPLESS.
THE LORD ALMIGHTY IS DETERMINED TO DO ALL THIS.

New Testament

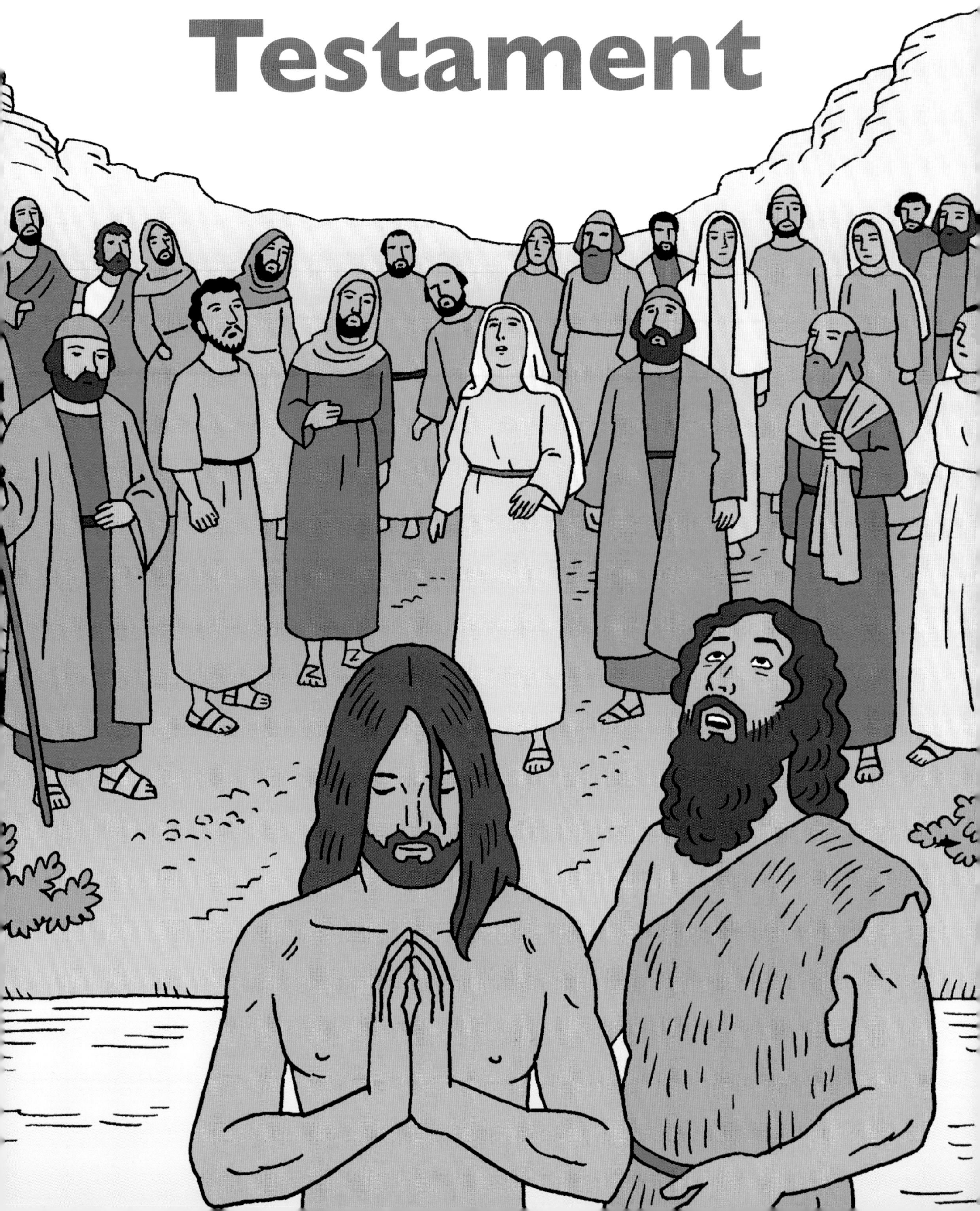

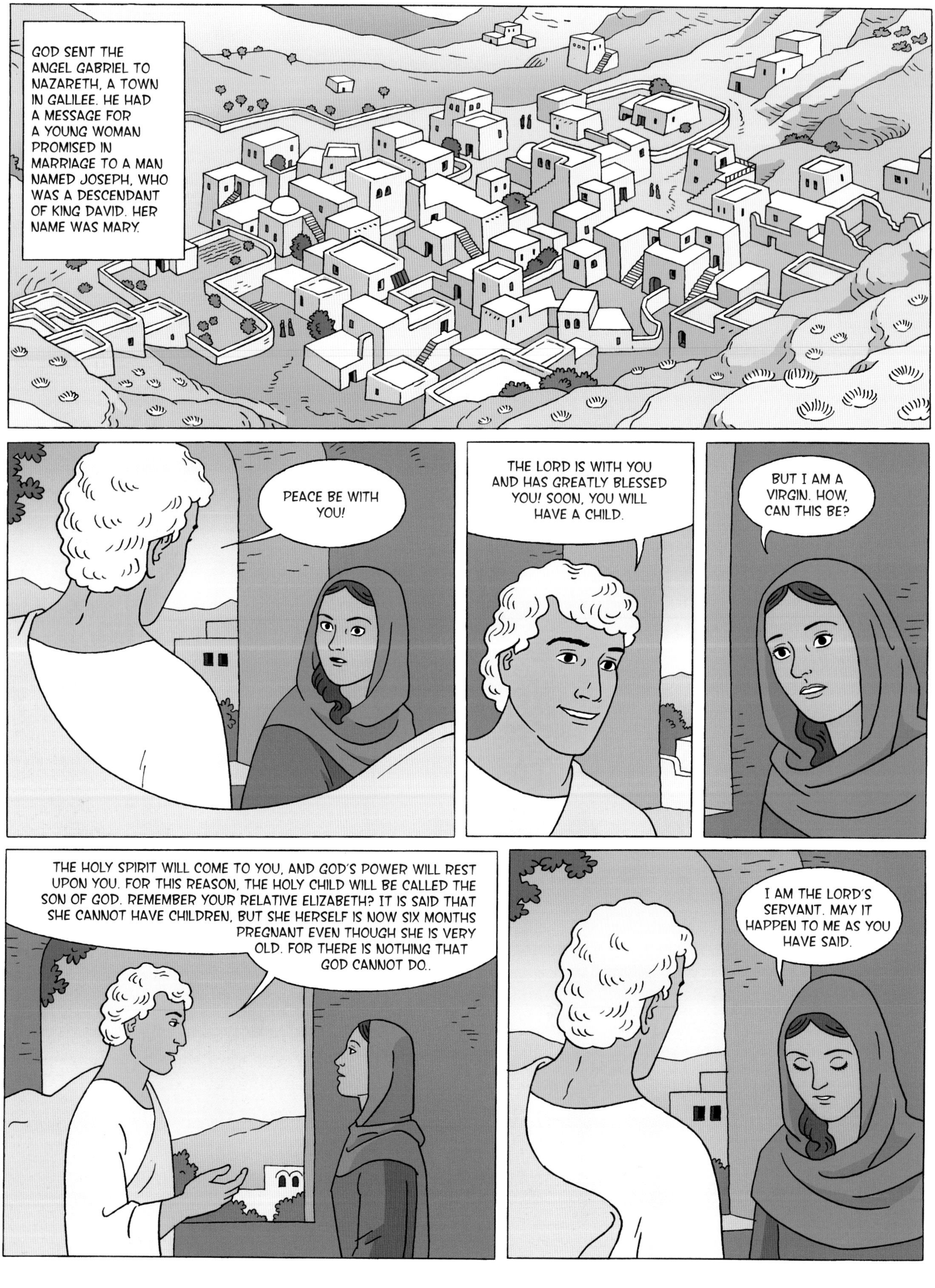
GOD SENT THE ANGEL GABRIEL TO NAZARETH, A TOWN IN GALILEE. HE HAD A MESSAGE FOR A YOUNG WOMAN PROMISED IN MARRIAGE TO A MAN NAMED JOSEPH, WHO WAS A DESCENDANT OF KING DAVID. HER NAME WAS MARY.
PEACE BE WITH YOU!
THE LORD IS WITH YOU AND HAS GREATLY BLESSED YOU! SOON, YOU WILL HAVE A CHILD.
BUT I AM A VIRGIN. HOW, CAN THIS BE?
THE HOLY SPIRIT WILL COME TO YOU, AND GOD'S POWER WILL REST UPON YOU. FOR THIS REASON, THE HOLY CHILD WILL BE CALLED THE SON OF GOD. REMEMBER YOUR RELATIVE ELIZABETH? IT IS SAID THAT SHE CANNOT HAVE CHILDREN, BUT SHE HERSELF IS NOW SIX MONTHS PREGNANT EVEN THOUGH SHE IS VERY OLD. FOR THERE IS NOTHING THAT GOD CANNOT DO..
I AM THE LORD'S SERVANT. MAY IT HAPPEN TO ME AS YOU HAVE SAID.

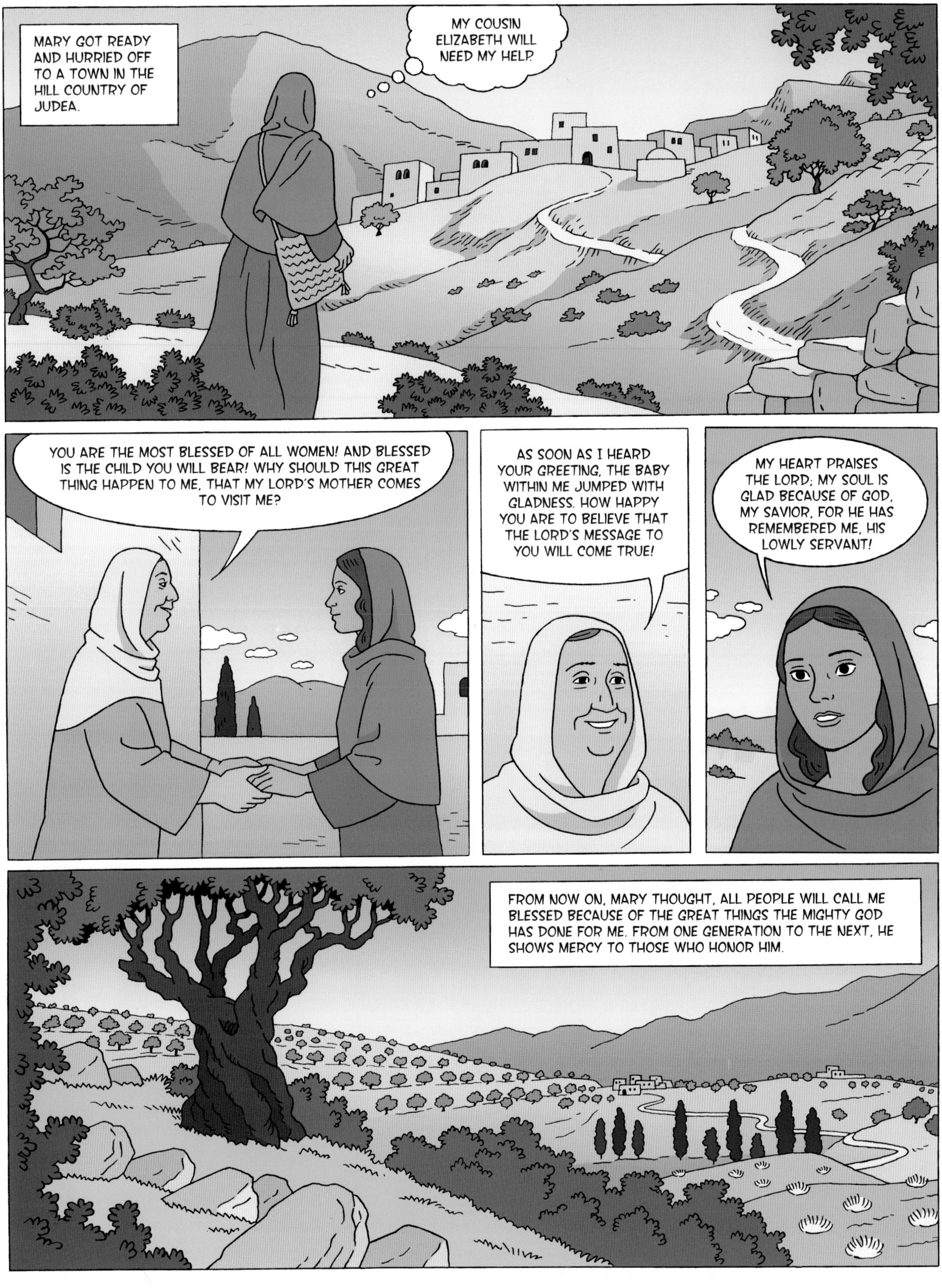
MARY GOT READY AND HURRIED OFF TO A TOWN IN THE HILL COUNTRY OF JUDEA.
MY COUSIN ELIZABETH WILL NEED MY HELP.
YOU ARE THE MOST BLESSED OF ALL WOMEN! AND BLESSED IS THE CHILD YOU WILL BEAR! WHY SHOULD THIS GREAT THING HAPPEN TO ME, THAT MY LORD'S MOTHER COMES TO VISIT ME?
AS SOON AS I HEARD YOUR GREETING, THE BABY WITHIN ME JUMPED WITH GLADNESS. HOW HAPPY YOU ARE TO BELIEVE THAT THE LORD'S MESSAGE TO YOU WILL COME TRUE!
MY HEART PRAISES THE LORD; MY SOUL IS GLAD BECAUSE OF GOD, MY SAVIOR, FOR HE HAS REMEMBERED ME, HIS LOWLY SERVANT!
FROM NOW ON, MARY THOUGHT, ALL PEOPLE WILL CALL ME BLESSED BECAUSE OF THE GREAT THINGS THE MIGHTY GOD HAS DONE FOR ME. FROM ONE GENERATION TO THE NEXT, HE SHOWS MERCY TO THOSE WHO HONOR HIM.

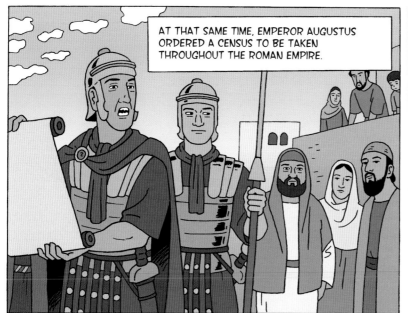

AT THAT SAME TIME, EMPEROR AUGUSTUS ORDERED A CENSUS TO BE TAKEN THROUGHOUT THE ROMAN EMPIRE.

JOSEPH AND MARY LEFT NAZARETH FOR THE CITY OF BETHLEHEM SO THEY COULD REGISTER.

BUT BECAUSE SO MANY PEOPLE HAD COME FOR THE CENSUS, THERE WERE NO ROOMS FOR THEM AT ANY LOCAL INNS.

SO THE COUPLE FOUND A STABLE WHERE THEY COULD REST FOR THE NIGHT.

WHILE THEY WERE IN BETHLEHEM, THE TIME CAME FOR MARY TO HAVE HER BABY.

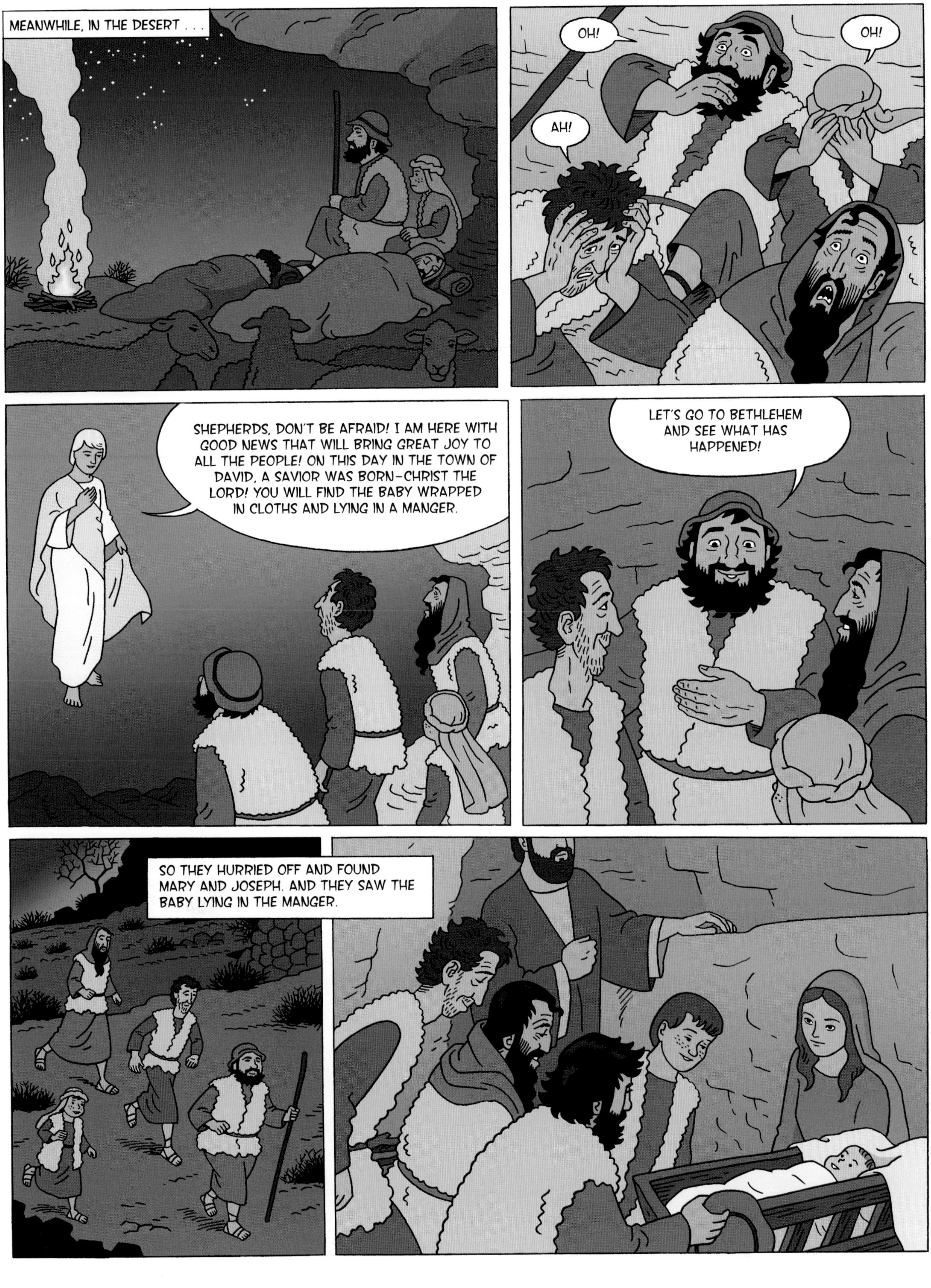
MEANWHILE, IN THE DESERT . . .
OH!
OH!
AH!
SHEPHERDS, DON'T BE AFRAID! I AM HERE WITH GOOD NEWS THAT WILL BRING GREAT JOY TO ALL THE PEOPLE! ON THIS DAY IN THE TOWN OF DAVID, A SAVIOR WAS BORN–CHRIST THE LORD! YOU WILL FIND THE BABY WRAPPED IN CLOTHS AND LYING IN A MANGER.
LET'S GO TO BETHLEHEM AND SEE WHAT HAS HAPPENED!
SO THEY HURRIED OFF AND FOUND MARY AND JOSEPH. AND THEY SAW THE BABY LYING IN THE MANGER.

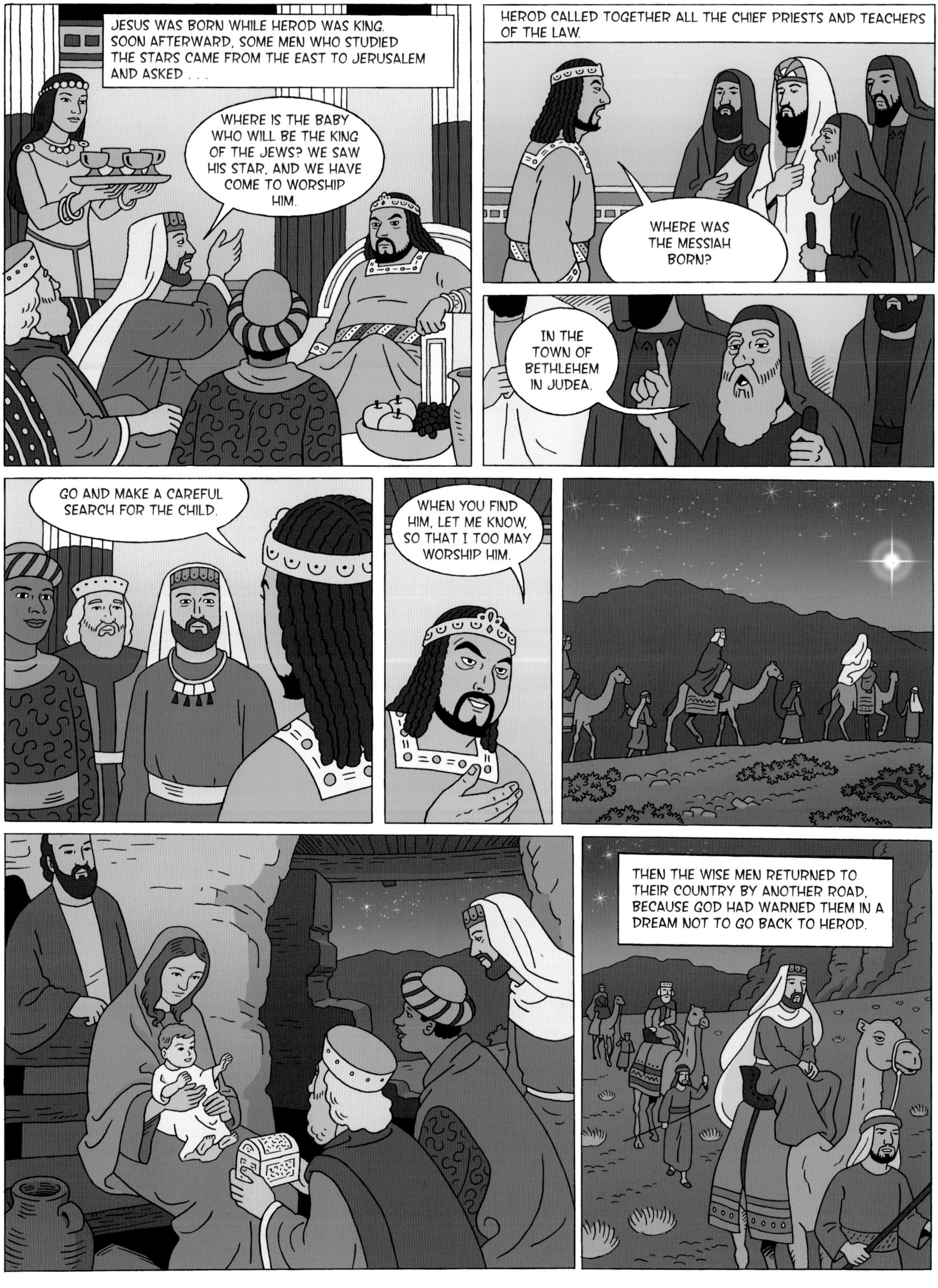
JESUS WAS BORN WHILE HEROD WAS KING. SOON AFTERWARD, SOME MEN WHO STUDIED THE STARS CAME FROM THE EAST TO JERUSALEM AND ASKED . . .
WHERE IS THE BABY WHO WILL BE THE KING OF THE JEWS? WE SAW HIS STAR, AND WE HAVE COME TO WORSHIP HIM.
HEROD CALLED TOGETHER ALL THE CHIEF PRIESTS AND TEACHERS OF THE LAW.
WHERE WAS THE MESSIAH BORN?
IN THE TOWN OF BETHLEHEM IN JUDEA.
GO AND MAKE A CAREFUL SEARCH FOR THE CHILD.
WHEN YOU FIND HIM, LET ME KNOW, SO THAT I TOO MAY WORSHIP HIM.
THEN THE WISE MEN RETURNED TO THEIR COUNTRY BY ANOTHER ROAD, BECAUSE GOD HAD WARNED THEM IN A DREAM NOT TO GO BACK TO HEROD.

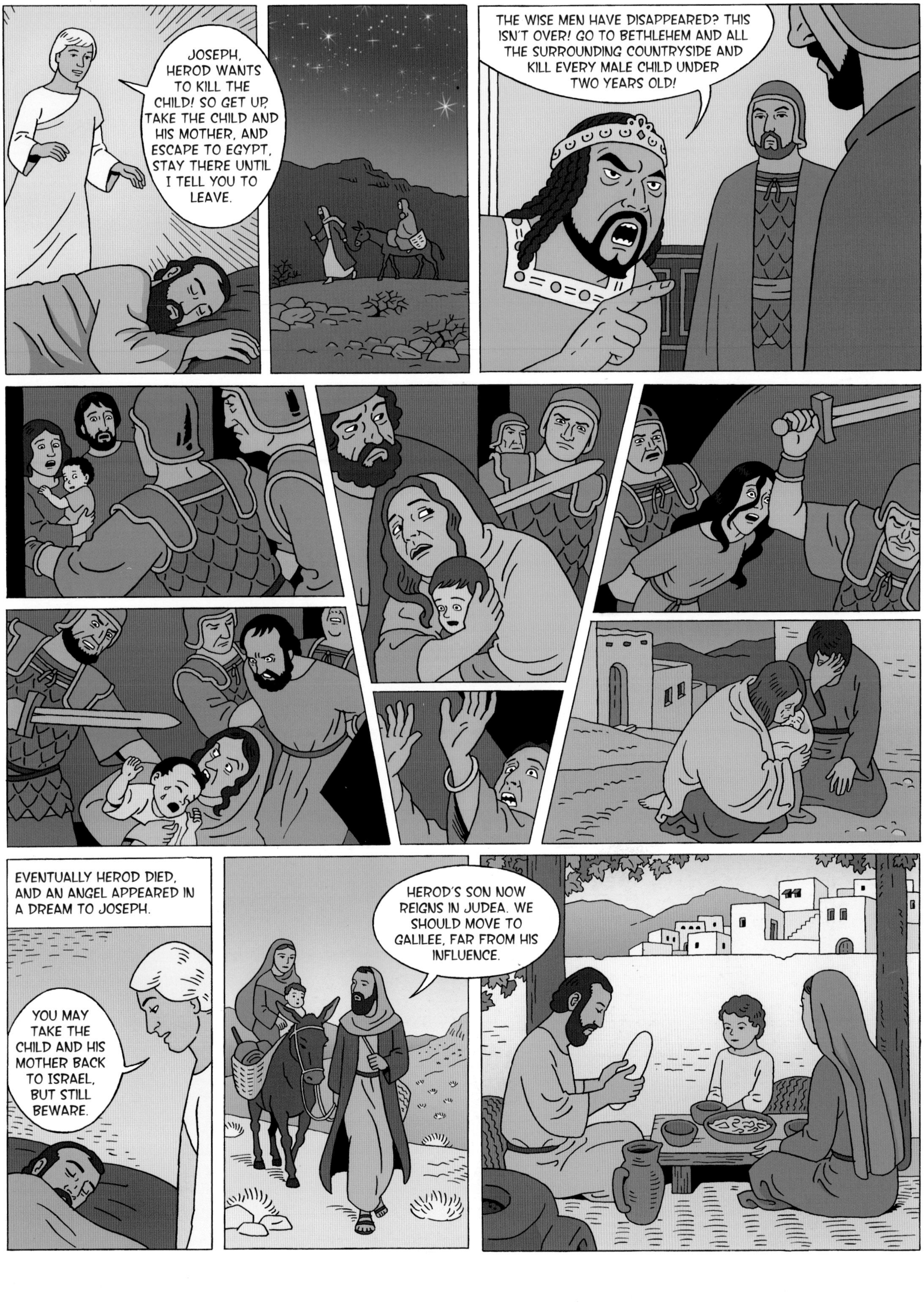
JOSEPH, HEROD WANTS TO KILL THE CHILD! SO GET UP, TAKE THE CHILD AND HIS MOTHER, AND ESCAPE TO EGYPT. STAY THERE UNTIL I TELL YOU TO LEAVE.
THE WISE MEN HAVE DISAPPEARED? THIS ISN'T OVER! GO TO BETHLEHEM AND ALL THE SURROUNDING COUNTRYSIDE AND KILL EVERY MALE CHILD UNDER TWO YEARS OLD!
EVENTUALLY HEROD DIED, AND AN ANGEL APPEARED IN A DREAM TO JOSEPH.
YOU MAY TAKE THE CHILD AND HIS MOTHER BACK TO ISRAEL, BUT STILL BEWARE.
HEROD'S SON NOW REIGNS IN JUDEA. WE SHOULD MOVE TO GALILEE, FAR FROM HIS INFLUENCE.

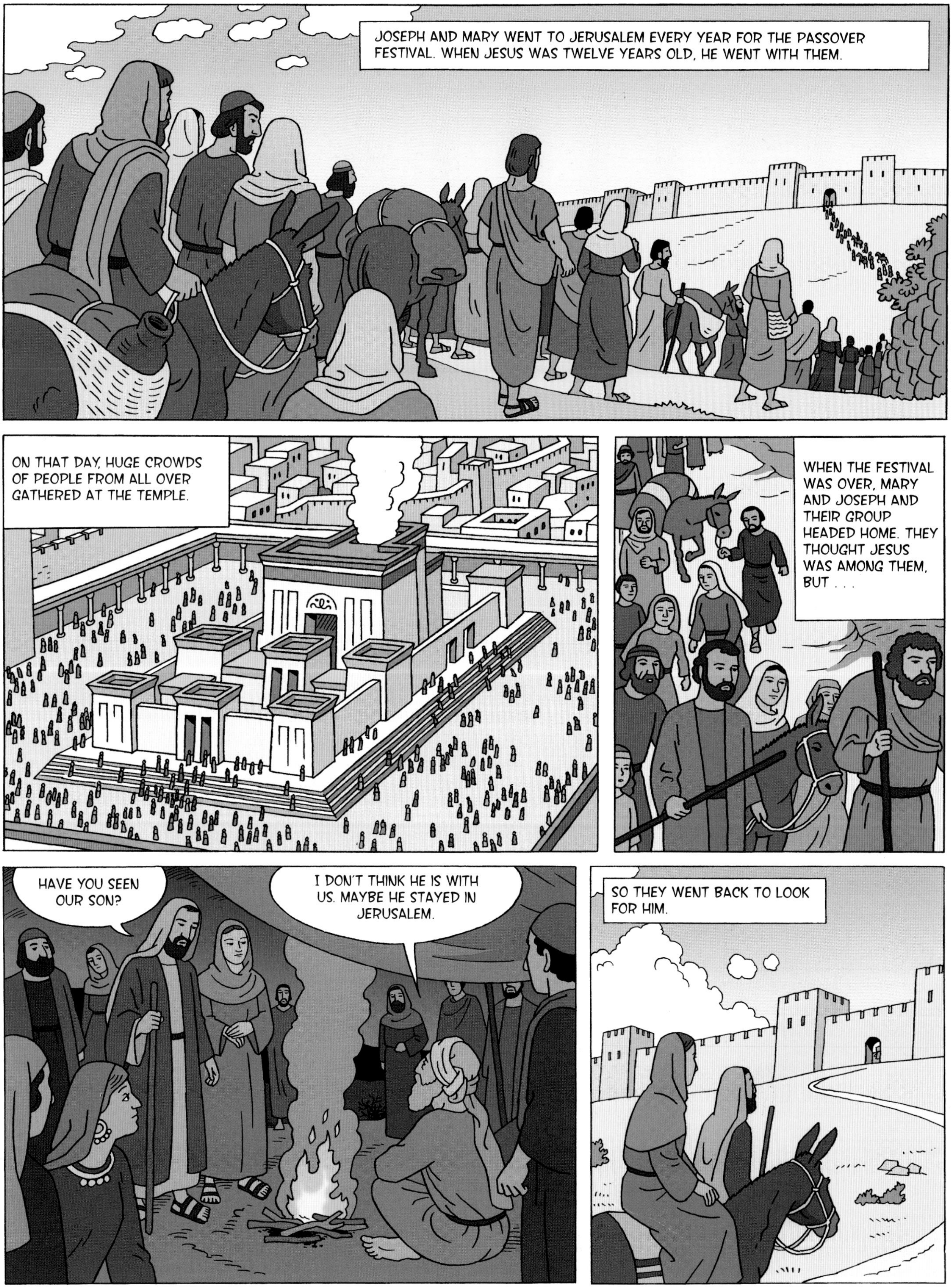
JOSEPH AND MARY WENT TO JERUSALEM EVERY YEAR FOR THE PASSOVER FESTIVAL. WHEN JESUS WAS TWELVE YEARS OLD, HE WENT WITH THEM.
ON THAT DAY, HUGE CROWDS OF PEOPLE FROM ALL OVER GATHERED AT THE TEMPLE.
WHEN THE FESTIVAL WAS OVER, MARY AND JOSEPH AND THEIR GROUP HEADED HOME. THEY THOUGHT JESUS WAS AMONG THEM, BUT . . .
HAVE YOU SEEN OUR SON?
I DON'T THINK HE IS WITH US. MAYBE HE STAYED IN JERUSALEM.
SO THEY WENT BACK TO LOOK FOR HIM.

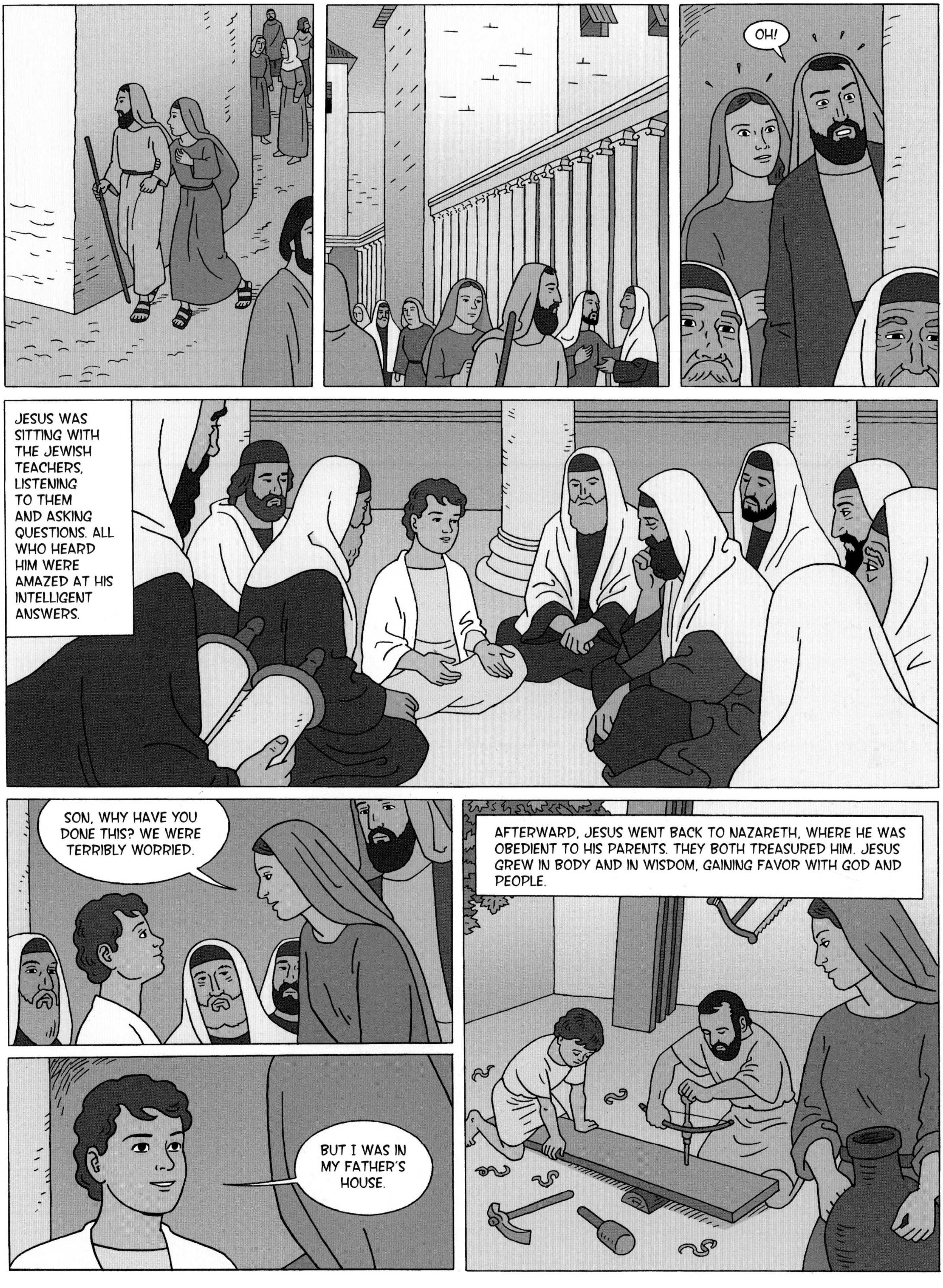
OH!
JESUS WAS SITTING WITH THE JEWISH TEACHERS, LISTENING TO THEM AND ASKING QUESTIONS. ALL WHO HEARD HIM WERE AMAZED AT HIS INTELLIGENT ANSWERS.
SON, WHY HAVE YOU DONE THIS? WE WERE TERRIBLY WORRIED.
BUT I WAS IN MY FATHER'S HOUSE.
AFTERWARD, JESUS WENT BACK TO NAZARETH, WHERE HE WAS OBEDIENT TO HIS PARENTS. THEY BOTH TREASURED HIM. JESUS GREW IN BODY AND IN WISDOM, GAINING FAVOR WITH GOD AND PEOPLE.

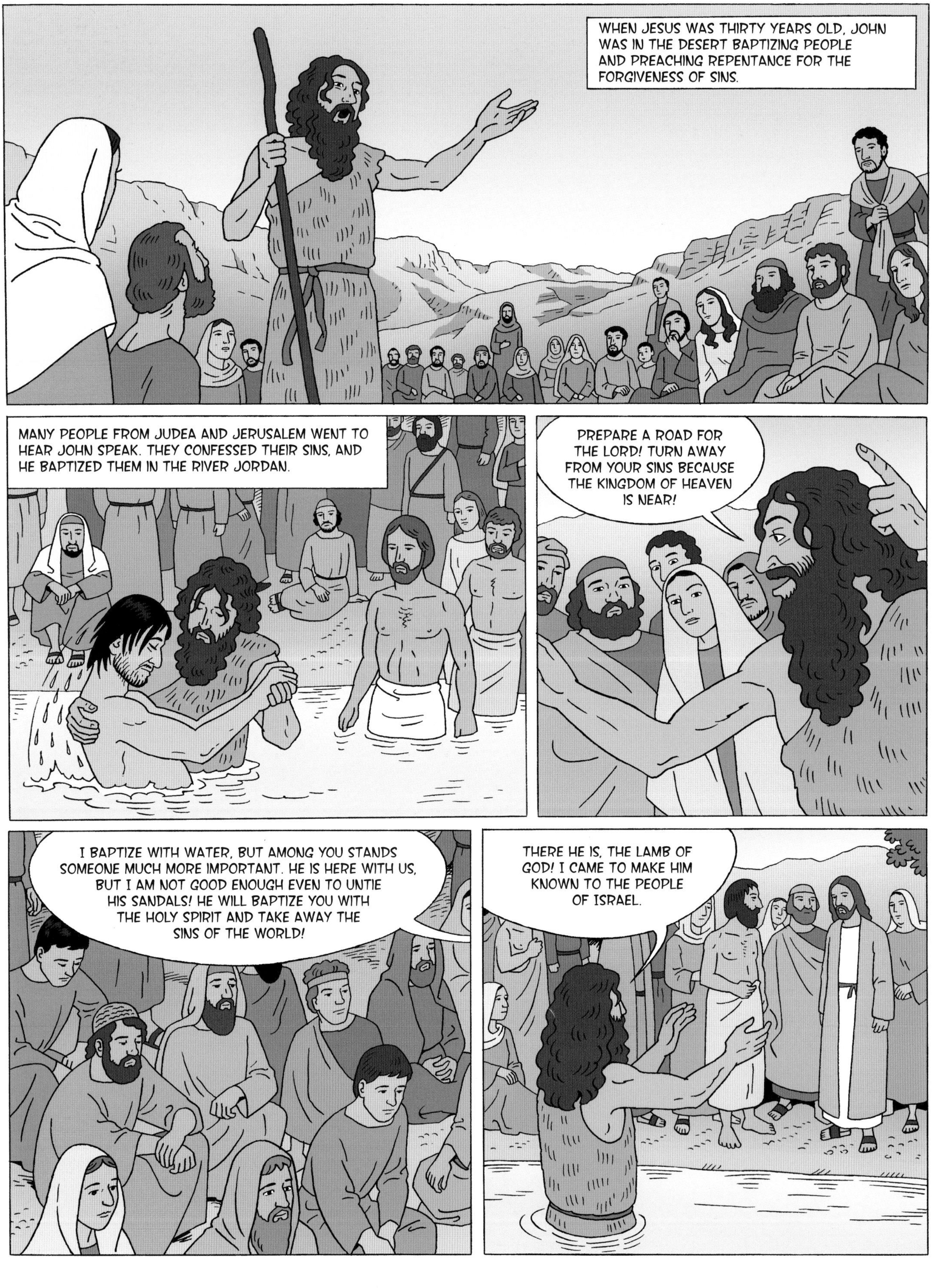
WHEN JESUS WAS THIRTY YEARS OLD, JOHN WAS IN THE DESERT BAPTIZING PEOPLE AND PREACHING REPENTANCE FOR THE FORGIVENESS OF SINS.
MANY PEOPLE FROM JUDEA AND JERUSALEM WENT TO HEAR JOHN SPEAK. THEY CONFESSED THEIR SINS, AND HE BAPTIZED THEM IN THE RIVER JORDAN.
PREPARE A ROAD FOR THE LORD! TURN AWAY FROM YOUR SINS BECAUSE THE KINGDOM OF HEAVEN IS NEAR!
I BAPTIZE WITH WATER, BUT AMONG YOU STANDS SOMEONE MUCH MORE IMPORTANT. HE IS HERE WITH US, BUT I AM NOT GOOD ENOUGH EVEN TO UNTIE HIS SANDALS! HE WILL BAPTIZE YOU WITH THE HOLY SPIRIT AND TAKE AWAY THE SINS OF THE WORLD!
THERE HE IS, THE LAMB OF GOD! I CAME TO MAKE HIM KNOWN TO THE PEOPLE OF ISRAEL.

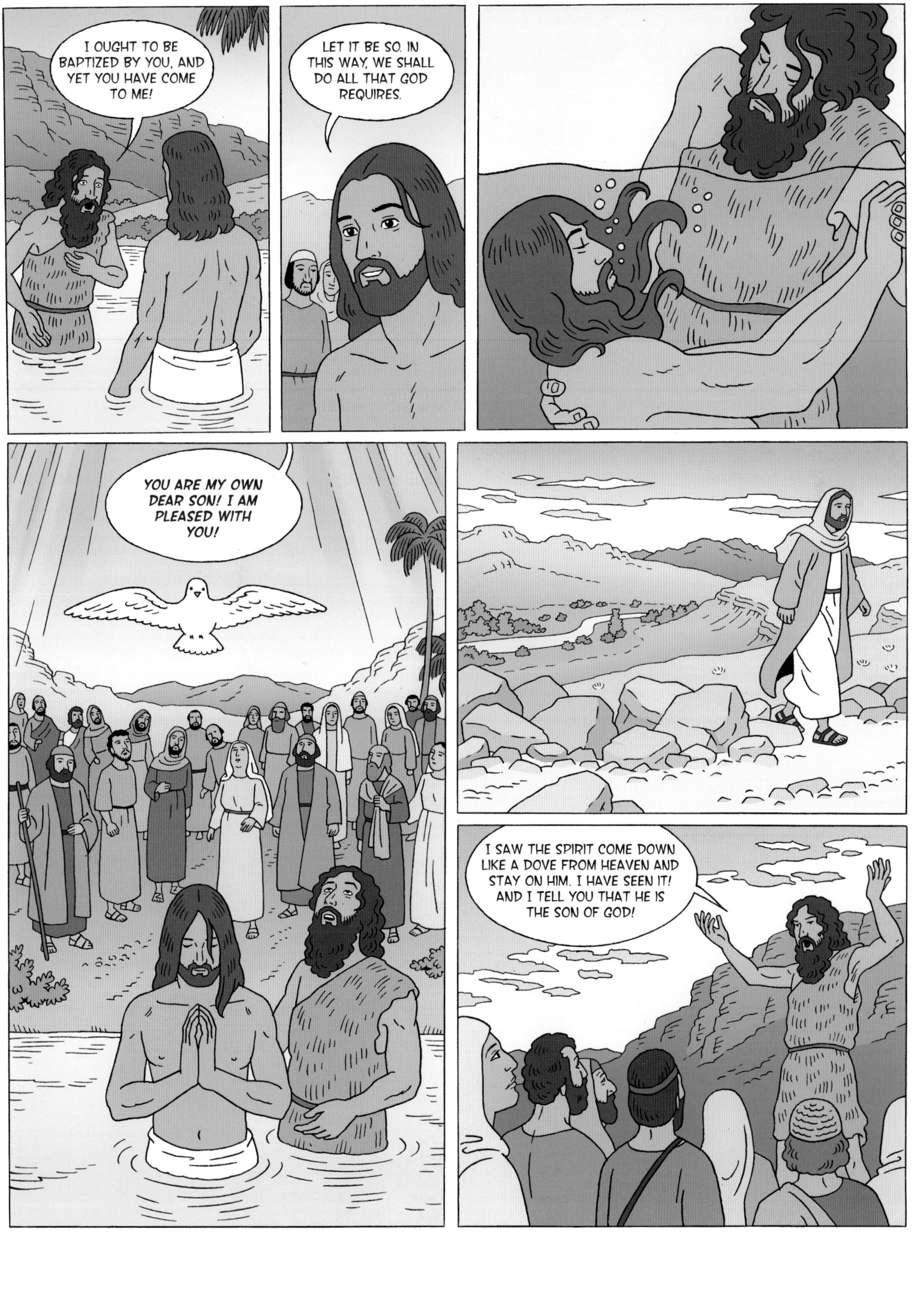
I OUGHT TO BE BAPTIZED BY YOU, AND YET YOU HAVE COME TO ME!
LET IT BE SO. IN THIS WAY, WE SHALL DO ALL THAT GOD REQUIRES.
YOU ARE MY OWN DEAR SON! I AM PLEASED WITH YOU!
I SAW THE SPIRIT COME DOWN LIKE A DOVE FROM HEAVEN AND STAY ON HIM. I HAVE SEEN IT! AND I TELL YOU THAT HE IS THE SON OF GOD!

AFTER BEING BAPTIZED IN THE RIVER JORDAN, JESUS WENT INTO THE DESERT WHERE HE WAS TEMPTED BY THE DEVIL.

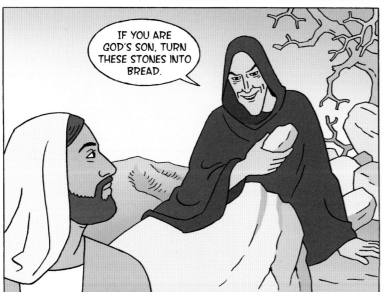

IF YOU ARE GOD'S SON, TURN THESE STONES INTO BREAD.

THE SCRIPTURE SAYS, "HUMAN BEINGS CANNOT LIVE ON BREAD ALONE, BUT NEED EVERY WORD THAT GOD SPEAKS."

THEN THE DEVIL TOOK JESUS TO JERUSALEM AND PUT HIM ON THE HIGHEST POINT OF THE TEMPLE.

IF YOU ARE GOD'S SON, THROW YOURSELF DOWN.

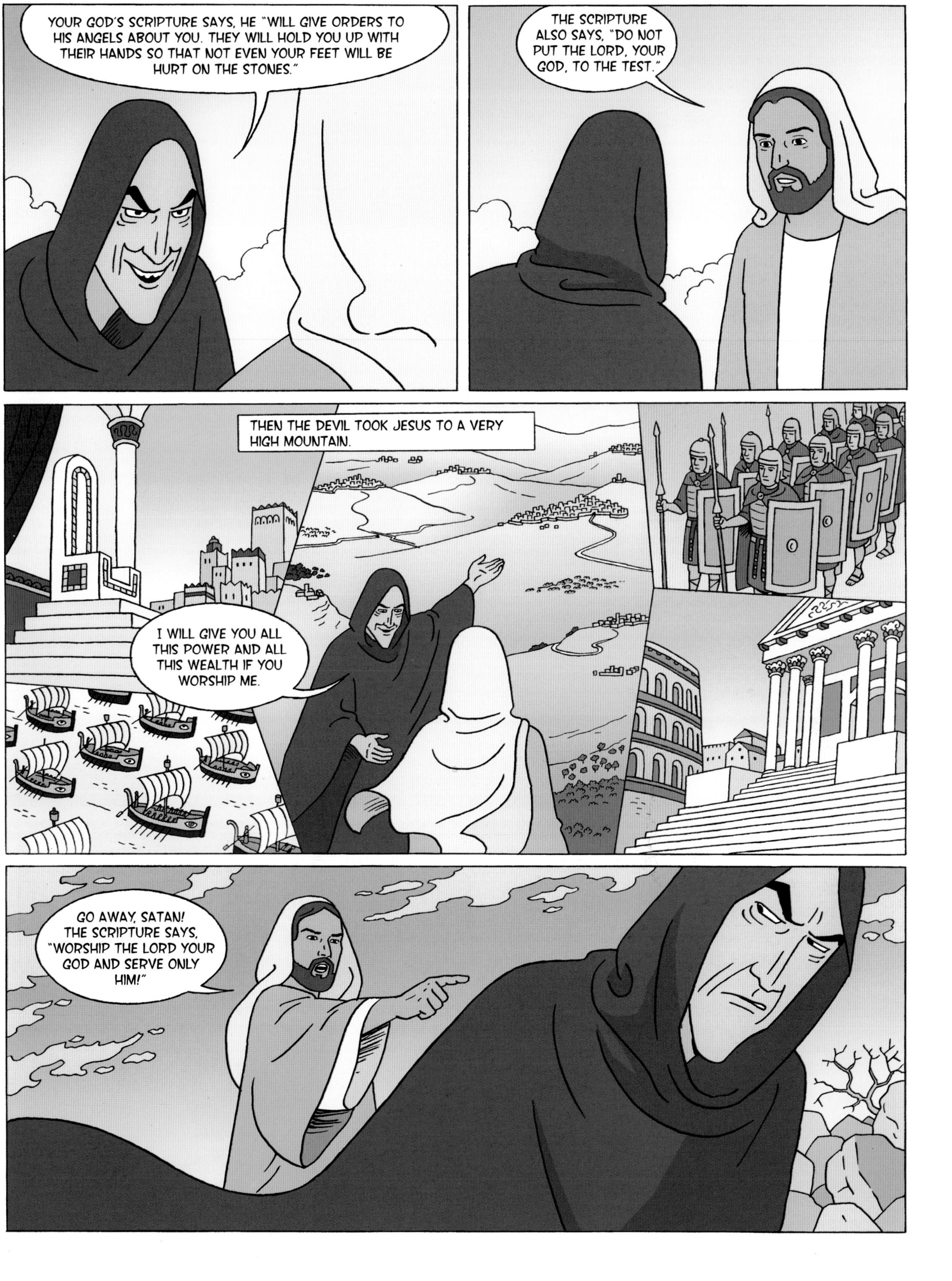
YOUR GOD'S SCRIPTURE SAYS, HE "WILL GIVE ORDERS TO HIS ANGELS ABOUT YOU. THEY WILL HOLD YOU UP WITH THEIR HANDS SO THAT NOT EVEN YOUR FEET WILL BE HURT ON THE STONES."
THE SCRIPTURE ALSO SAYS, "DO NOT PUT THE LORD, YOUR GOD, TO THE TEST."
THEN THE DEVIL TOOK JESUS TO A VERY HIGH MOUNTAIN.
I WILL GIVE YOU ALL THIS POWER AND ALL THIS WEALTH IF YOU WORSHIP ME.
GO AWAY, SATAN! THE SCRIPTURE SAYS, "WORSHIP THE LORD YOUR GOD AND SERVE ONLY HIM!"

JESUS TRAVELED ALL OVER GALILEE, TEACHING IN THE TEMPLES, PREACHING GOOD NEWS ABOUT THE KINGDOM, AND HEALING PEOPLE WHO HAD ALL KINDS OF DISEASES AND SICKNESSES.

THE TIME HAS COME, AND THE KINGDOM OF GOD IS NEAR! TURN AWAY FROM YOUR SINS AND BELIEVE THE GOOD NEWS!

PUSH THE BOAT INTO THE WATER, AND RELEASE YOUR NETS.

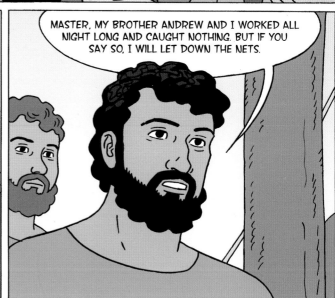

MASTER, MY BROTHER ANDREW AND I WORKED ALL NIGHT LONG AND CAUGHT NOTHING. BUT IF YOU SAY SO, I WILL LET DOWN THE NETS.

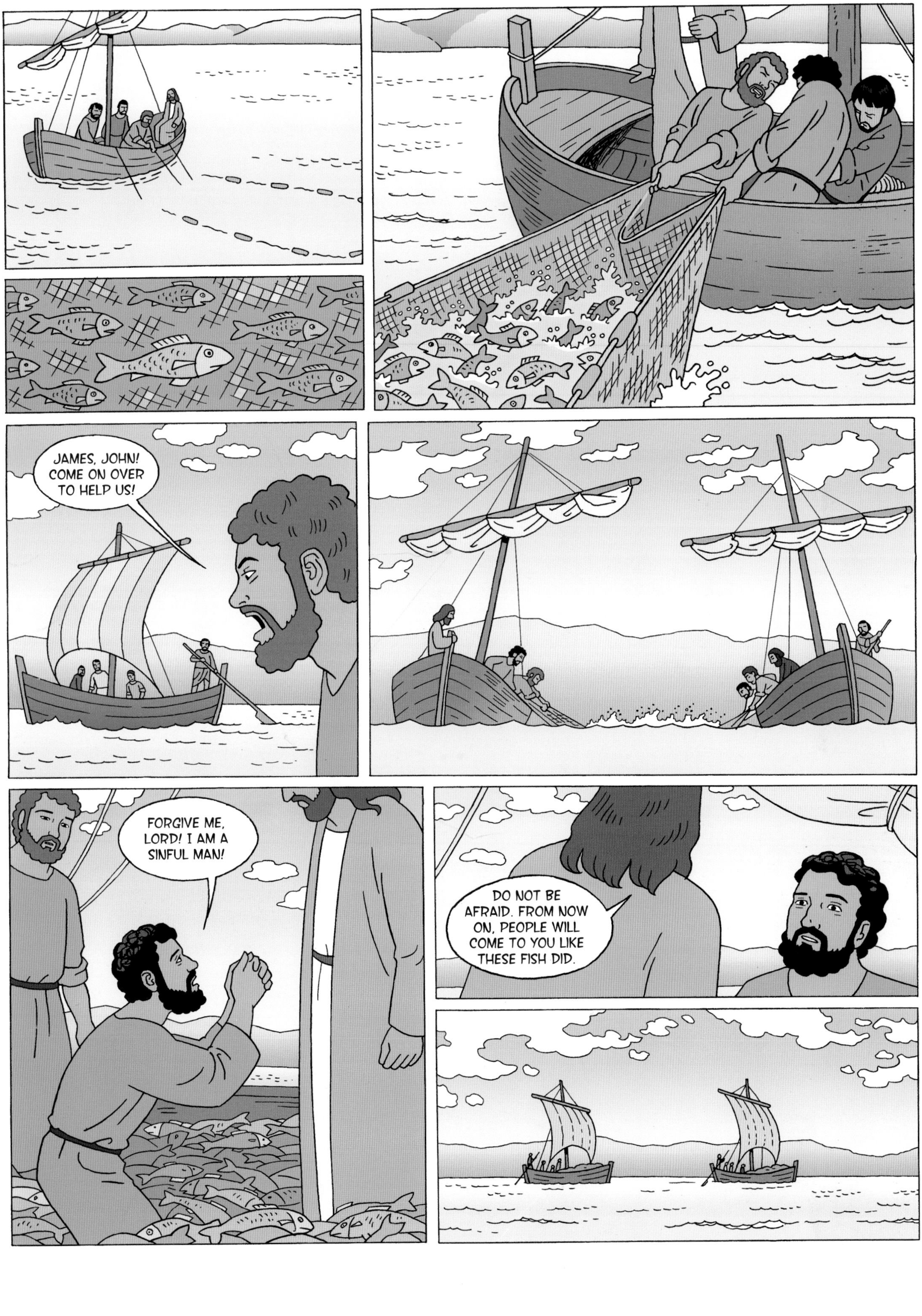
JAMES, JOHN! COME ON OVER TO HELP US!
FORGIVE ME, LORD! I AM A SINFUL MAN!
DO NOT BE AFRAID. FROM NOW ON, PEOPLE WILL COME TO YOU LIKE THESE FISH DID.

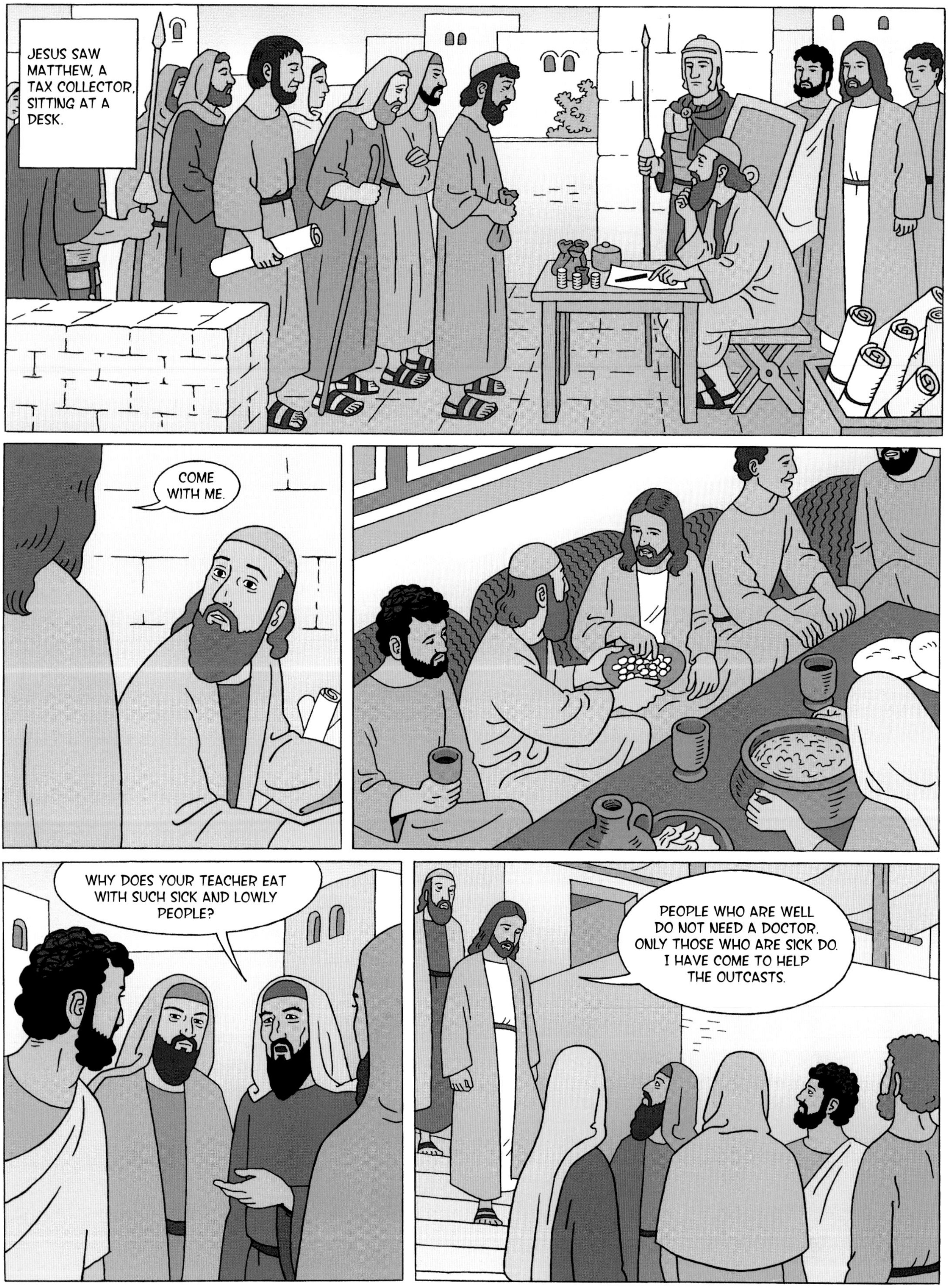
JESUS SAW MATTHEW, A TAX COLLECTOR, SITTING AT A DESK.
COME WITH ME.
WHY DOES YOUR TEACHER EAT WITH SUCH SICK AND LOWLY PEOPLE?
PEOPLE WHO ARE WELL DO NOT NEED A DOCTOR. ONLY THOSE WHO ARE SICK DO. I HAVE COME TO HELP THE OUTCASTS.

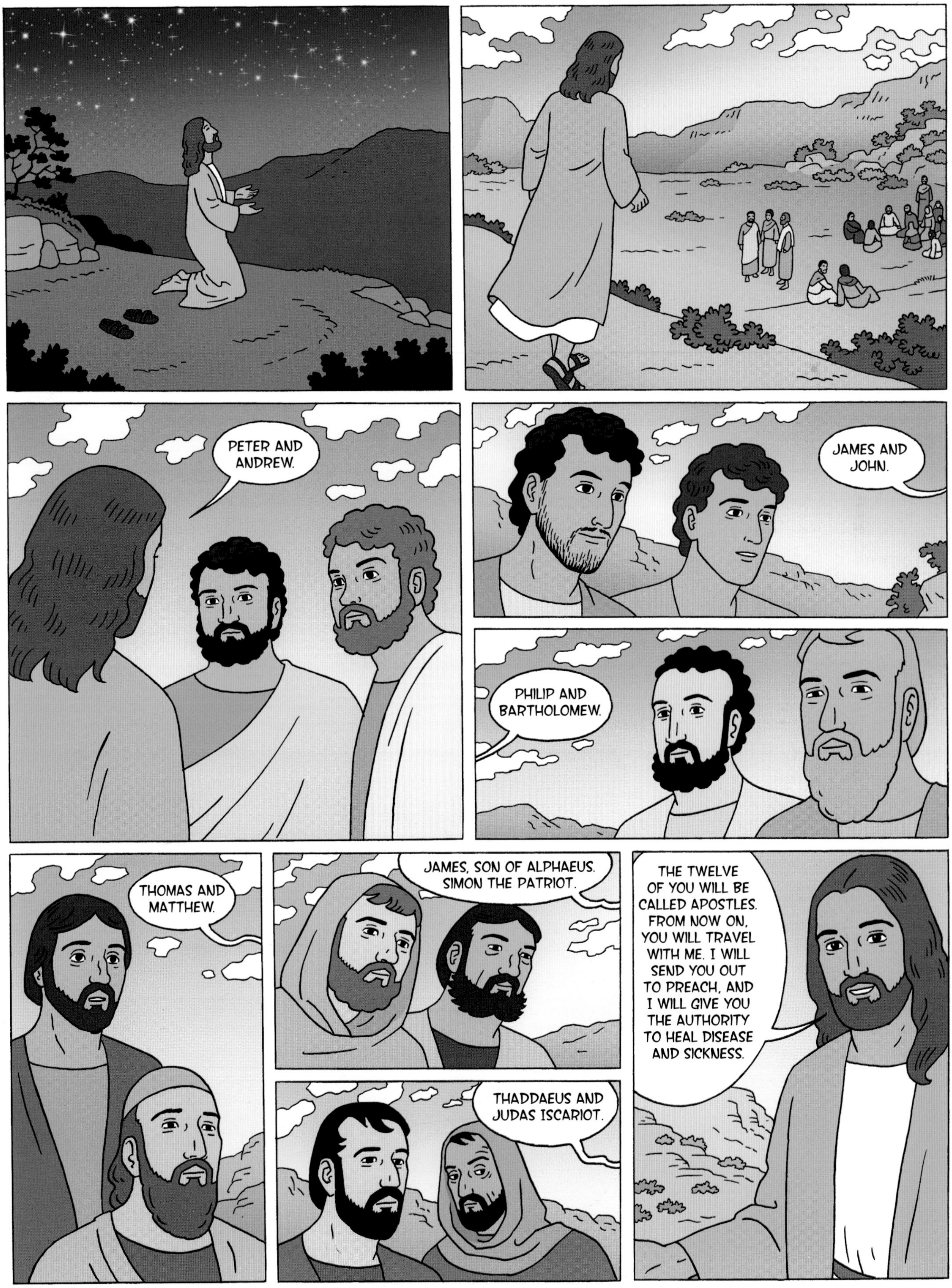
PETER AND ANDREW.
JAMES AND JOHN.
PHILIP AND BARTHOLOMEW.
THOMAS AND MATTHEW.
JAMES, SON OF ALPHAEUS. SIMON THE PATRIOT.
THADDAEUS AND JUDAS ISCARIOT.
THE TWELVE OF YOU WILL BE CALLED APOSTLES. FROM NOW ON, YOU WILL TRAVEL WITH ME. I WILL SEND YOU OUT TO PREACH, AND I WILL GIVE YOU THE AUTHORITY TO HEAL DISEASE AND SICKNESS.

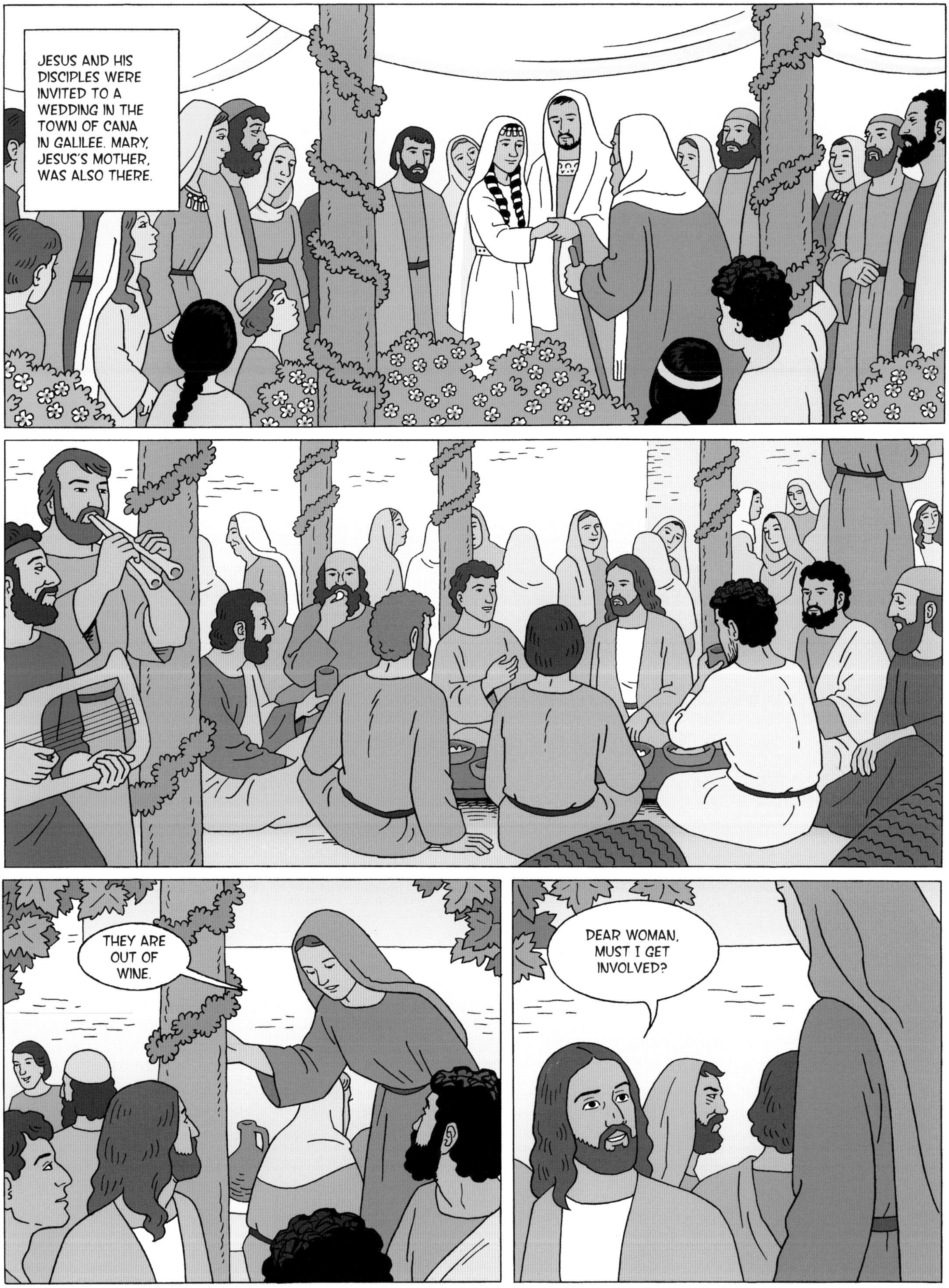
JESUS AND HIS DISCIPLES WERE INVITED TO A WEDDING IN THE TOWN OF CANA IN GALILEE. MARY, JESUS'S MOTHER, WAS ALSO THERE.
THEY ARE OUT OF WINE.
DEAR WOMAN, MUST I GET INVOLVED?

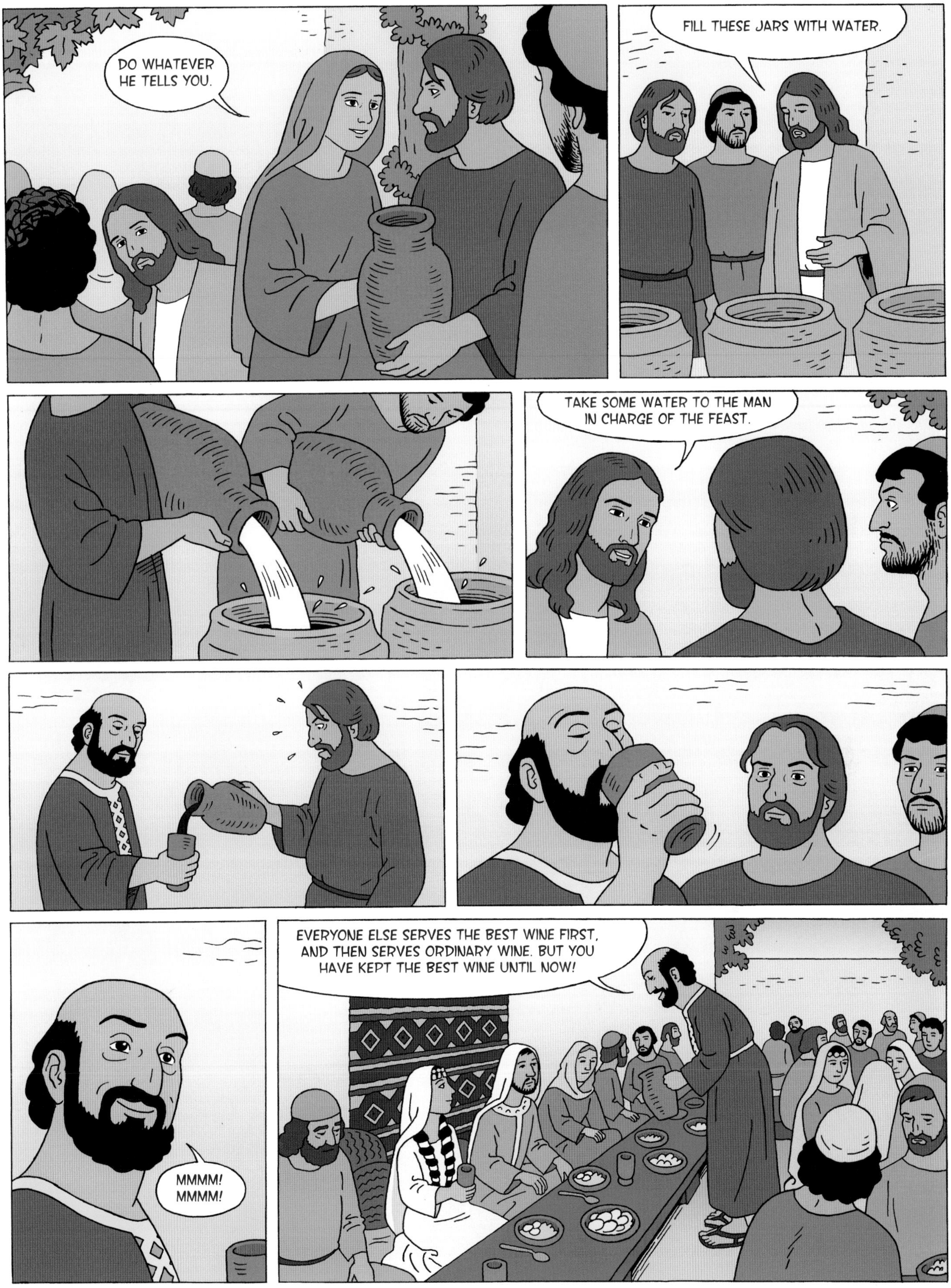
DO WHATEVER HE TELLS YOU.
FILL THESE JARS WITH WATER.
TAKE SOME WATER TO THE MAN IN CHARGE OF THE FEAST.
MMMM! MMMM!
EVERYONE ELSE SERVES THE BEST WINE FIRST, AND THEN SERVES ORDINARY WINE. BUT YOU HAVE KEPT THE BEST WINE UNTIL NOW!

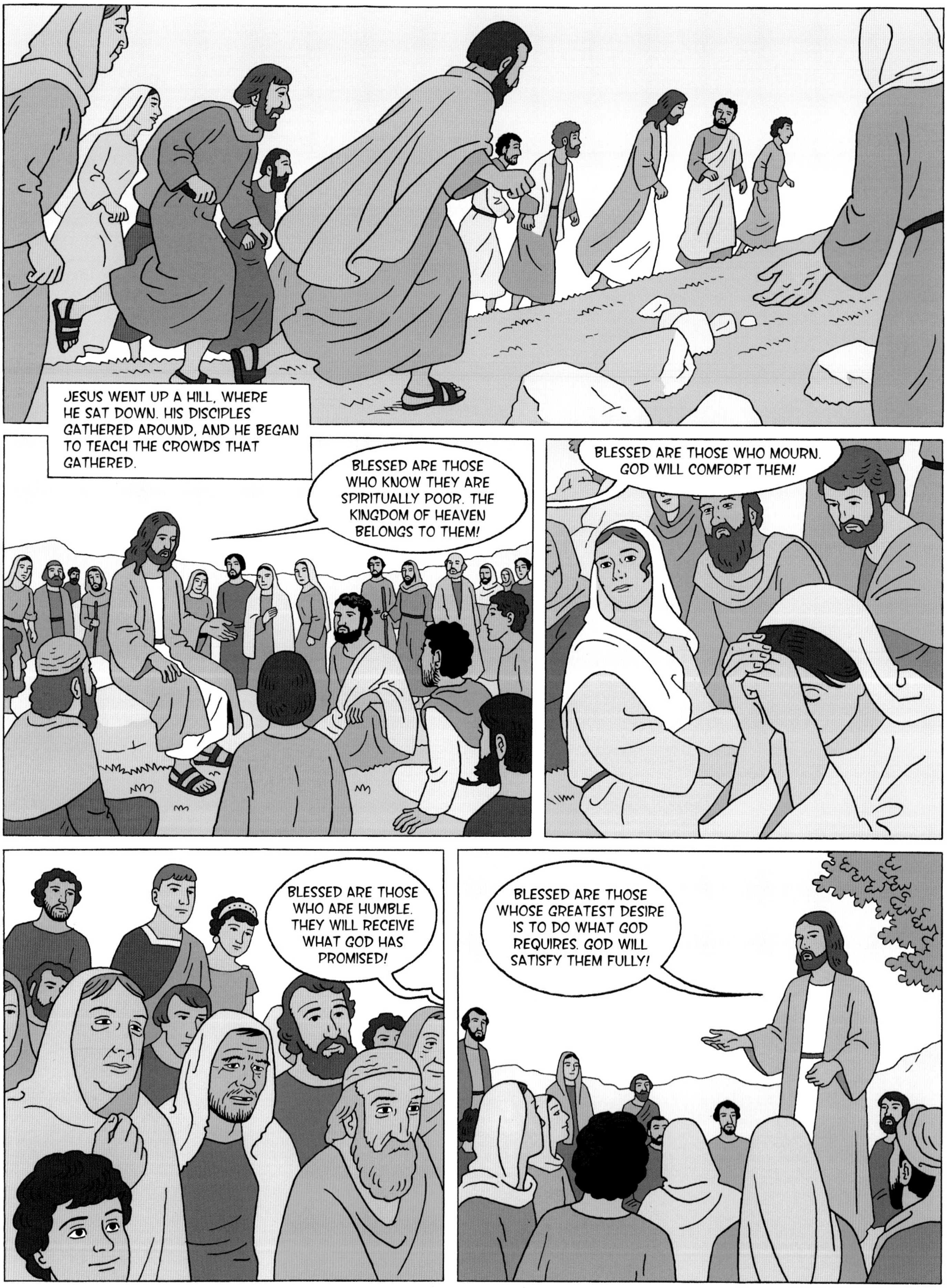
JESUS WENT UP A HILL, WHERE HE SAT DOWN. HIS DISCIPLES GATHERED AROUND, AND HE BEGAN TO TEACH THE CROWDS THAT GATHERED.
BLESSED ARE THOSE WHO KNOW THEY ARE SPIRITUALLY POOR. THE KINGDOM OF HEAVEN BELONGS TO THEM!
BLESSED ARE THOSE WHO MOURN. GOD WILL COMFORT THEM!
BLESSED ARE THOSE WHO ARE HUMBLE. THEY WILL RECEIVE WHAT GOD HAS PROMISED!
BLESSED ARE THOSE WHOSE GREATEST DESIRE IS TO DO WHAT GOD REQUIRES. GOD WILL SATISFY THEM FULLY!

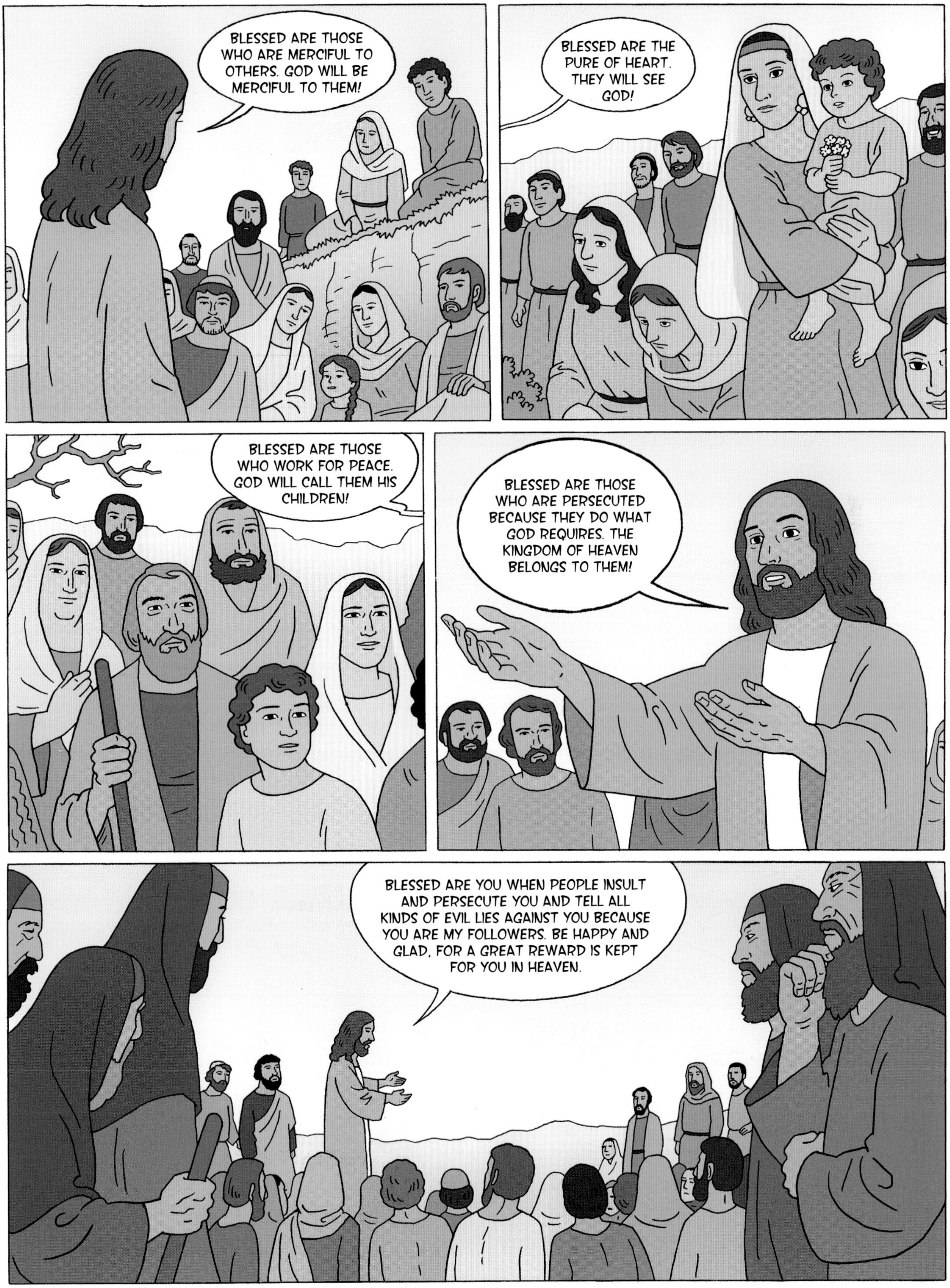
BLESSED ARE THOSE WHO ARE MERCIFUL TO OTHERS. GOD WILL BE MERCIFUL TO THEM!
BLESSED ARE THE PURE OF HEART. THEY WILL SEE GOD!
BLESSED ARE THOSE WHO WORK FOR PEACE. GOD WILL CALL THEM HIS CHILDREN!
BLESSED ARE THOSE WHO ARE PERSECUTED BECAUSE THEY DO WHAT GOD REQUIRES. THE KINGDOM OF HEAVEN BELONGS TO THEM!
BLESSED ARE YOU WHEN PEOPLE INSULT AND PERSECUTE YOU AND TELL ALL KINDS OF EVIL LIES AGAINST YOU BECAUSE YOU ARE MY FOLLOWERS. BE HAPPY AND GLAD, FOR A GREAT REWARD IS KEPT FOR YOU IN HEAVEN.

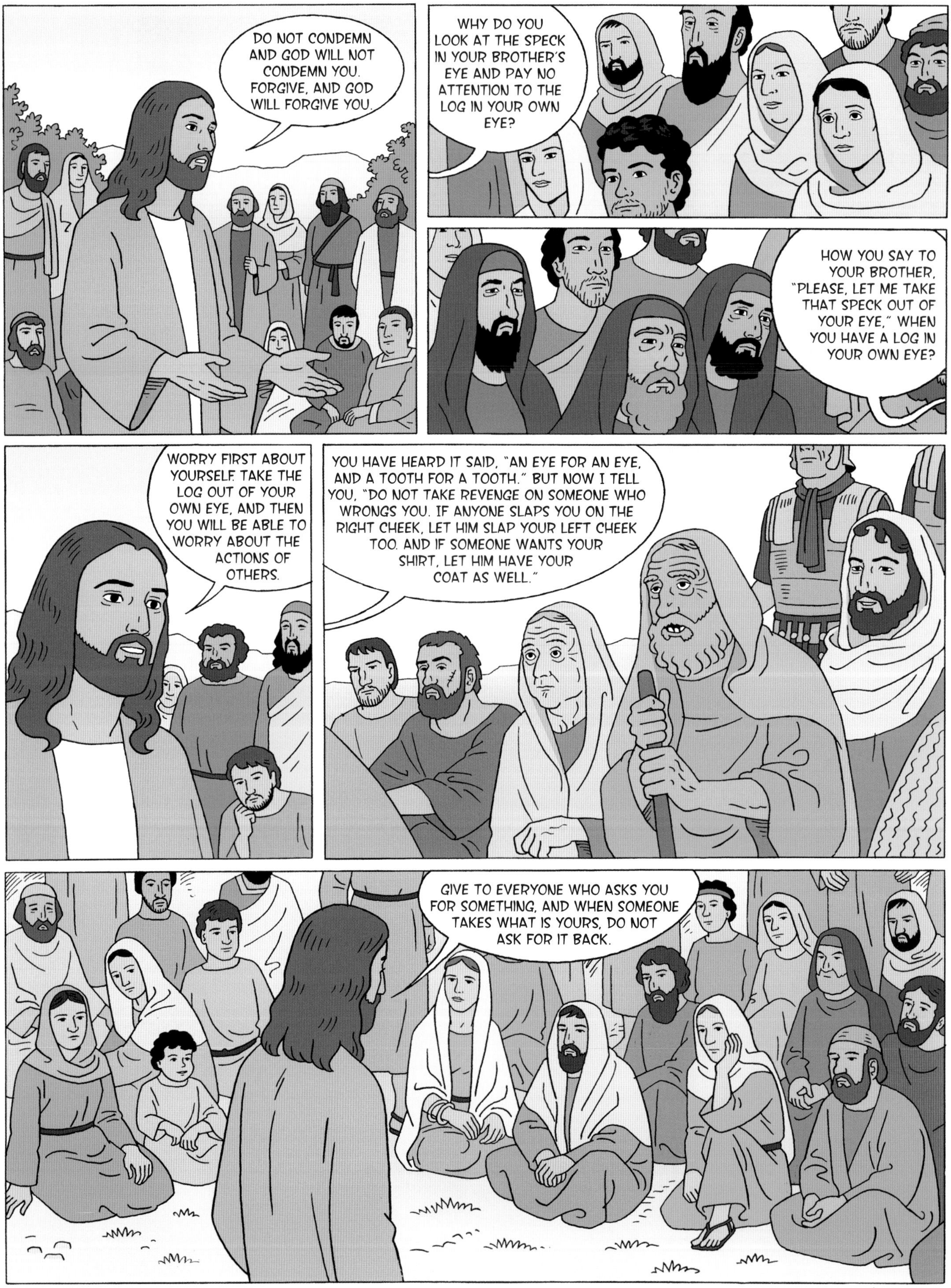
DO NOT CONDEMN AND GOD WILL NOT CONDEMN YOU. FORGIVE, AND GOD WILL FORGIVE YOU.
WHY DO YOU LOOK AT THE SPECK IN YOUR BROTHER'S EYE AND PAY NO ATTENTION TO THE LOG IN YOUR OWN EYE?
HOW YOU SAY TO YOUR BROTHER, "PLEASE, LET ME TAKE THAT SPECK OUT OF YOUR EYE," WHEN YOU HAVE A LOG IN YOUR OWN EYE?
WORRY FIRST ABOUT YOURSELF. TAKE THE LOG OUT OF YOUR OWN EYE, AND THEN YOU WILL BE ABLE TO WORRY ABOUT THE ACTIONS OF OTHERS.
YOU HAVE HEARD IT SAID, "AN EYE FOR AN EYE, AND A TOOTH FOR A TOOTH." BUT NOW I TELL YOU, "DO NOT TAKE REVENGE ON SOMEONE WHO WRONGS YOU. IF ANYONE SLAPS YOU ON THE RIGHT CHEEK, LET HIM SLAP YOUR LEFT CHEEK TOO. AND IF SOMEONE WANTS YOUR SHIRT, LET HIM HAVE YOUR COAT AS WELL."
GIVE TO EVERYONE WHO ASKS YOU FOR SOMETHING, AND WHEN SOMEONE TAKES WHAT IS YOURS, DO NOT ASK FOR IT BACK.

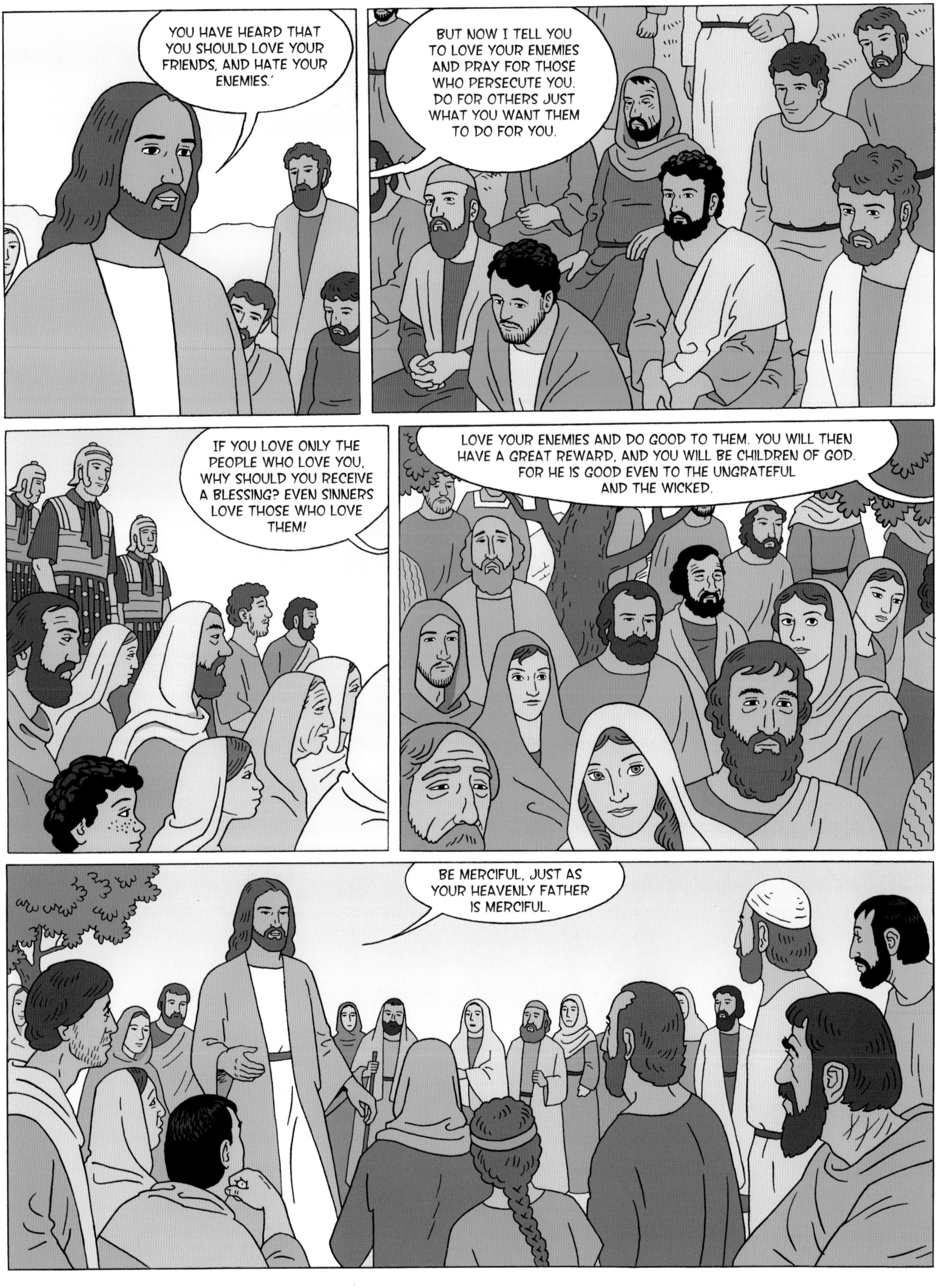
YOU HAVE HEARD THAT YOU SHOULD LOVE YOUR FRIENDS, AND HATE YOUR ENEMIES.'
BUT NOW I TELL YOU TO LOVE YOUR ENEMIES AND PRAY FOR THOSE WHO PERSECUTE YOU. DO FOR OTHERS JUST WHAT YOU WANT THEM TO DO FOR YOU.
IF YOU LOVE ONLY THE PEOPLE WHO LOVE YOU, WHY SHOULD YOU RECEIVE A BLESSING? EVEN SINNERS LOVE THOSE WHO LOVE THEM!
LOVE YOUR ENEMIES AND DO GOOD TO THEM. YOU WILL THEN HAVE A GREAT REWARD, AND YOU WILL BE CHILDREN OF GOD. FOR HE IS GOOD EVEN TO THE UNGRATEFUL AND THE WICKED.
BE MERCIFUL, JUST AS YOUR HEAVENLY FATHER IS MERCIFUL.

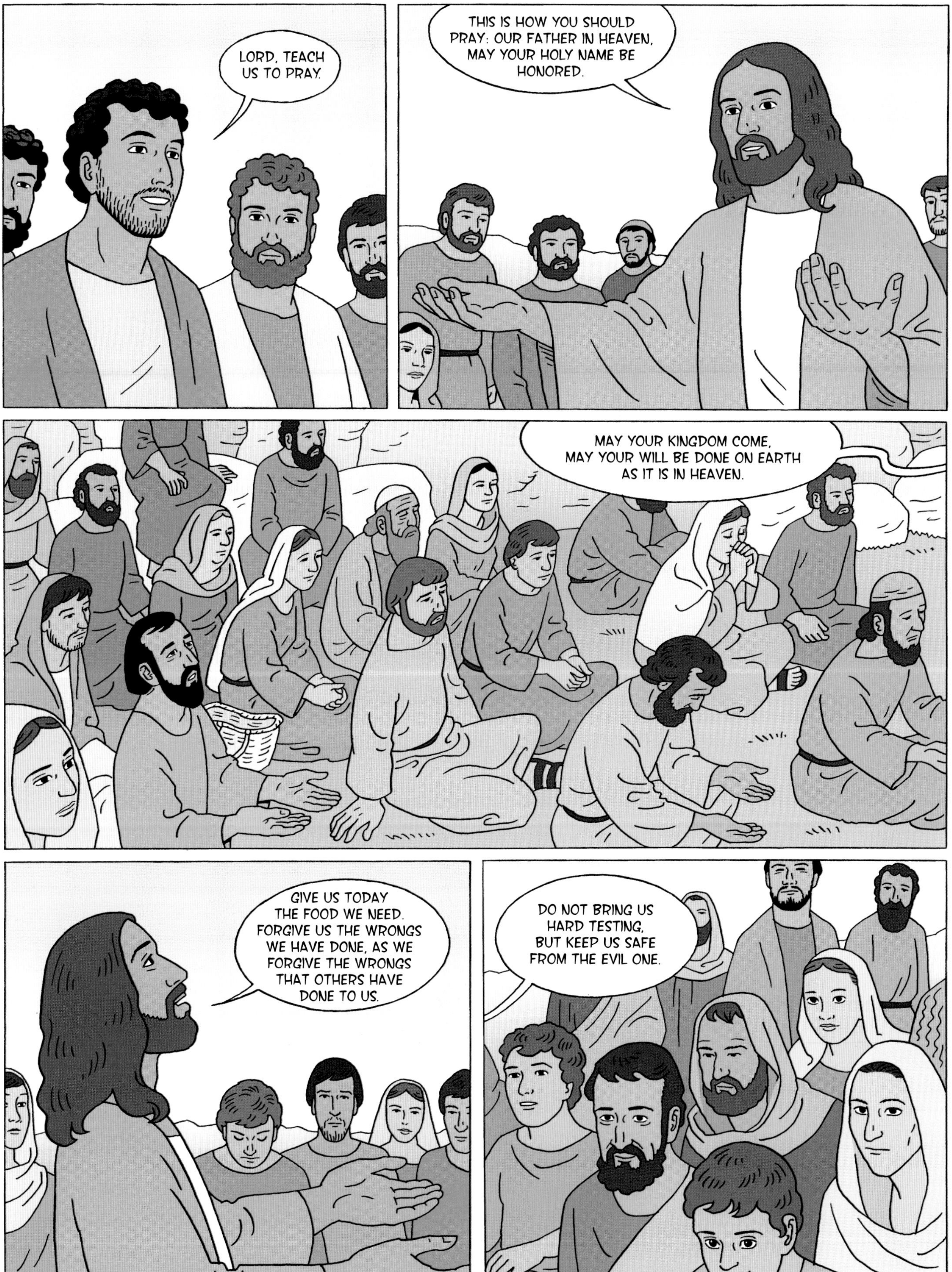
LORD, TEACH US TO PRAY.
THIS IS HOW YOU SHOULD PRAY: OUR FATHER IN HEAVEN, MAY YOUR HOLY NAME BE HONORED.
MAY YOUR KINGDOM COME, MAY YOUR WILL BE DONE ON EARTH AS IT IS IN HEAVEN.
GIVE US TODAY THE FOOD WE NEED. FORGIVE US THE WRONGS WE HAVE DONE, AS WE FORGIVE THE WRONGS THAT OTHERS HAVE DONE TO US.
DO NOT BRING US HARD TESTING, BUT KEEP US SAFE FROM THE EVIL ONE.

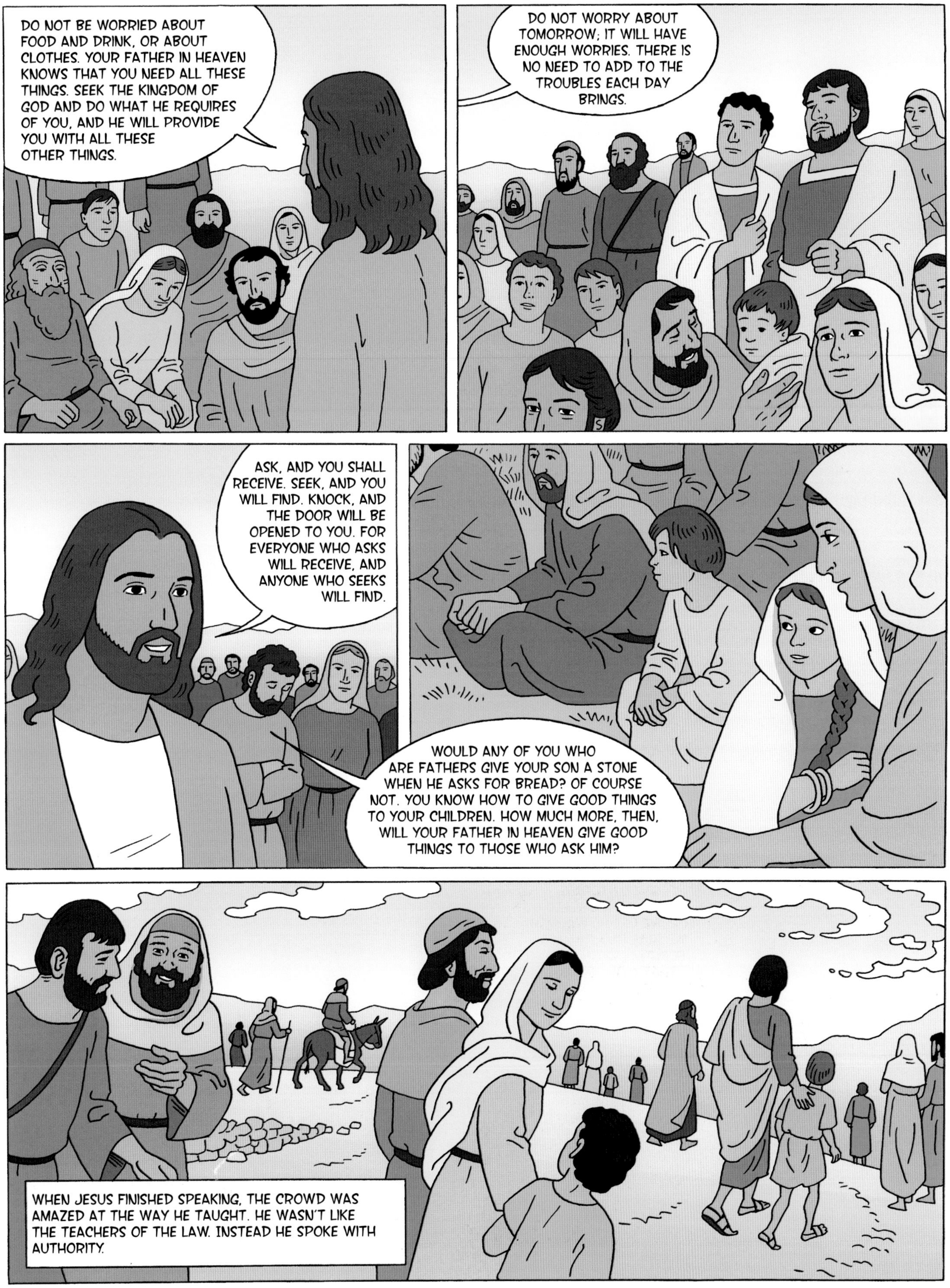
DO NOT BE WORRIED ABOUT FOOD AND DRINK, OR ABOUT CLOTHES. YOUR FATHER IN HEAVEN KNOWS THAT YOU NEED ALL THESE THINGS. SEEK THE KINGDOM OF GOD AND DO WHAT HE REQUIRES OF YOU, AND HE WILL PROVIDE YOU WITH ALL THESE OTHER THINGS.
DO NOT WORRY ABOUT TOMORROW; IT WILL HAVE ENOUGH WORRIES. THERE IS NO NEED TO ADD TO THE TROUBLES EACH DAY BRINGS.
ASK, AND YOU SHALL RECEIVE. SEEK, AND YOU WILL FIND. KNOCK, AND THE DOOR WILL BE OPENED TO YOU. FOR EVERYONE WHO ASKS WILL RECEIVE, AND ANYONE WHO SEEKS WILL FIND.
WOULD ANY OF YOU WHO ARE FATHERS GIVE YOUR SON A STONE WHEN HE ASKS FOR BREAD? OF COURSE NOT. YOU KNOW HOW TO GIVE GOOD THINGS TO YOUR CHILDREN. HOW MUCH MORE, THEN, WILL YOUR FATHER IN HEAVEN GIVE GOOD THINGS TO THOSE WHO ASK HIM?
WHEN JESUS FINISHED SPEAKING, THE CROWD WAS AMAZED AT THE WAY HE TAUGHT. HE WASN'T LIKE THE TEACHERS OF THE LAW. INSTEAD HE SPOKE WITH AUTHORITY.

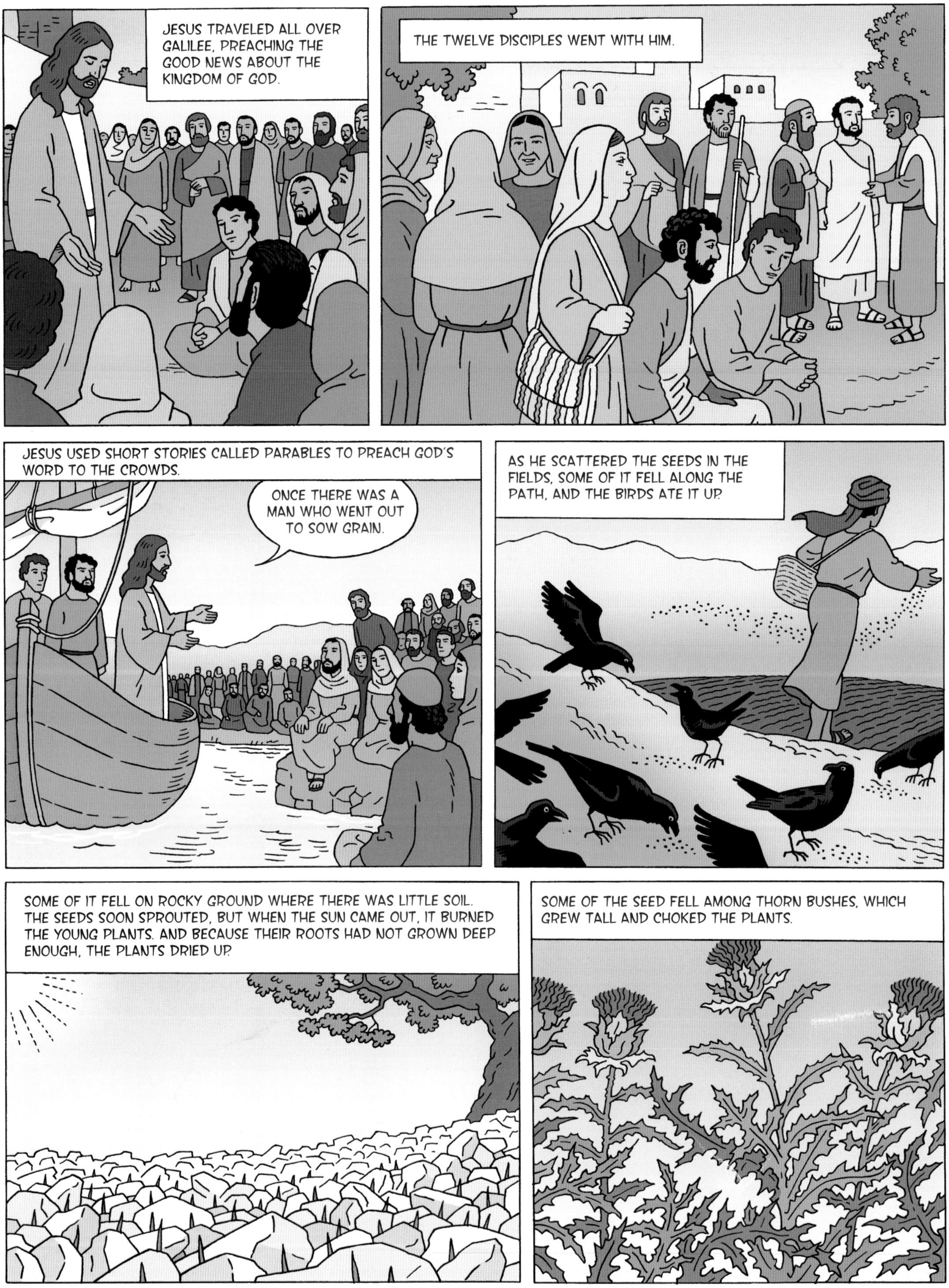
JESUS TRAVELED ALL OVER GALILEE, PREACHING THE GOOD NEWS ABOUT THE KINGDOM OF GOD.
THE TWELVE DISCIPLES WENT WITH HIM.
JESUS USED SHORT STORIES CALLED PARABLES TO PREACH GOD'S WORD TO THE CROWDS.
ONCE THERE WAS A MAN WHO WENT OUT TO SOW GRAIN.
AS HE SCATTERED THE SEEDS IN THE FIELDS, SOME OF IT FELL ALONG THE PATH, AND THE BIRDS ATE IT UP.
SOME OF IT FELL ON ROCKY GROUND WHERE THERE WAS LITTLE SOIL. THE SEEDS SOON SPROUTED, BUT WHEN THE SUN CAME OUT, IT BURNED THE YOUNG PLANTS. AND BECAUSE THEIR ROOTS HAD NOT GROWN DEEP ENOUGH, THE PLANTS DRIED UP.
SOME OF THE SEED FELL AMONG THORN BUSHES, WHICH GREW TALL AND CHOKED THE PLANTS.

BUT SOME SEEDS FELL IN GOOD SOIL, AND THE PLANTS BORE GRAIN. SOME EVEN HAD ONE HUNDRED GRAINS. OTHERS HAD SIXTY, AND OTHERS HAD THIRTY.

WHY DO YOU USE PARABLES?

SOMETIMES, PEOPLE WHO ARE ON THE OUTSIDE OF THE KINGDOM OF GOD LEARN BEST THROUGH PARABLES.

HERE IS WHAT THE PARABLE MEANS. THE SEED IS THE WORD OF GOD. THOSE WHO HEAR IT BUT DO NOT UNDERSTAND IT, ARE LIKE THE SEEDS THAT FELL ALONG THE PATH. THE DEVIL COMES AND SNATCHES AWAY WHAT WAS SOWN IN THEM.

THE SEEDS THAT FELL ON ROCKY GROUND STAND FOR THOSE WHO RECEIVE THE MESSAGE GLADLY AS SOON AS THEY HEAR IT, BUT IT DOES NOT SINK DEEPLY INTO THEM. THEY BELIEVE FOR AWHILE, BUT WHEN HARDSHIPS COME, THEY FALL AWAY.

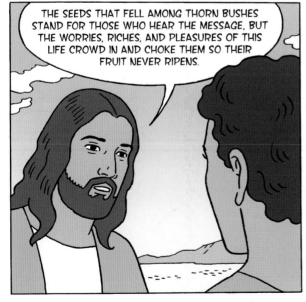

THE SEEDS THAT FELL AMONG THORN BUSHES STAND FOR THOSE WHO HEAR THE MESSAGE, BUT THE WORRIES, RICHES, AND PLEASURES OF THIS LIFE CROWD IN AND CHOKE THEM SO THEIR FRUIT NEVER RIPENS.

THE SEEDS SOWN IN THE GOOD SOIL REPRESENT THOSE WHO HEAR THE MESSAGE AND RETAIN IT IN A GOOD HEART. THEY PERSIST UNTIL THEY BEAR FRUIT.

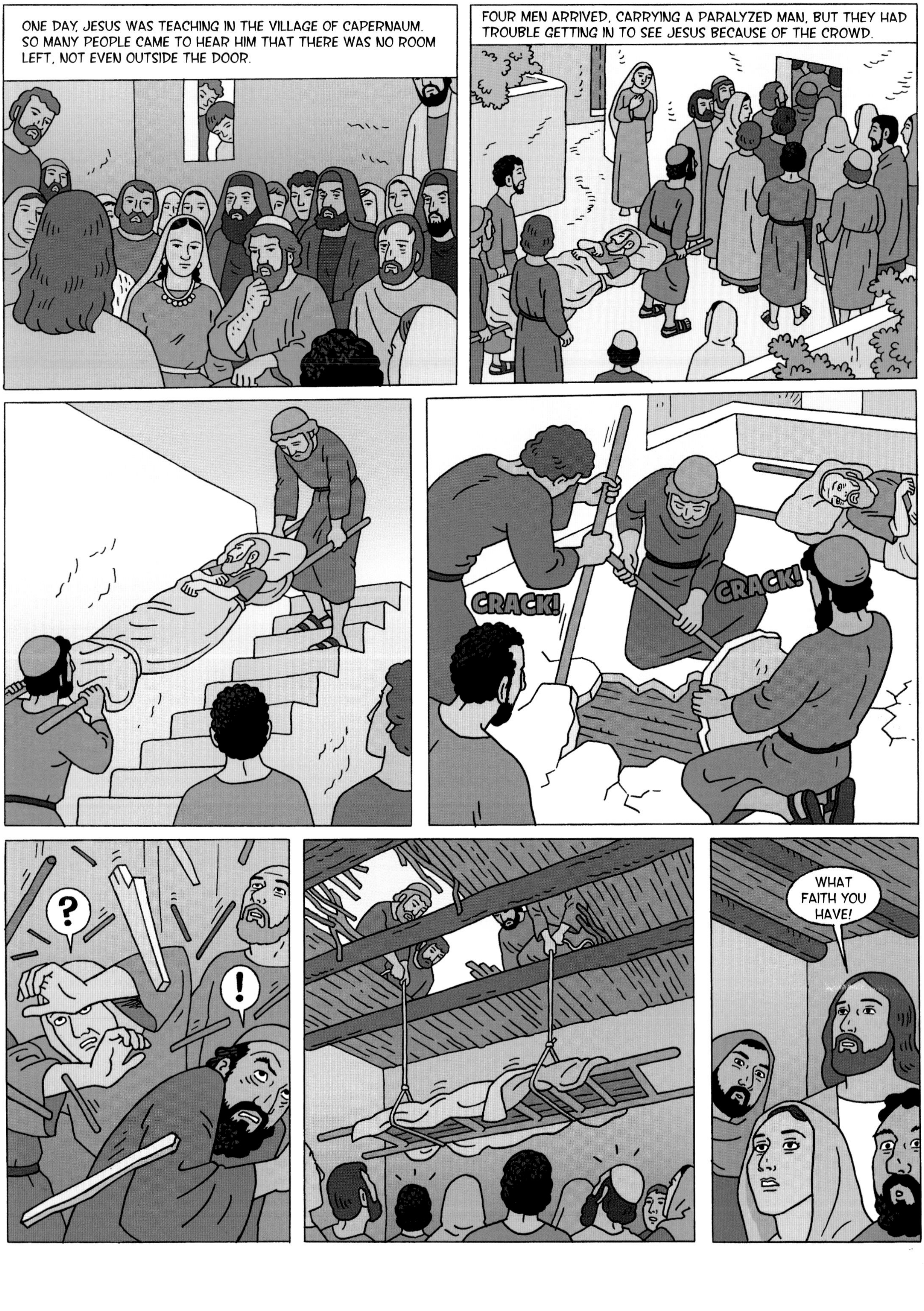
ONE DAY, JESUS WAS TEACHING IN THE VILLAGE OF CAPERNAUM. SO MANY PEOPLE CAME TO HEAR HIM THAT THERE WAS NO ROOM LEFT, NOT EVEN OUTSIDE THE DOOR.
FOUR MEN ARRIVED, CARRYING A PARALYZED MAN, BUT THEY HAD TROUBLE GETTING IN TO SEE JESUS BECAUSE OF THE CROWD.
CRACK!
CRACK!
?
!
WHAT FAITH YOU HAVE!

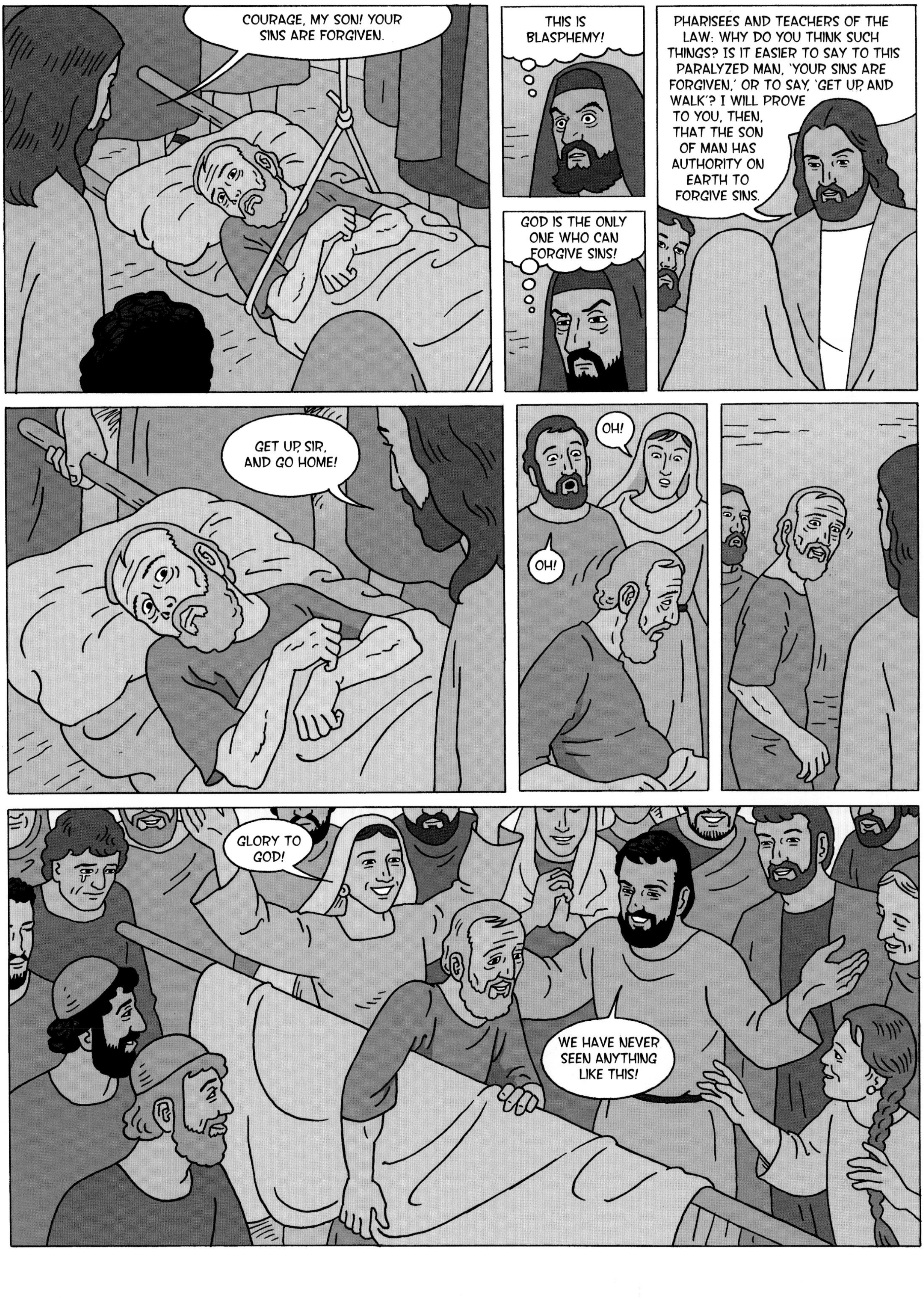
COURAGE, MY SON! YOUR SINS ARE FORGIVEN.
THIS IS BLASPHEMY!
GOD IS THE ONLY ONE WHO CAN FORGIVE SINS!
PHARISEES AND TEACHERS OF THE LAW: WHY DO YOU THINK SUCH THINGS? IS IT EASIER TO SAY TO THIS PARALYZED MAN, 'YOUR SINS ARE FORGIVEN,' OR TO SAY, 'GET UP, AND WALK'? I WILL PROVE TO YOU, THEN, THAT THE SON OF MAN HAS AUTHORITY ON EARTH TO FORGIVE SINS.
GET UP, SIR, AND GO HOME!
OH!
OH!
GLORY TO GOD!
WE HAVE NEVER SEEN ANYTHING LIKE THIS!

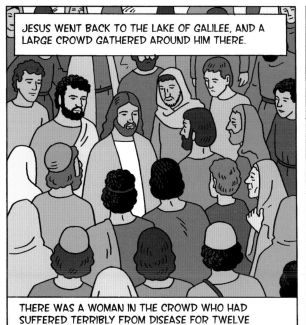

JESUS WENT BACK TO THE LAKE OF GALILEE, AND A LARGE CROWD GATHERED AROUND HIM THERE.

THERE WAS A WOMAN IN THE CROWD WHO HAD SUFFERED TERRIBLY FROM DISEASE FOR TWELVE YEARS.

THEN, JAIRUS, AN OFFICIAL AT THE LOCAL SYNAGOGUE, ARRIVED.

MY DAUGHTER IS VERY SICK. PLEASE COME AND PLACE YOUR HANDS ON HER SO THAT SHE WILL GET WELL AND LIVE!

IF I JUST TOUCH HIS CLOAK, I WILL GET WELL!

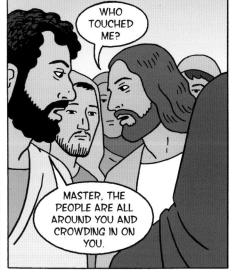

WHO TOUCHED ME?

MASTER, THE PEOPLE ARE ALL AROUND YOU AND CROWDING IN ON YOU.

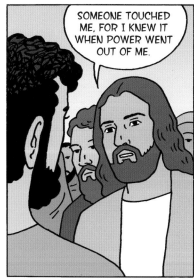

SOMEONE TOUCHED ME, FOR I KNEW IT WHEN POWER WENT OUT OF ME.

MASTER, IT WAS ME. I HAVE TOUCHED THE GARMENT, AND I HEALED.

WOMAN, YOUR FAITH HAS MADE YOU WELL. GO IN PEACE, AND BE HEALED OF YOUR TROUBLE.

YOUR DAUGHTER HAS DIED. WHY BOTHER THE TEACHER ANY LONGER?

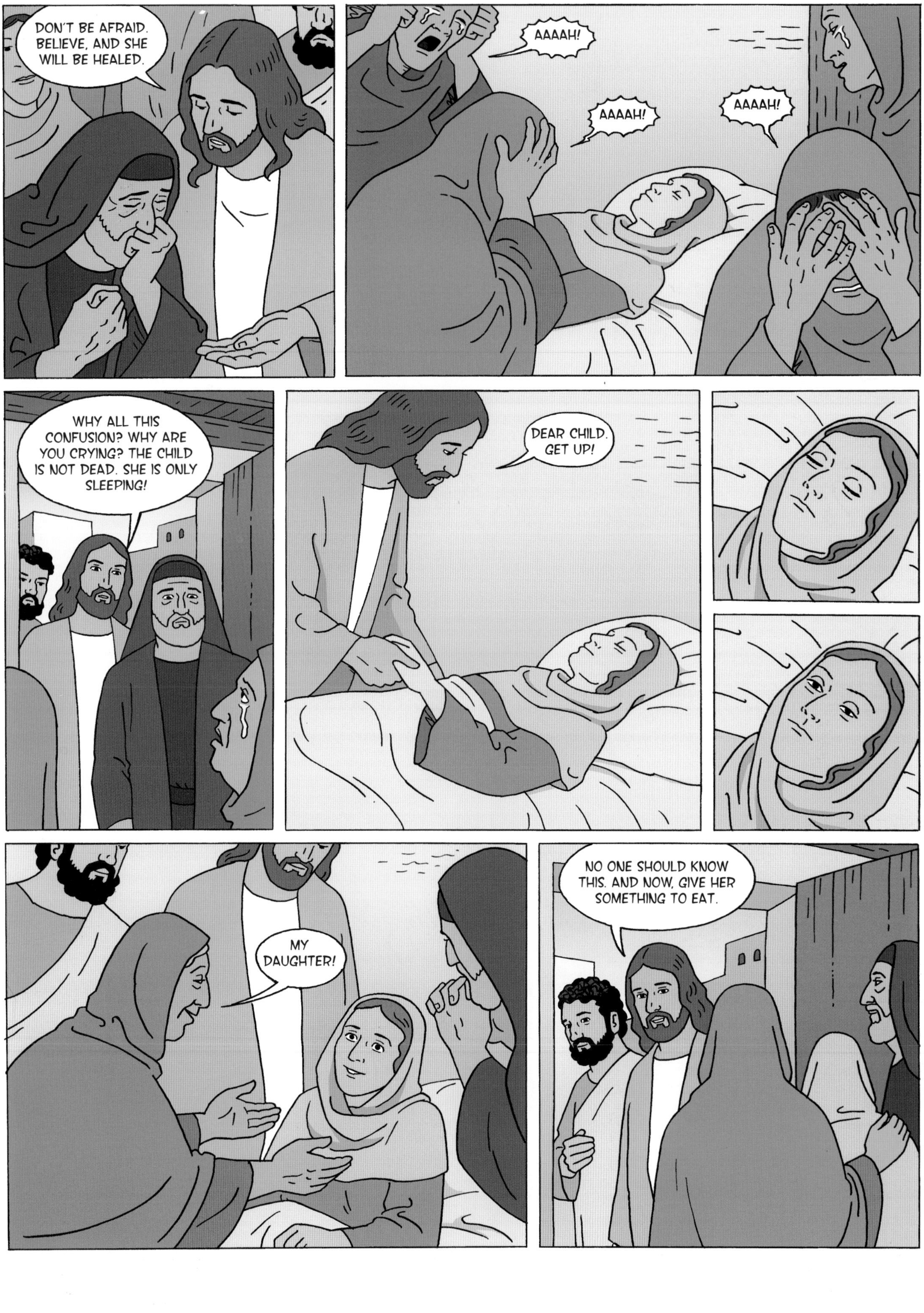
DON'T BE AFRAID. BELIEVE, AND SHE WILL BE HEALED.
AAAAH!
AAAAH!
AAAAH!
WHY ALL THIS CONFUSION? WHY ARE YOU CRYING? THE CHILD IS NOT DEAD. SHE IS ONLY SLEEPING!
DEAR CHILD. GET UP!
MY DAUGHTER!
NO ONE SHOULD KNOW THIS. AND NOW, GIVE HER SOMETHING TO EAT.

JESUS AND HIS DISCIPLES HEADED OUT IN A BOAT BY THEMSELVES TO AN ISOLATED PLACE WHERE THEY COULD REST AWHILE. BUT THE PEOPLE HEARD HE WAS THERE AND FOLLOWED HIM BY LAND.

WHEN JESUS GOT OUT OF THE BOAT, HE SAW THE LARGE CROWD, AND HIS HEART WAS FILLED WITH PITY FOR THEM. THEY WERE LIKE SHEEP WITHOUT A SHEPHERD.

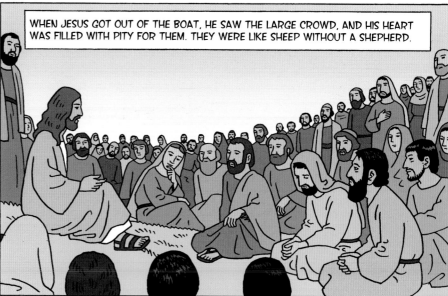

IT IS ALREADY VERY LATE, AND THIS IS A LONELY PLACE. SEND THE PEOPLE AWAY, AND LET THEM GO TO THE NEARBY FARMS AND VILLAGES TO BUY THEMSELVES SOMETHING TO EAT.

WE WILL GIVE THEM SOMETHING TO EAT.

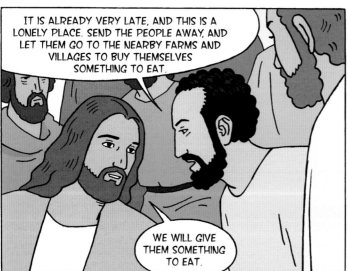

FOR EVERYONE TO HAVE EVEN A LITTLE, IT WOULD TAKE MORE THAN TWO HUNDRED SILVER COINS TO BUY ENOUGH BREAD.

HOW MUCH BREAD DO YOU HAVE?

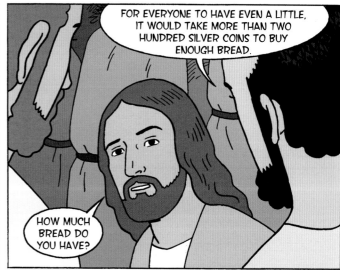

THIS BOY HAS FIVE LOAVES OF BARLEY BREAD AND TWO FISH. BUT THEY WILL CERTAINLY NOT BE ENOUGH FOR ALL THESE PEOPLE.

HAVE THE PEOPLE SIT DOWN.

BLESSED ARE YOU, LORD, GOD OF ALL CREATION. THROUGH YOUR GOODNESS, WE HAVE THIS BREAD TO OFFER, WHICH EARTH HAS GIVEN AND HUMAN HANDS HAVE MADE.

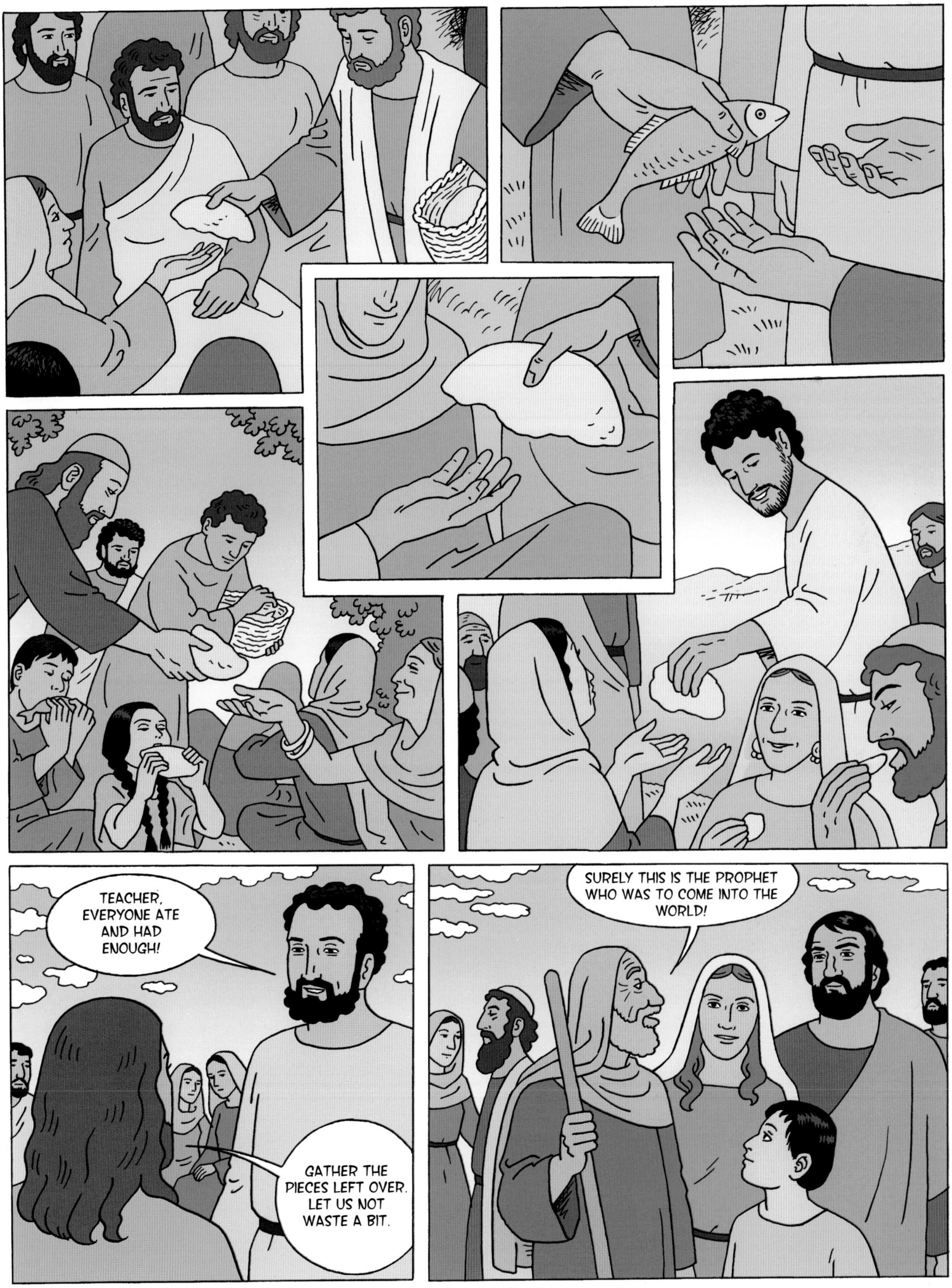
TEACHER, EVERYONE ATE AND HAD ENOUGH!
GATHER THE PIECES LEFT OVER. LET US NOT WASTE A BIT.
SURELY THIS IS THE PROPHET WHO WAS TO COME INTO THE WORLD!

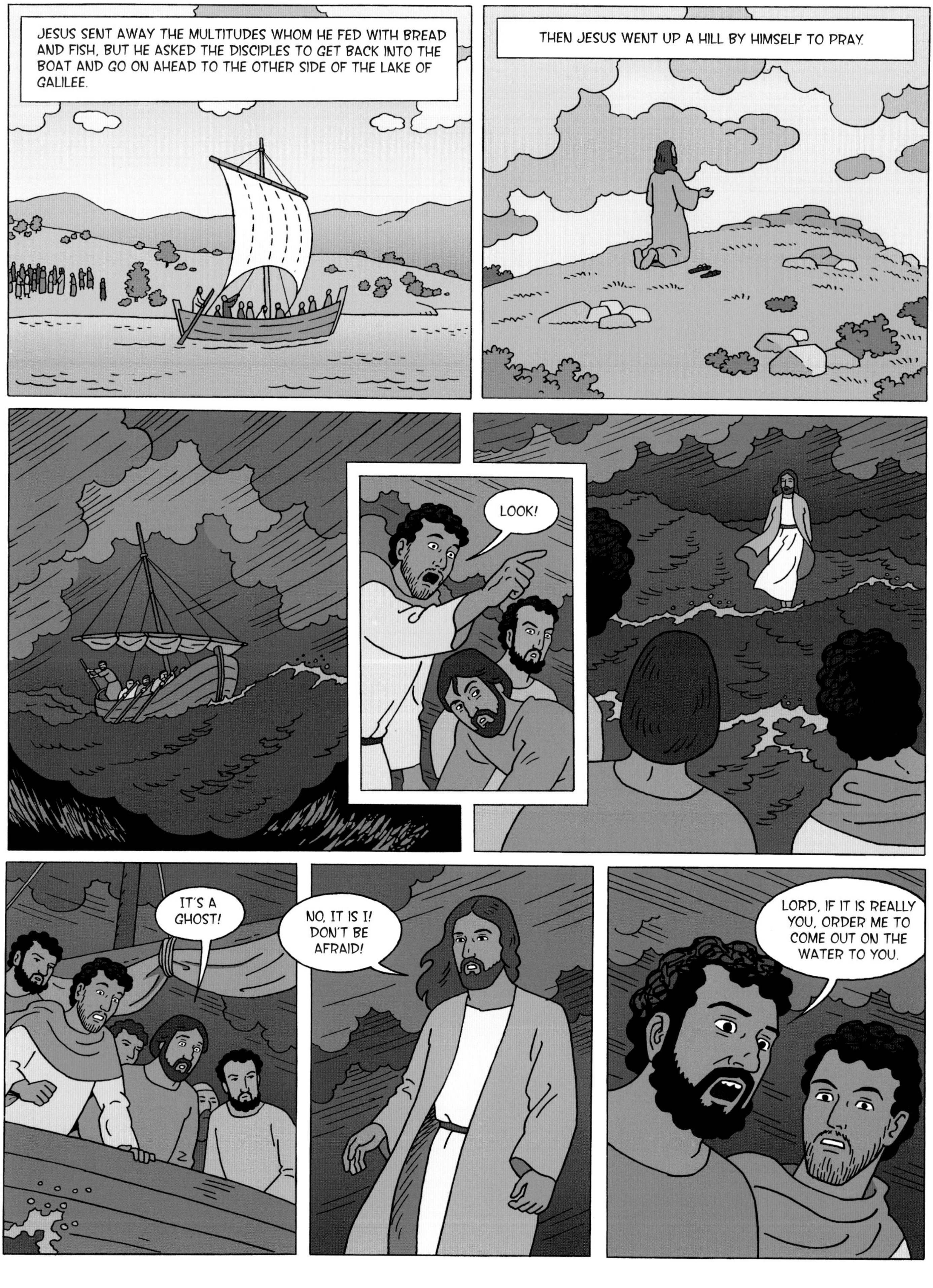
JESUS SENT AWAY THE MULTITUDES WHOM HE FED WITH BREAD AND FISH, BUT HE ASKED THE DISCIPLES TO GET BACK INTO THE BOAT AND GO ON AHEAD TO THE OTHER SIDE OF THE LAKE OF GALILEE.
THEN JESUS WENT UP A HILL BY HIMSELF TO PRAY.
LOOK!
IT'S A GHOST!
NO, IT IS I! DON'T BE AFRAID!
LORD, IF IT IS REALLY YOU, ORDER ME TO COME OUT ON THE WATER TO YOU.

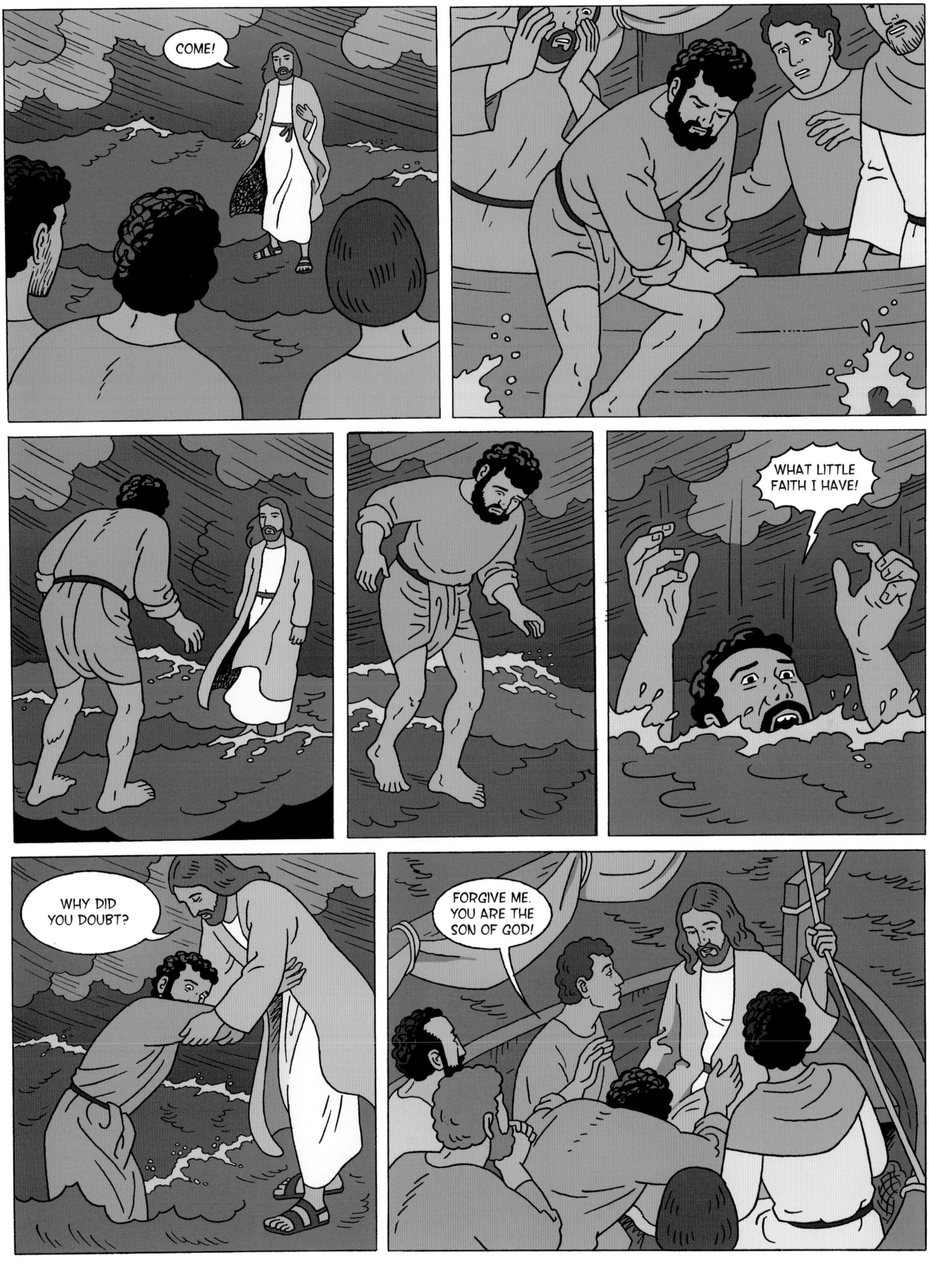
COME!
WHAT LITTLE FAITH I HAVE!
WHY DID YOU DOUBT?
FORGIVE ME. YOU ARE THE SON OF GOD!

JESUS LED PETER, JAMES, AND JOHN UP A HIGH MOUNTAIN TO PRAY.

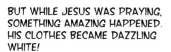

BUT WHILE JESUS WAS PRAYING, SOMETHING AMAZING HAPPENED. HIS CLOTHES BECAME DAZZLING WHITE!

THEN THE THREE DISCIPLES SAW MOSES AND ELIJAH TALKING WITH JESUS.

LORD, HOW GOOD IT IS THAT WE ARE HERE! IF YOU WISH, I WILL SET UP THREE TENTS: ONE FOR YOU, ONE FOR MOSES, AND ONE FOR ELIJAH.
THIS IS MY OWN DEAR SON, WITH WHOM I AM VERY PLEASED. LISTEN TO HIM!
GET UP. DON'T BE AFRAID!
DON'T TELL ANYONE ABOUT THIS VISION UNTIL THE SON OF MAN HAS BEEN RAISED FROM DEATH.

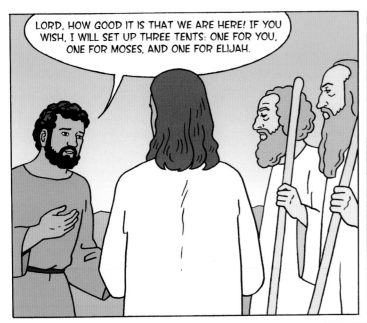

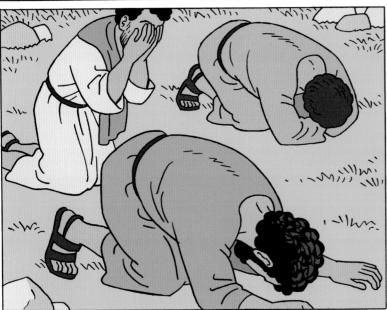

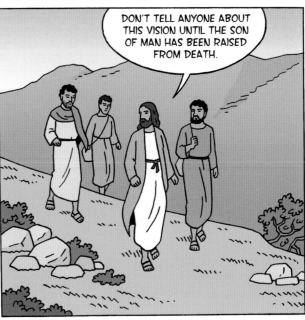

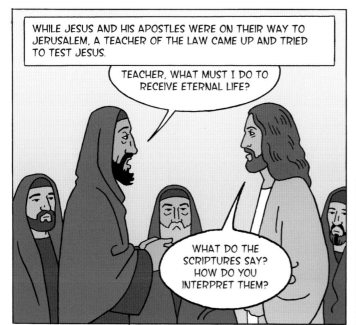

WHILE JESUS AND HIS APOSTLES WERE ON THEIR WAY TO JERUSALEM, A TEACHER OF THE LAW CAME UP AND TRIED TO TEST JESUS.

TEACHER, WHAT MUST I DO TO RECEIVE ETERNAL LIFE?

WHAT DO THE SCRIPTURES SAY? HOW DO YOU INTERPRET THEM?

"LOVE THE LORD, YOUR GOD, WITH ALL YOUR HEART, WITH ALL YOUR SOUL, WITH ALL YOUR STRENGTH, AND WITH ALL YOUR MIND." AND "LOVE YOUR NEIGHBOR AS YOU LOVE YOURSELF."

YOU ARE RIGHT. DO AS IT SAYS.

BUT WHO IS MY NEIGHBOR?

THERE WAS ONCE A MAN WHO WAS GOING DOWN FROM JERUSALEM TO JERICHO WHEN ROBBERS ATTACKED HIM.

THEY STRIPPED HIM AND BEAT HIM UP, LEAVING HIM HALF DEAD.

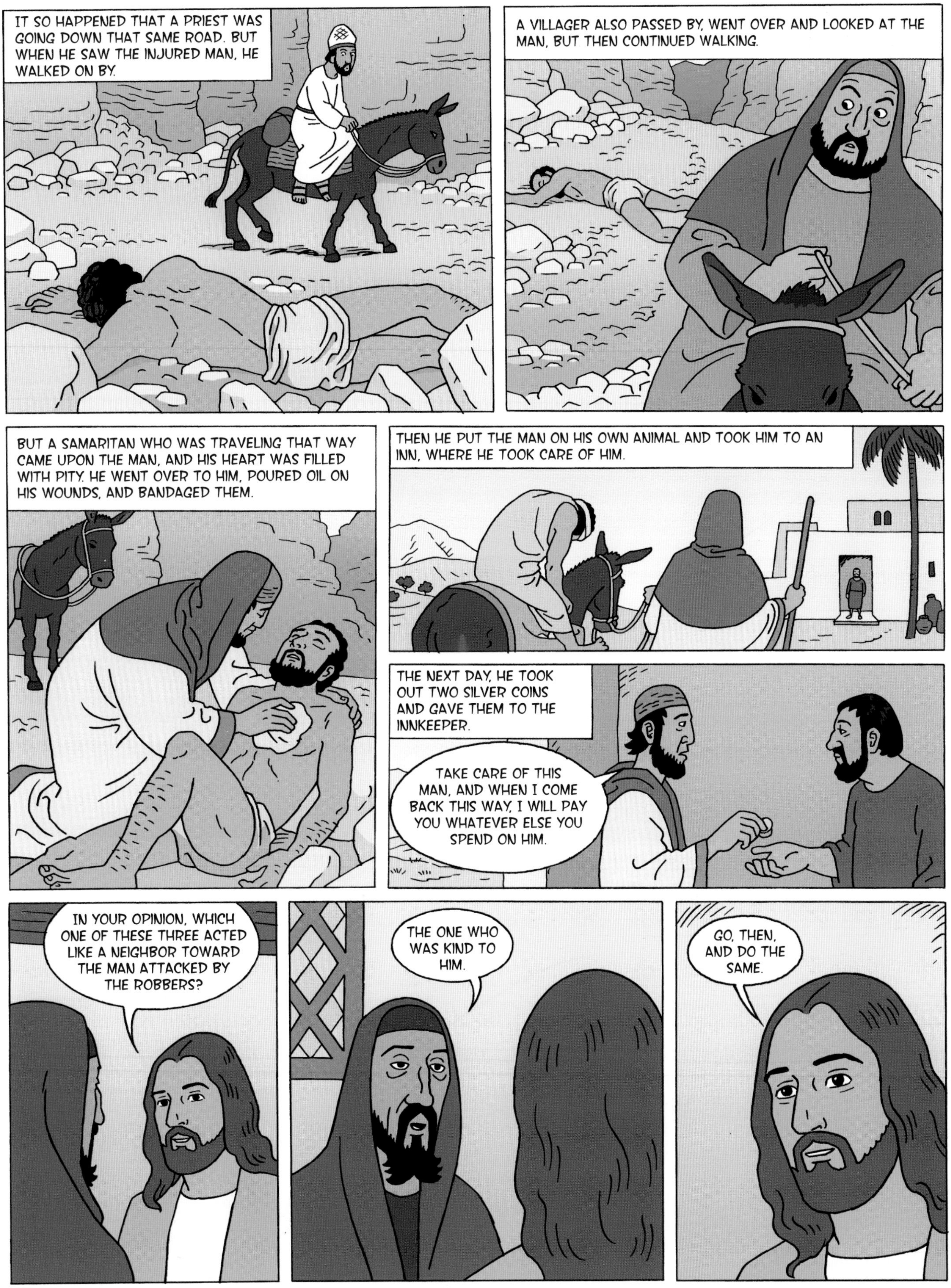
IT SO HAPPENED THAT A PRIEST WAS GOING DOWN THAT SAME ROAD. BUT WHEN HE SAW THE INJURED MAN, HE WALKED ON BY.
A VILLAGER ALSO PASSED BY, WENT OVER AND LOOKED AT THE MAN, BUT THEN CONTINUED WALKING.
BUT A SAMARITAN WHO WAS TRAVELING THAT WAY CAME UPON THE MAN, AND HIS HEART WAS FILLED WITH PITY. HE WENT OVER TO HIM, POURED OIL ON HIS WOUNDS, AND BANDAGED THEM.
THEN HE PUT THE MAN ON HIS OWN ANIMAL AND TOOK HIM TO AN INN, WHERE HE TOOK CARE OF HIM.
THE NEXT DAY, HE TOOK OUT TWO SILVER COINS AND GAVE THEM TO THE INNKEEPER.
TAKE CARE OF THIS MAN, AND WHEN I COME BACK THIS WAY, I WILL PAY YOU WHATEVER ELSE YOU SPEND ON HIM.
IN YOUR OPINION, WHICH ONE OF THESE THREE ACTED LIKE A NEIGHBOR TOWARD THE MAN ATTACKED BY THE ROBBERS?
THE ONE WHO WAS KIND TO HIM.
GO, THEN, AND DO THE SAME.

SOME PEOPLE BROUGHT CHILDREN TO JESUS SO HE COULD PLACE HIS HANDS ON THEM. THE DISCIPLES SCOLDED THEM, BUT JESUS SAID . . .

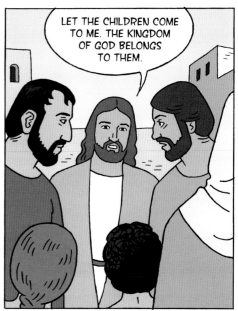

LET THE CHILDREN COME TO ME. THE KINGDOM OF GOD BELONGS TO THEM.

I ASSURE YOU THAT WHOEVER DOES NOT RECEIVE THE KINGDOM OF GOD LIKE A CHILD WILL NEVER ENTER IT.

GOOD TEACHER, WHAT MUST I DO TO RECEIVE ETERNAL LIFE?

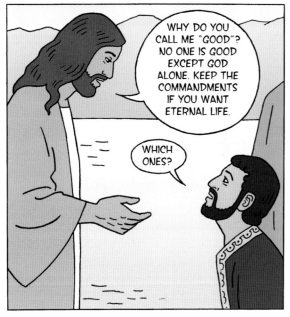

WHY DO YOU CALL ME "GOOD"? NO ONE IS GOOD EXCEPT GOD ALONE. KEEP THE COMMANDMENTS IF YOU WANT ETERNAL LIFE.

WHICH ONES?

ALL OF THEM. DO NOT COMMIT MURDER. DO NOT COMMIT ADULTERY. DO NOT STEAL. DO NOT ACCUSE ANYONE FALSELY, AND ALL THE REST.

TEACHER, I HAVE OBEYED ALL THESE COMMANDMENTS. WHAT ELSE MUST I DO?

GO AND SELL ALL YOU HAVE AND GIVE THE MONEY TO THE POOR. YOU WILL HAVE RICHES IN HEAVEN; THEN FOLLOW ME.

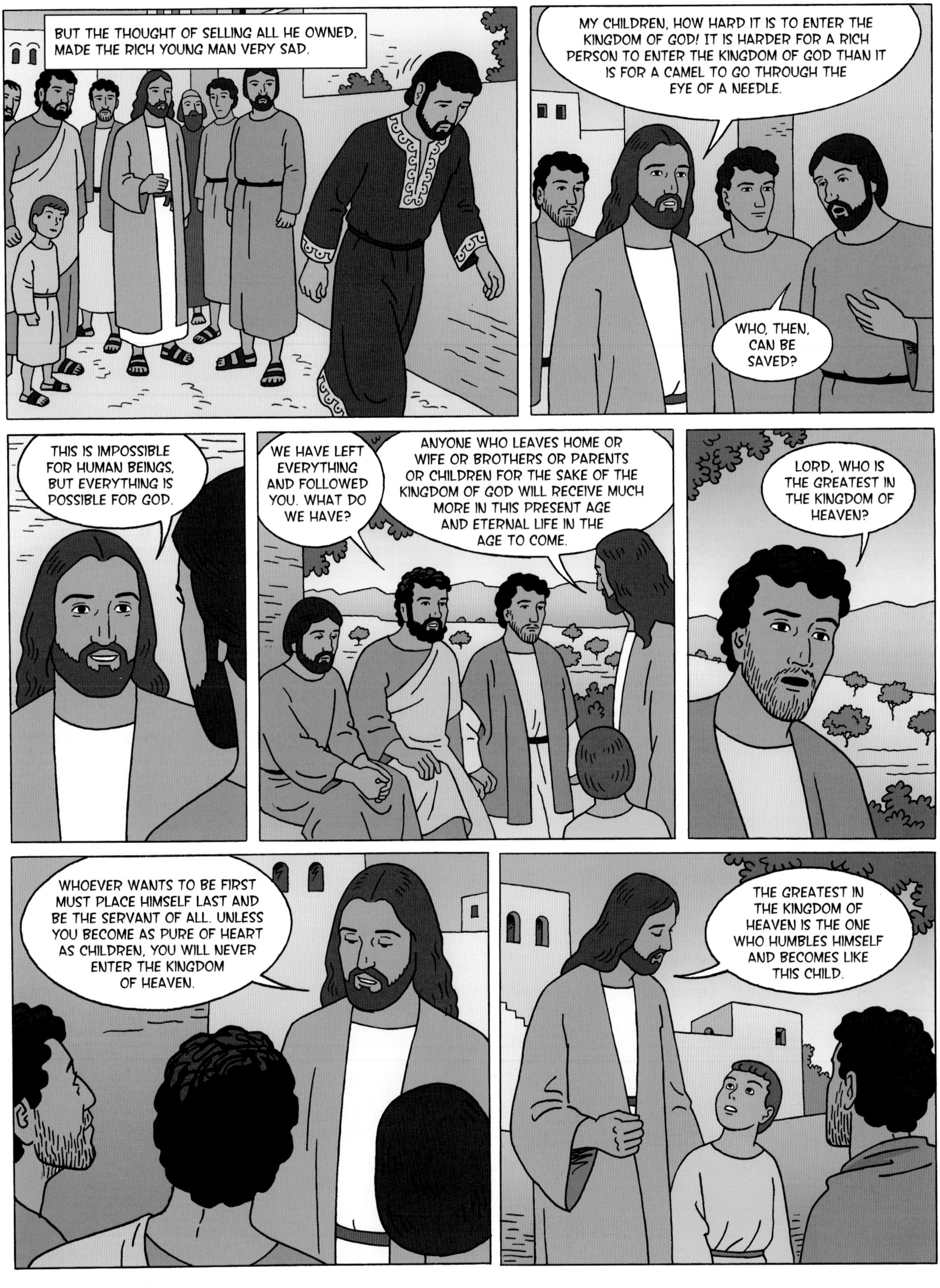
BUT THE THOUGHT OF SELLING ALL HE OWNED, MADE THE RICH YOUNG MAN VERY SAD.
MY CHILDREN, HOW HARD IT IS TO ENTER THE KINGDOM OF GOD! IT IS HARDER FOR A RICH PERSON TO ENTER THE KINGDOM OF GOD THAN IT IS FOR A CAMEL TO GO THROUGH THE EYE OF A NEEDLE.
WHO, THEN, CAN BE SAVED?
THIS IS IMPOSSIBLE FOR HUMAN BEINGS, BUT EVERYTHING IS POSSIBLE FOR GOD.
WE HAVE LEFT EVERYTHING AND FOLLOWED YOU. WHAT DO WE HAVE?
ANYONE WHO LEAVES HOME OR WIFE OR BROTHERS OR PARENTS OR CHILDREN FOR THE SAKE OF THE KINGDOM OF GOD WILL RECEIVE MUCH MORE IN THIS PRESENT AGE AND ETERNAL LIFE IN THE AGE TO COME.
LORD, WHO IS THE GREATEST IN THE KINGDOM OF HEAVEN?
WHOEVER WANTS TO BE FIRST MUST PLACE HIMSELF LAST AND BE THE SERVANT OF ALL. UNLESS YOU BECOME AS PURE OF HEART AS CHILDREN, YOU WILL NEVER ENTER THE KINGDOM OF HEAVEN.
THE GREATEST IN THE KINGDOM OF HEAVEN IS THE ONE WHO HUMBLES HIMSELF AND BECOMES LIKE THIS CHILD.

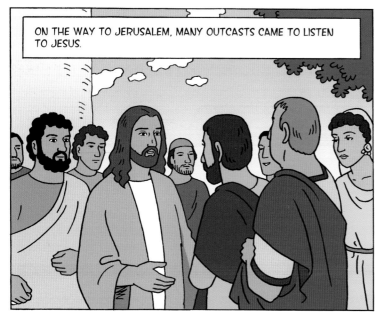

ON THE WAY TO JERUSALEM, MANY OUTCASTS CAME TO LISTEN TO JESUS.

THIS MAN WELCOMES OUTCASTS AND EVEN EATS WITH THEM!

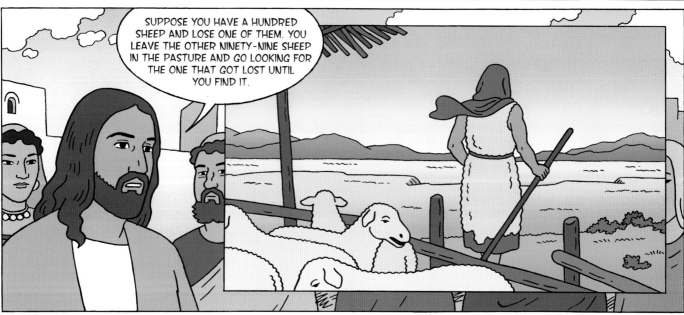

SUPPOSE YOU HAVE A HUNDRED SHEEP AND LOSE ONE OF THEM. YOU LEAVE THE OTHER NINETY-NINE SHEEP IN THE PASTURE AND GO LOOKING FOR THE ONE THAT GOT LOST UNTIL YOU FIND IT.

WHEN YOU FIND IT, YOU ARE SO HAPPY THAT YOU PUT IT ON YOUR SHOULDERS AND CARRY IT BACK HOME. THEN YOU CALL YOUR FRIENDS AND NEIGHBORS TOGETHER AND SAY TO THEM, "I AM SO HAPPY! I FOUND MY LOST SHEEP!"

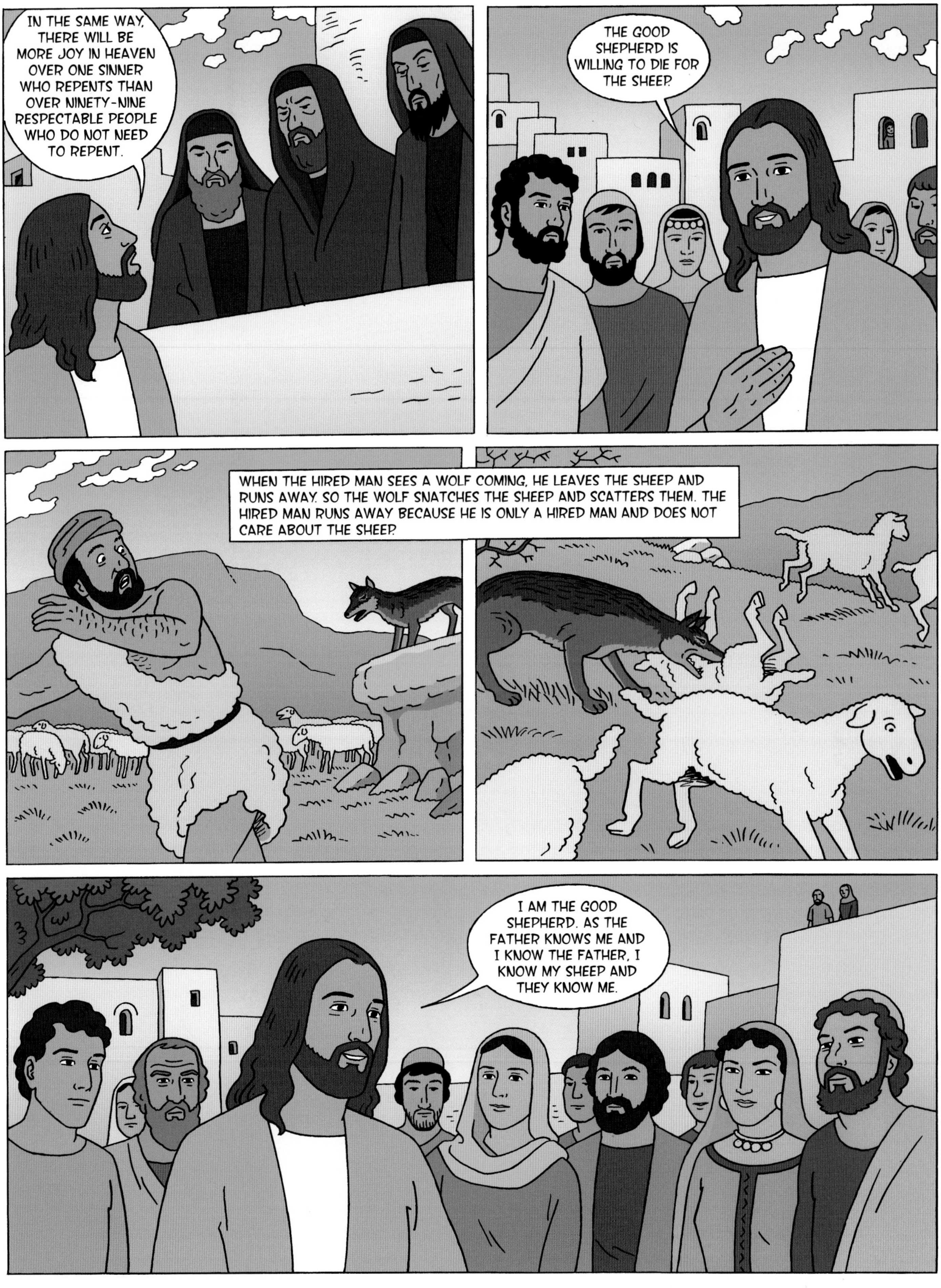
IN THE SAME WAY, THERE WILL BE MORE JOY IN HEAVEN OVER ONE SINNER WHO REPENTS THAN OVER NINETY-NINE RESPECTABLE PEOPLE WHO DO NOT NEED TO REPENT.
THE GOOD SHEPHERD IS WILLING TO DIE FOR THE SHEEP.
WHEN THE HIRED MAN SEES A WOLF COMING, HE LEAVES THE SHEEP AND RUNS AWAY. SO THE WOLF SNATCHES THE SHEEP AND SCATTERS THEM. THE HIRED MAN RUNS AWAY BECAUSE HE IS ONLY A HIRED MAN AND DOES NOT CARE ABOUT THE SHEEP.
I AM THE GOOD SHEPHERD. AS THE FATHER KNOWS ME AND I KNOW THE FATHER, I KNOW MY SHEEP AND THEY KNOW ME.

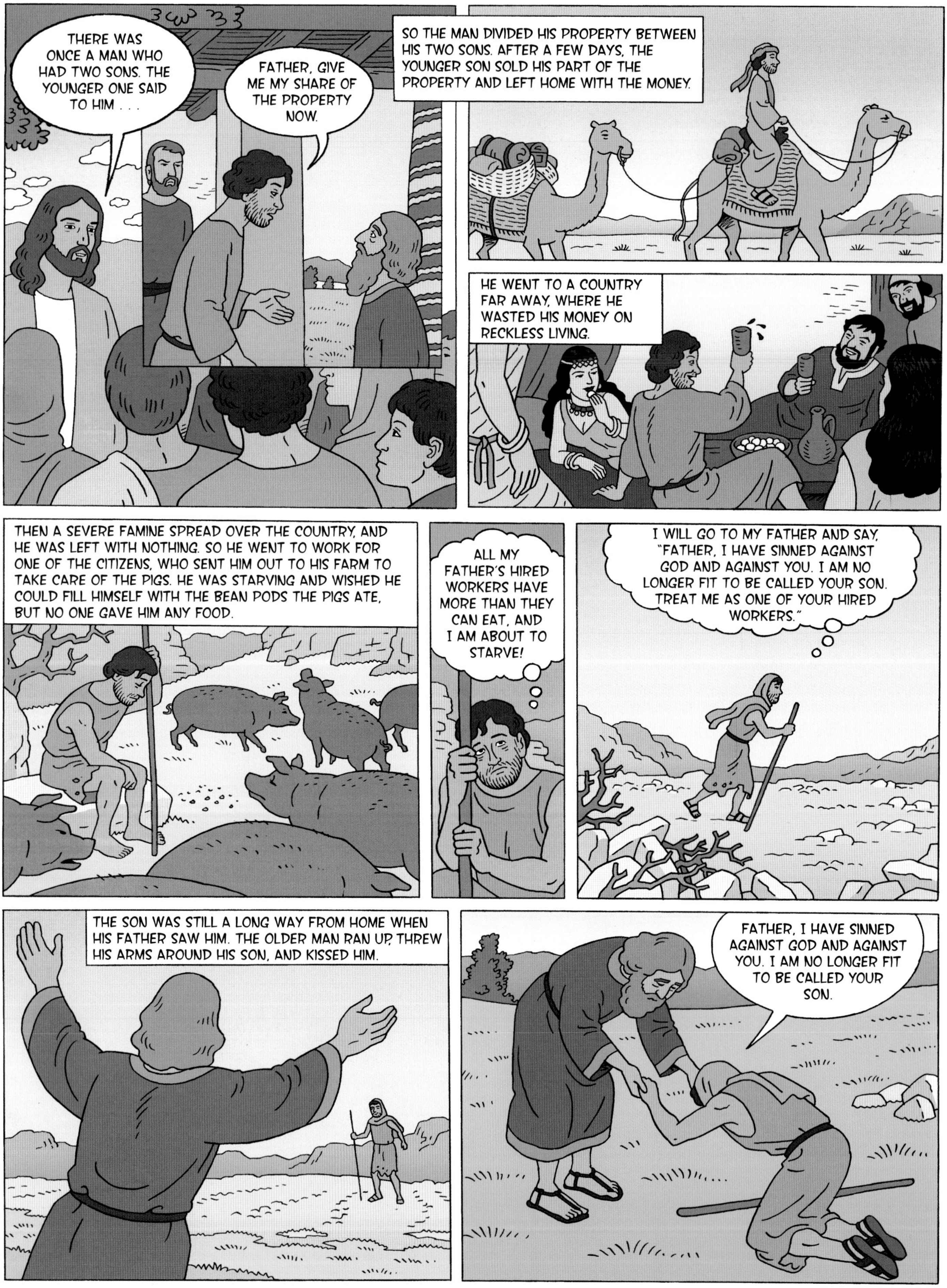
THERE WAS ONCE A MAN WHO HAD TWO SONS. THE YOUNGER ONE SAID TO HIM . . .
FATHER, GIVE ME MY SHARE OF THE PROPERTY NOW.
SO THE MAN DIVIDED HIS PROPERTY BETWEEN HIS TWO SONS. AFTER A FEW DAYS, THE YOUNGER SON SOLD HIS PART OF THE PROPERTY AND LEFT HOME WITH THE MONEY.
HE WENT TO A COUNTRY FAR AWAY, WHERE HE WASTED HIS MONEY ON RECKLESS LIVING.
THEN A SEVERE FAMINE SPREAD OVER THE COUNTRY, AND HE WAS LEFT WITH NOTHING. SO HE WENT TO WORK FOR ONE OF THE CITIZENS, WHO SENT HIM OUT TO HIS FARM TO TAKE CARE OF THE PIGS. HE WAS STARVING AND WISHED HE COULD FILL HIMSELF WITH THE BEAN PODS THE PIGS ATE, BUT NO ONE GAVE HIM ANY FOOD.
ALL MY FATHER'S HIRED WORKERS HAVE MORE THAN THEY CAN EAT, AND I AM ABOUT TO STARVE!
I WILL GO TO MY FATHER AND SAY, "FATHER, I HAVE SINNED AGAINST GOD AND AGAINST YOU. I AM NO LONGER FIT TO BE CALLED YOUR SON. TREAT ME AS ONE OF YOUR HIRED WORKERS."
THE SON WAS STILL A LONG WAY FROM HOME WHEN HIS FATHER SAW HIM. THE OLDER MAN RAN UP, THREW HIS ARMS AROUND HIS SON, AND KISSED HIM.
FATHER, I HAVE SINNED AGAINST GOD AND AGAINST YOU. I AM NO LONGER FIT TO BE CALLED YOUR SON.

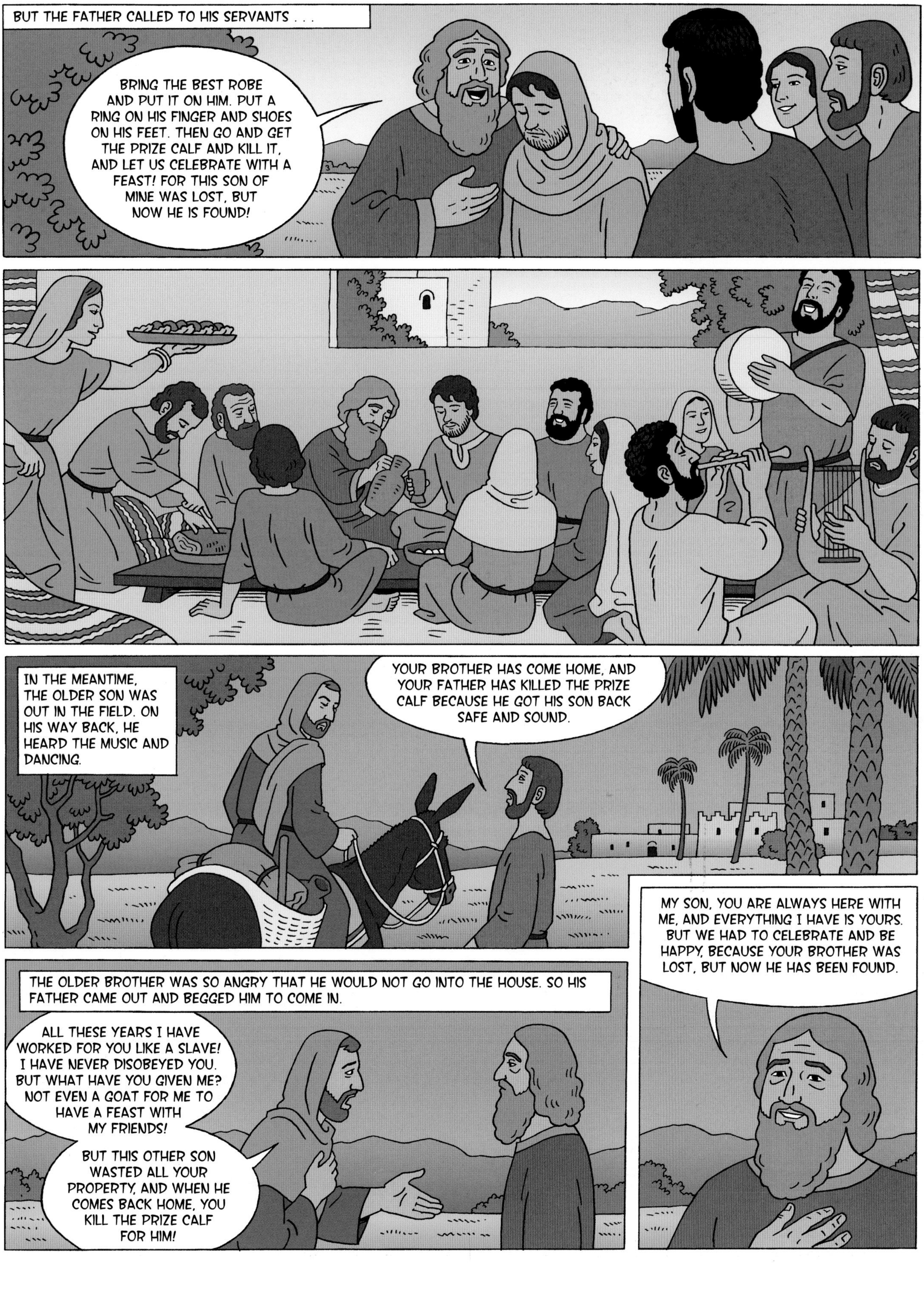
BUT THE FATHER CALLED TO HIS SERVANTS . . .
BRING THE BEST ROBE AND PUT IT ON HIM. PUT A RING ON HIS FINGER AND SHOES ON HIS FEET. THEN GO AND GET THE PRIZE CALF AND KILL IT, AND LET US CELEBRATE WITH A FEAST! FOR THIS SON OF MINE WAS LOST, BUT NOW HE IS FOUND!
IN THE MEANTIME, THE OLDER SON WAS OUT IN THE FIELD. ON HIS WAY BACK, HE HEARD THE MUSIC AND DANCING.
YOUR BROTHER HAS COME HOME, AND YOUR FATHER HAS KILLED THE PRIZE CALF BECAUSE HE GOT HIS SON BACK SAFE AND SOUND.
THE OLDER BROTHER WAS SO ANGRY THAT HE WOULD NOT GO INTO THE HOUSE. SO HIS FATHER CAME OUT AND BEGGED HIM TO COME IN.
ALL THESE YEARS I HAVE WORKED FOR YOU LIKE A SLAVE! I HAVE NEVER DISOBEYED YOU. BUT WHAT HAVE YOU GIVEN ME? NOT EVEN A GOAT FOR ME TO HAVE A FEAST WITH MY FRIENDS!
BUT THIS OTHER SON WASTED ALL YOUR PROPERTY, AND WHEN HE COMES BACK HOME, YOU KILL THE PRIZE CALF FOR HIM!
MY SON, YOU ARE ALWAYS HERE WITH ME, AND EVERYTHING I HAVE IS YOURS. BUT WE HAD TO CELEBRATE AND BE HAPPY, BECAUSE YOUR BROTHER WAS LOST, BUT NOW HE HAS BEEN FOUND.

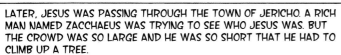

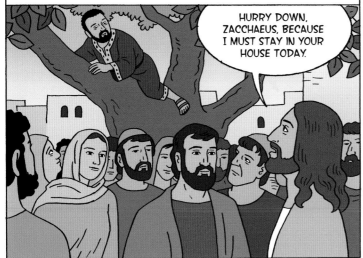

LATER, JESUS WAS PASSING THROUGH THE TOWN OF JERICHO. A RICH MAN NAMED ZACCHAEUS WAS TRYING TO SEE WHO JESUS WAS. BUT THE CROWD WAS SO LARGE AND HE WAS SO SHORT THAT HE HAD TO CLIMB UP A TREE.

HURRY DOWN, ZACCHAEUS, BECAUSE I MUST STAY IN YOUR HOUSE TODAY.

THIS MAN HAS GONE AS A GUEST TO THE HOME OF A SINNER, A TAX COLLECTOR!

SIR, I WILL GIVE HALF MY BELONGINGS TO THE POOR, AND IF I HAVE CHEATED ANYONE, I WILL PAY BACK FOUR TIMES AS MUCH.

SALVATION HAS COME TO THIS HOUSE TODAY. I CAME TO SEEK AND TO SAVE THE LOST. CONSIDER THIS TALE.

ONCE THERE WAS A MAN WHO WAS ABOUT TO LEAVE HOME ON A TRIP. HE CALLED HIS SERVANTS AND PUT THEM IN CHARGE OF HIS PROPERTY. HE GAVE TO EACH ONE ACCORDING TO HIS ABILITY: FIVE THOUSAND GOLD COINS, TWO THOUSAND, AND ONE THOUSAND.

THE SERVANT WHO HAD RECEIVED FIVE THOUSAND COINS WENT AT ONCE AND INVESTED HIS MONEY AND EARNED ANOTHER FIVE THOUSAND.

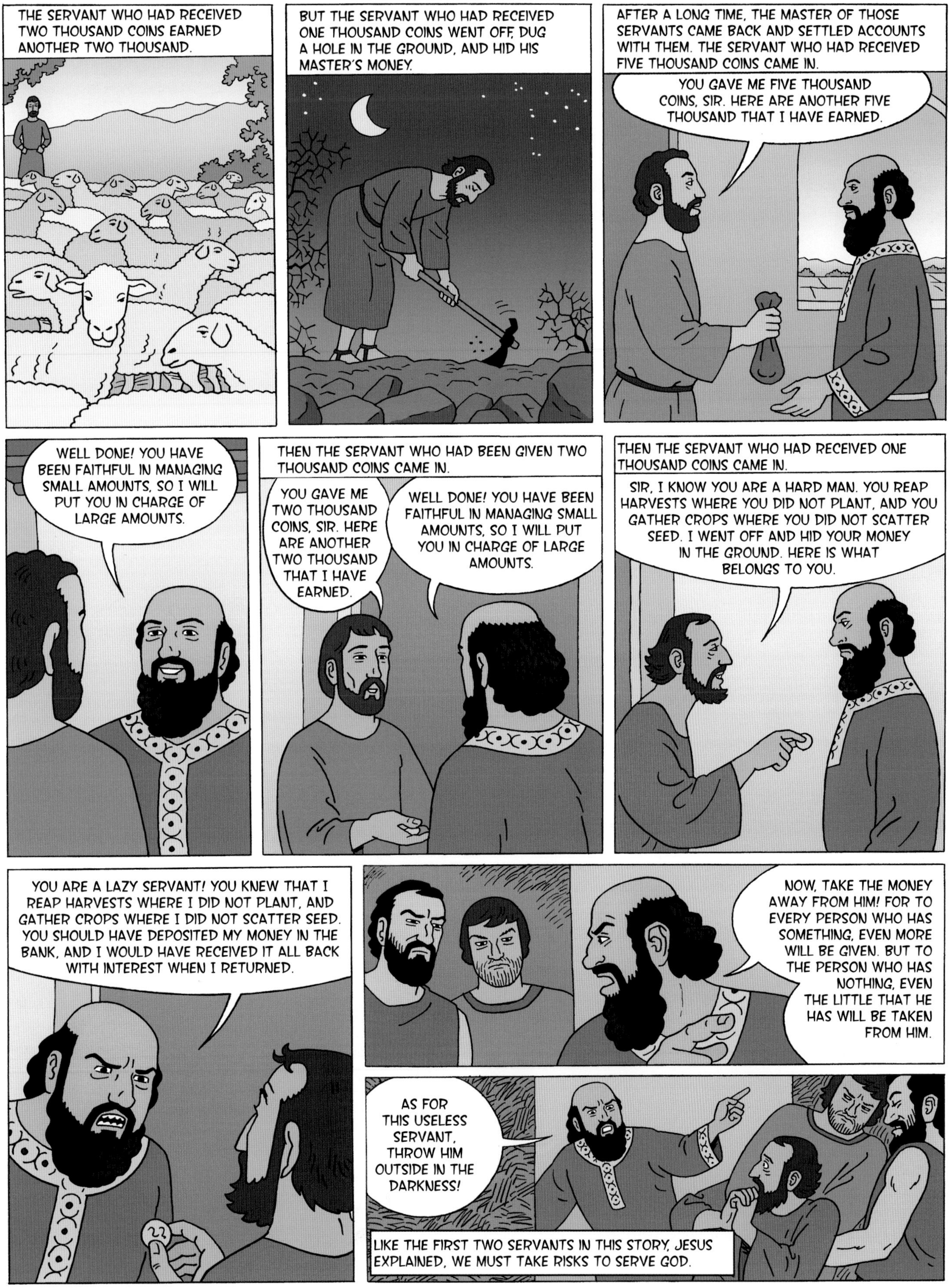
THE SERVANT WHO HAD RECEIVED TWO THOUSAND COINS EARNED ANOTHER TWO THOUSAND.
BUT THE SERVANT WHO HAD RECEIVED ONE THOUSAND COINS WENT OFF, DUG A HOLE IN THE GROUND, AND HID HIS MASTER'S MONEY.
AFTER A LONG TIME, THE MASTER OF THOSE SERVANTS CAME BACK AND SETTLED ACCOUNTS WITH THEM. THE SERVANT WHO HAD RECEIVED FIVE THOUSAND COINS CAME IN.
YOU GAVE ME FIVE THOUSAND COINS, SIR. HERE ARE ANOTHER FIVE THOUSAND THAT I HAVE EARNED.
WELL DONE! YOU HAVE BEEN FAITHFUL IN MANAGING SMALL AMOUNTS, SO I WILL PUT YOU IN CHARGE OF LARGE AMOUNTS.
THEN THE SERVANT WHO HAD BEEN GIVEN TWO THOUSAND COINS CAME IN.
YOU GAVE ME TWO THOUSAND COINS, SIR. HERE ARE ANOTHER TWO THOUSAND THAT I HAVE EARNED.
WELL DONE! YOU HAVE BEEN FAITHFUL IN MANAGING SMALL AMOUNTS, SO I WILL PUT YOU IN CHARGE OF LARGE AMOUNTS.
THEN THE SERVANT WHO HAD RECEIVED ONE THOUSAND COINS CAME IN.
SIR, I KNOW YOU ARE A HARD MAN. YOU REAP HARVESTS WHERE YOU DID NOT PLANT, AND YOU GATHER CROPS WHERE YOU DID NOT SCATTER SEED. I WENT OFF AND HID YOUR MONEY IN THE GROUND. HERE IS WHAT BELONGS TO YOU.
YOU ARE A LAZY SERVANT! YOU KNEW THAT I REAP HARVESTS WHERE I DID NOT PLANT, AND GATHER CROPS WHERE I DID NOT SCATTER SEED. YOU SHOULD HAVE DEPOSITED MY MONEY IN THE BANK, AND I WOULD HAVE RECEIVED IT ALL BACK WITH INTEREST WHEN I RETURNED.
NOW, TAKE THE MONEY AWAY FROM HIM! FOR TO EVERY PERSON WHO HAS SOMETHING, EVEN MORE WILL BE GIVEN. BUT TO THE PERSON WHO HAS NOTHING, EVEN THE LITTLE THAT HE HAS WILL BE TAKEN FROM HIM.
AS FOR THIS USELESS SERVANT, THROW HIM OUTSIDE IN THE DARKNESS!
LIKE THE FIRST TWO SERVANTS IN THIS STORY, JESUS EXPLAINED, WE MUST TAKE RISKS TO SERVE GOD.

AS JESUS CONTINUED ON HIS WAY, HE CAME TO A VILLAGE CALLED BETHANY, LOCATED NEAR JERUSALEM. THERE, A WOMAN NAMED MARTHA WELCOMED HIM INTO HER HOME.

LORD, MY SISTER MARY SPENDS ALL HER TIME LISTENING TO YOU, BUT SHE HAS LEFT ME TO DO ALL THE WORK BY MYSELF. PLEASE TELL HER TO HELP ME!

MARTHA, MARTHA! YOU ARE WORRIED AND TROUBLED OVER SO MANY THINGS, BUT JUST ONE IS NEEDED. MARY HAS CHOSEN THE RIGHT PATH, AND IT WILL NOT BE TAKEN AWAY FROM HER.

SOME TIME LATER, LAZARUS, THE BROTHER OF MARTHA AND MARY, BECAME SICK.

THE SISTERS WARNED JESUS.

LORD, YOUR DEAR FRIEND IS SICK.

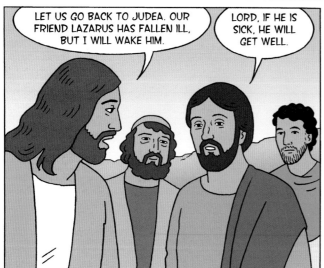

LET US GO BACK TO JUDEA. OUR FRIEND LAZARUS HAS FALLEN ILL, BUT I WILL WAKE HIM.

LORD, IF HE IS SICK, HE WILL GET WELL.

LAZARUS IS DEAD, BUT FOR YOUR SAKE I AM GLAD THAT I WAS NOT WITH HIM SO THAT YOU WILL BELIEVE. LET US GO TO HIM.

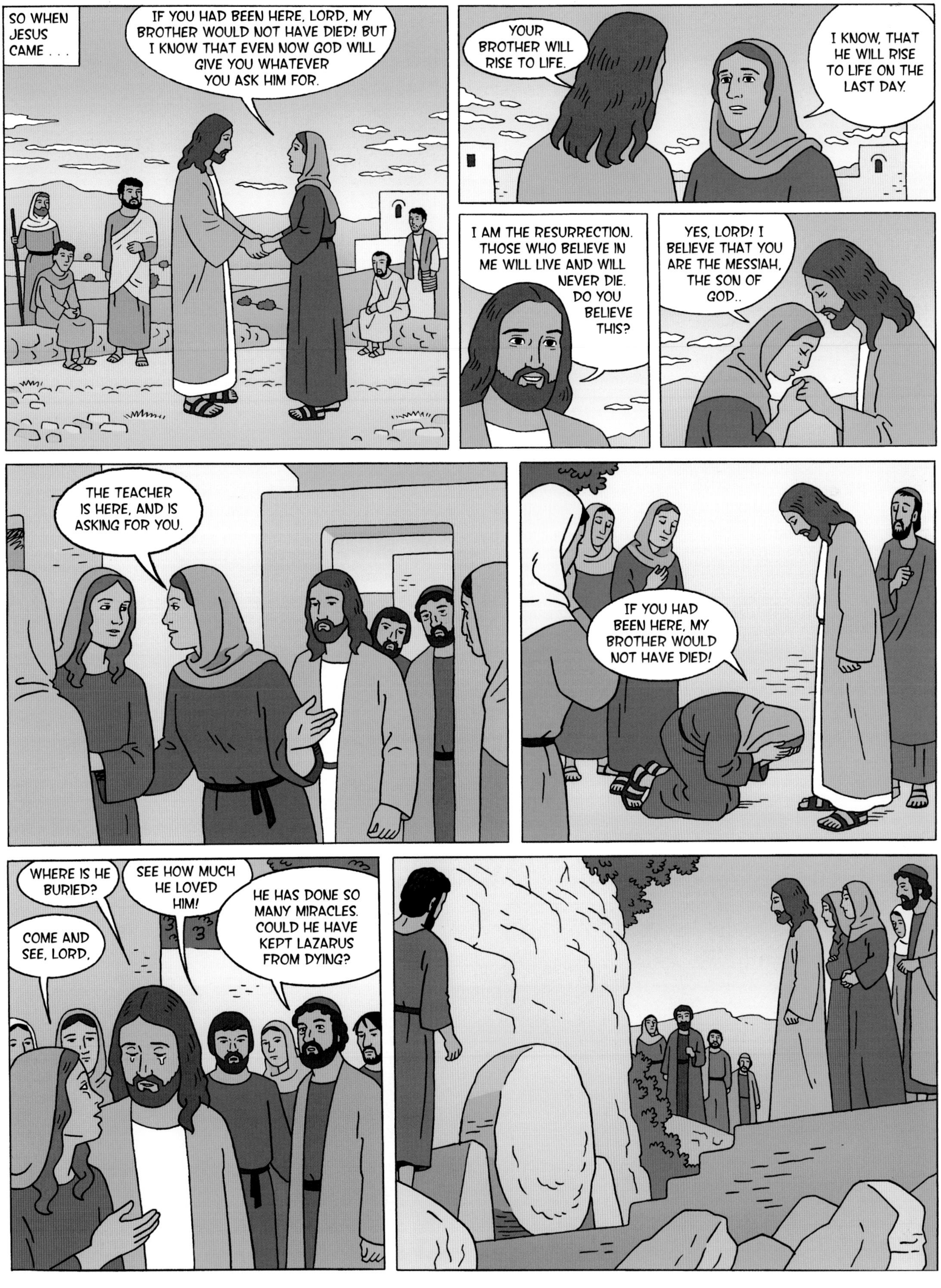
SO WHEN JESUS CAME . . .
IF YOU HAD BEEN HERE, LORD, MY BROTHER WOULD NOT HAVE DIED! BUT I KNOW THAT EVEN NOW GOD WILL GIVE YOU WHATEVER YOU ASK HIM FOR.
YOUR BROTHER WILL RISE TO LIFE.
I KNOW, THAT HE WILL RISE TO LIFE ON THE LAST DAY.
I AM THE RESURRECTION. THOSE WHO BELIEVE IN ME WILL LIVE AND WILL NEVER DIE. DO YOU BELIEVE THIS?
YES, LORD! I BELIEVE THAT YOU ARE THE MESSIAH, THE SON OF GOD..
THE TEACHER IS HERE, AND IS ASKING FOR YOU.
IF YOU HAD BEEN HERE, MY BROTHER WOULD NOT HAVE DIED!
WHERE IS HE BURIED?
COME AND SEE, LORD,
SEE HOW MUCH HE LOVED HIM!
HE HAS DONE SO MANY MIRACLES. COULD HE HAVE KEPT LAZARUS FROM DYING?

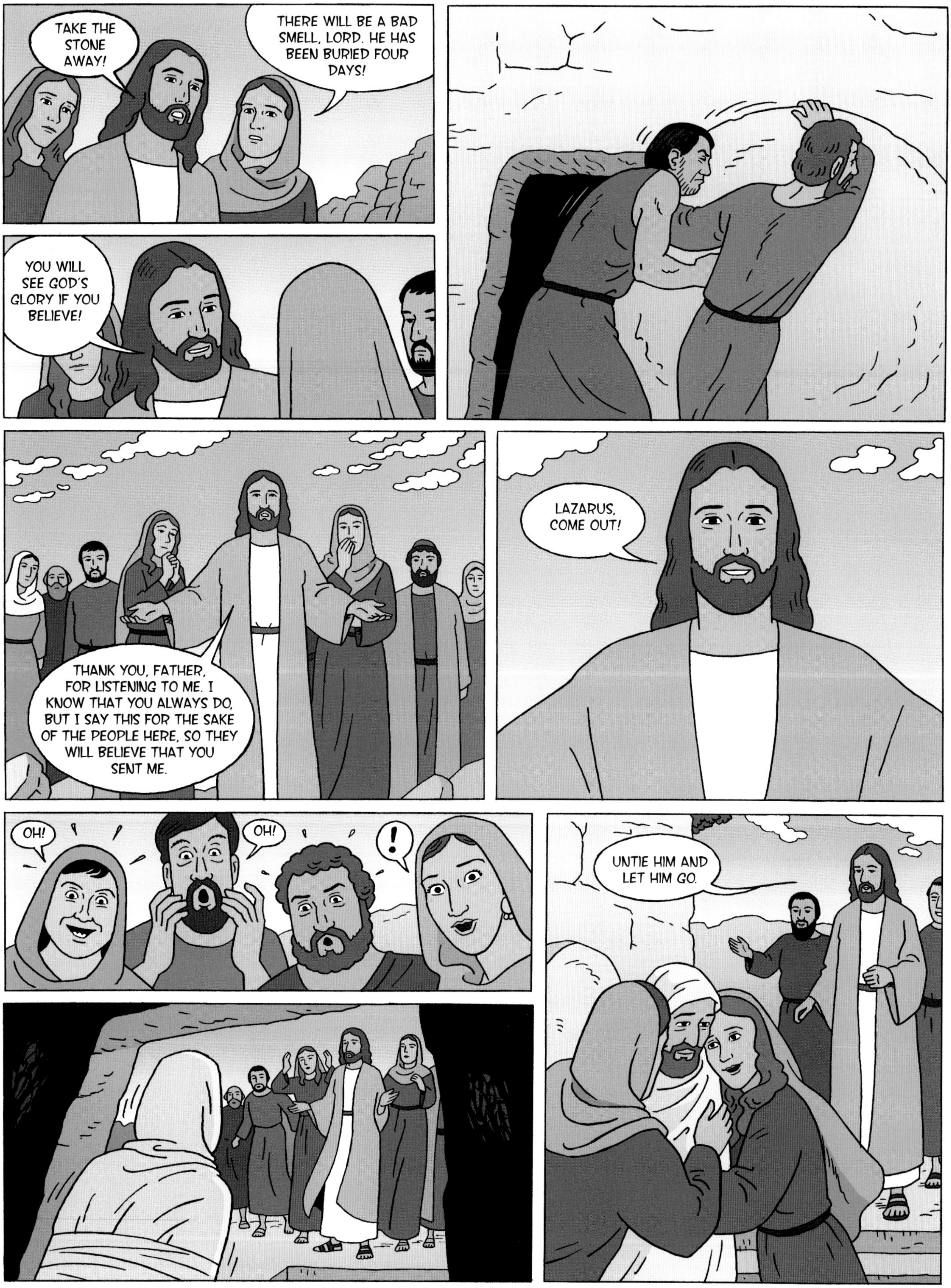
TAKE THE STONE AWAY!
THERE WILL BE A BAD SMELL, LORD. HE HAS BEEN BURIED FOUR DAYS!
YOU WILL SEE GOD'S GLORY IF YOU BELIEVE!
THANK YOU, FATHER, FOR LISTENING TO ME. I KNOW THAT YOU ALWAYS DO, BUT I SAY THIS FOR THE SAKE OF THE PEOPLE HERE, SO THEY WILL BELIEVE THAT YOU SENT ME.
LAZARUS, COME OUT!
OH!
OH!
!
UNTIE HIM AND LET HIM GO.

MANY OF THE PEOPLE WHO HAD COME TO VISIT MARY SAW WHAT JESUS HAD DONE, AND THEY BELIEVED IN HIM. BUT SOME RETURNED TO THE PHARISEES AND TOLD THEM WHAT HAD HAPPENED.

LOOK AT ALL THE MIRACLES THIS MAN IS PERFORMING! IF WE LET HIM GO ON IN THIS WAY, EVERYONE WILL BELIEVE IN HIM, AND THE ROMAN AUTHORITIES WILL DESTROY OUR TEMPLE AND OUR NATION!

FOOLS! DON'T YOU REALIZE THAT IT IS BETTER TO HAVE ONE MAN DIE FOR THE PEOPLE, INSTEAD OF HAVING THE WHOLE NATION DESTROYED?

HE HAS TO DIE!

HE MUST DIE!

JESUS, KNOWING THEY THEY WERE MAKING PLANS TO KILL HIM, DID NOT TRAVEL OPENLY IN JUDEA.

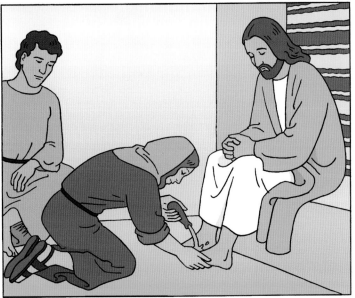

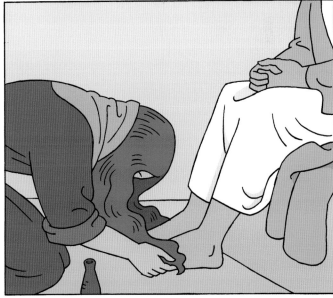

WHY WASN'T THIS PERFUME SOLD FOR THREE HUNDRED SILVER COINS AND THE MONEY GIVEN TO THE POOR?

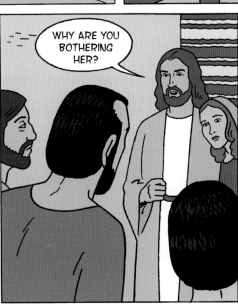

WHY ARE YOU BOTHERING HER?

SHE HAS DONE A BEAUTIFUL THING FOR ME. YOU WILL ALWAYS HAVE POOR PEOPLE WITH YOU, AND YOU CAN HELP THEM AT ANY TIME. BUT YOU WILL NOT ALWAYS HAVE ME. SHE DID WHAT SHE COULD. SHE POURED PERFUME ON MY FEET AND BODY TO PREPARE ME AHEAD OF TIME FOR BURIAL.

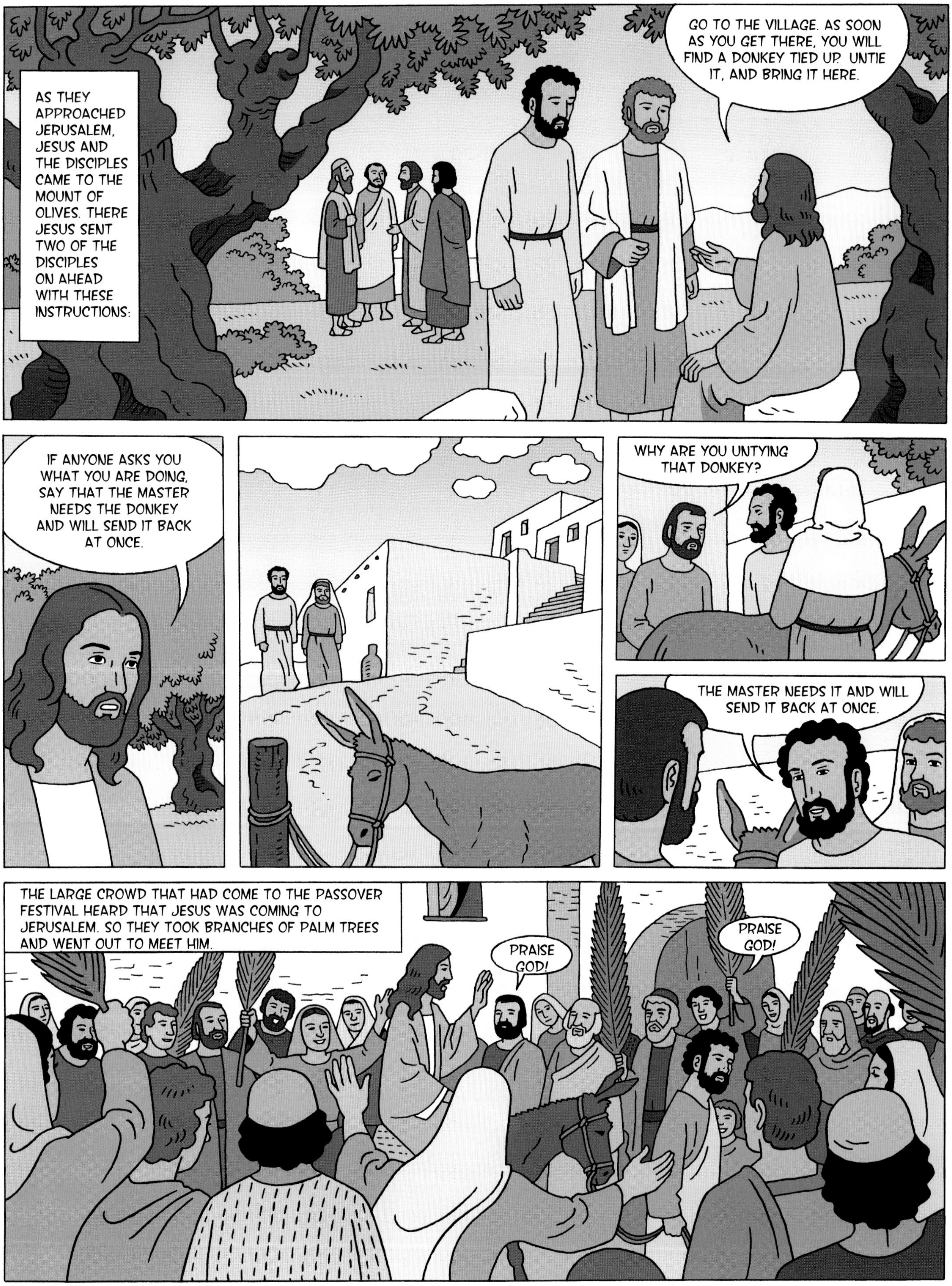
AS THEY APPROACHED JERUSALEM, JESUS AND THE DISCIPLES CAME TO THE MOUNT OF OLIVES. THERE JESUS SENT TWO OF THE DISCIPLES ON AHEAD WITH THESE INSTRUCTIONS:
GO TO THE VILLAGE. AS SOON AS YOU GET THERE, YOU WILL FIND A DONKEY TIED UP. UNTIE IT, AND BRING IT HERE.
IF ANYONE ASKS YOU WHAT YOU ARE DOING, SAY THAT THE MASTER NEEDS THE DONKEY AND WILL SEND IT BACK AT ONCE.
WHY ARE YOU UNTYING THAT DONKEY?
THE MASTER NEEDS IT AND WILL SEND IT BACK AT ONCE.
THE LARGE CROWD THAT HAD COME TO THE PASSOVER FESTIVAL HEARD THAT JESUS WAS COMING TO JERUSALEM. SO THEY TOOK BRANCHES OF PALM TREES AND WENT OUT TO MEET HIM.
PRAISE GOD!
PRAISE GOD!

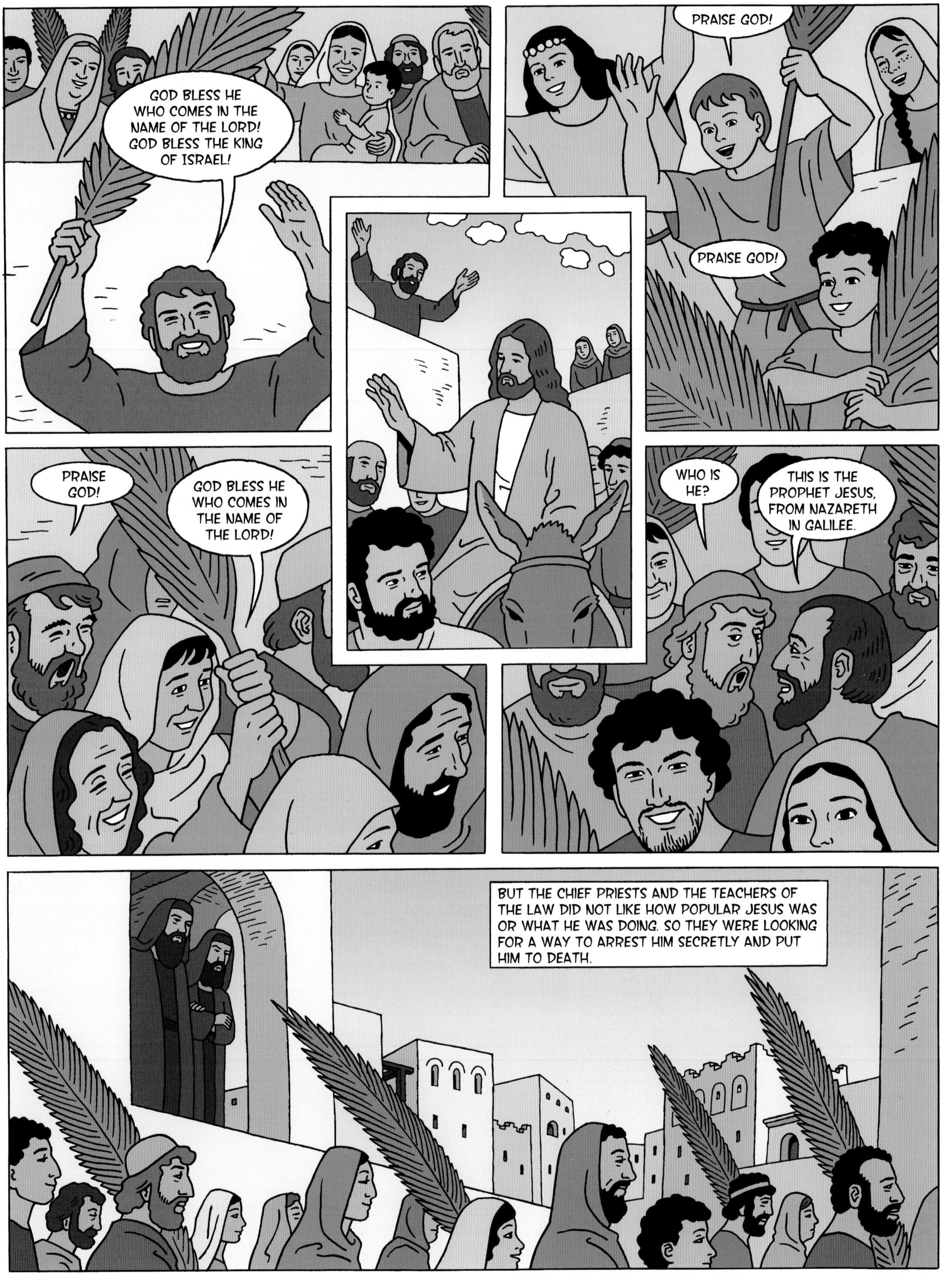
GOD BLESS HE WHO COMES IN THE NAME OF THE LORD! GOD BLESS THE KING OF ISRAEL!
PRAISE GOD!
PRAISE GOD!
PRAISE GOD!
GOD BLESS HE WHO COMES IN THE NAME OF THE LORD!
WHO IS HE?
THIS IS THE PROPHET JESUS, FROM NAZARETH IN GALILEE.
BUT THE CHIEF PRIESTS AND THE TEACHERS OF THE LAW DID NOT LIKE HOW POPULAR JESUS WAS OR WHAT HE WAS DOING. SO THEY WERE LOOKING FOR A WAY TO ARREST HIM SECRETLY AND PUT HIM TO DEATH.

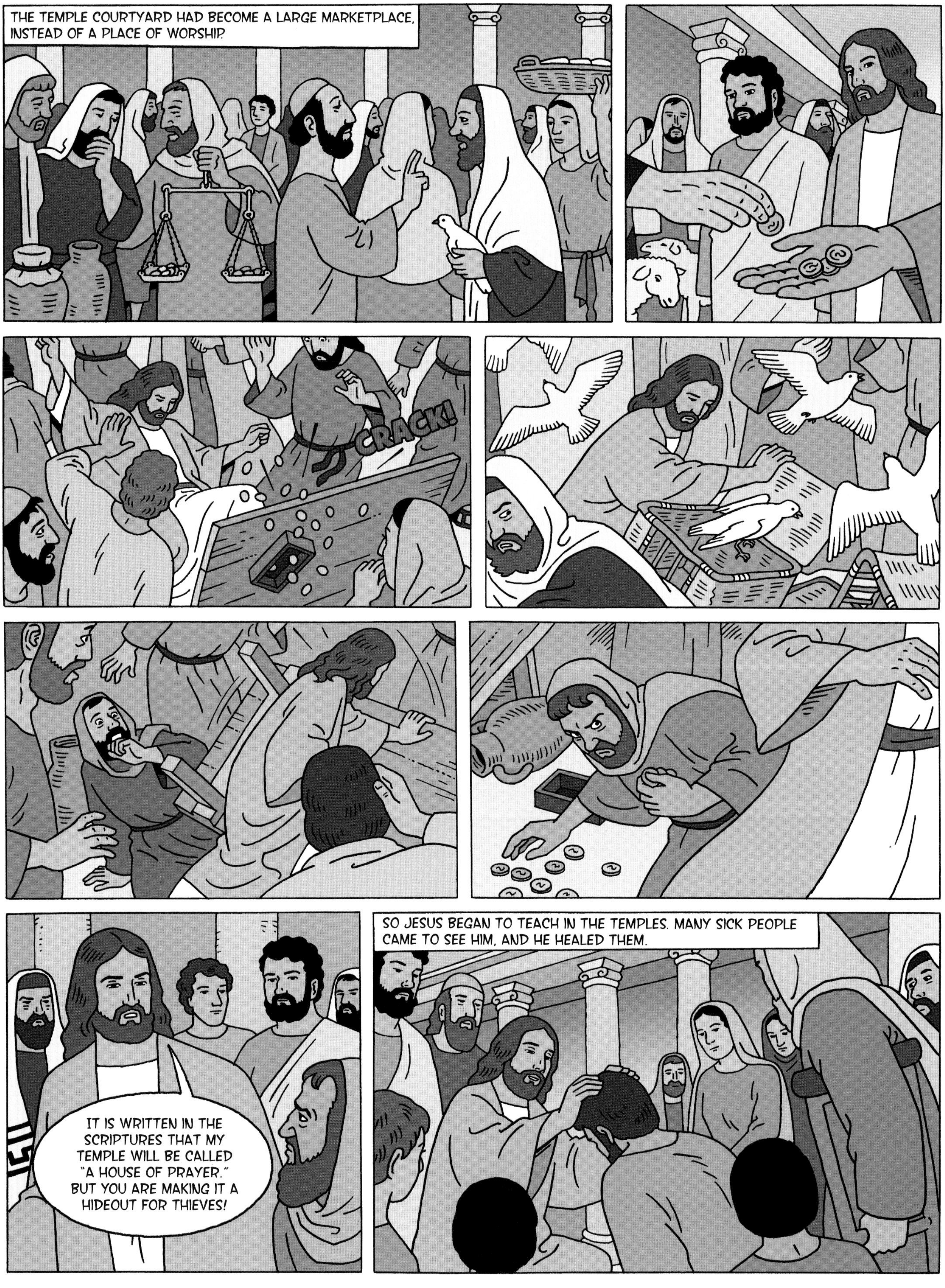
THE TEMPLE COURTYARD HAD BECOME A LARGE MARKETPLACE, INSTEAD OF A PLACE OF WORSHIP.
CRACK!
IT IS WRITTEN IN THE SCRIPTURES THAT MY TEMPLE WILL BE CALLED "A HOUSE OF PRAYER." BUT YOU ARE MAKING IT A HIDEOUT FOR THIEVES!
SO JESUS BEGAN TO TEACH IN THE TEMPLES. MANY SICK PEOPLE CAME TO SEE HIM, AND HE HEALED THEM.

OUSIDE THE TEMPLE'S TREASURY WAS AN OFFERING BOX WHERE PEOPLE DROPPED IN THEIR MONEY.

CLANK
CLANK
CLANK
CLANK

THIS POOR WIDOW PUT MORE IN THE OFFERING BOX THAN ALL THE OTHERS. THEY PUT IN ONLY WHAT THEY HAD TO SPARE. BUT POOR AS SHE IS, SHE PUT IN ALL SHE HAD.

MEANWHILE, THE CHIEF PRIESTS AND TEACHERS OF THE LAW CAME UP WITH A PLAN TO TRICK JESUS.

TEACHER, YOU TELL THE TRUTH WITHOUT WORRYING WHAT PEOPLE THINK. SO TELL US: IS IT AGAINST OUR LAW TO PAY TAXES TO THE ROMAN EMPEROR?

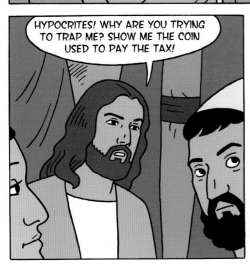

HYPOCRITES! WHY ARE YOU TRYING TO TRAP ME? SHOW ME THE COIN USED TO PAY THE TAX!

WHOSE FACE AND NAME ARE THESE?

THE EMPEROR'S.

THEN, PAY TO THE EMPEROR WHAT BELONGS TO HIM, AND PAY TO GOD WHAT BELONGS TO GOD.

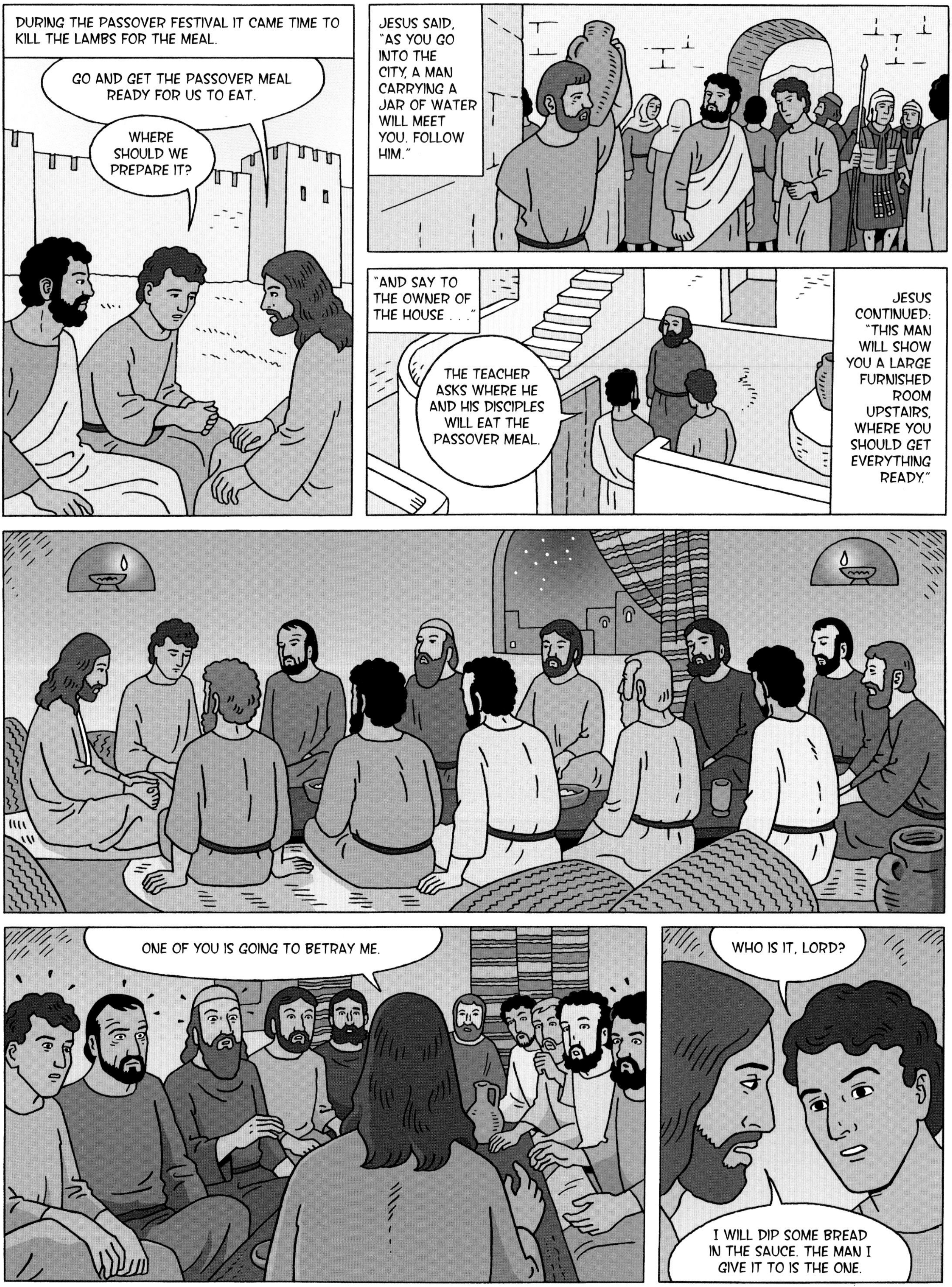
DURING THE PASSOVER FESTIVAL IT CAME TIME TO KILL THE LAMBS FOR THE MEAL.
GO AND GET THE PASSOVER MEAL READY FOR US TO EAT.
WHERE SHOULD WE PREPARE IT?
JESUS SAID, "AS YOU GO INTO THE CITY, A MAN CARRYING A JAR OF WATER WILL MEET YOU. FOLLOW HIM."
"AND SAY TO THE OWNER OF THE HOUSE . . ."
THE TEACHER ASKS WHERE HE AND HIS DISCIPLES WILL EAT THE PASSOVER MEAL.
JESUS CONTINUED: "THIS MAN WILL SHOW YOU A LARGE FURNISHED ROOM UPSTAIRS, WHERE YOU SHOULD GET EVERYTHING READY."
ONE OF YOU IS GOING TO BETRAY ME.
WHO IS IT, LORD?
I WILL DIP SOME BREAD IN THE SAUCE. THE MAN I GIVE IT TO IS THE ONE.

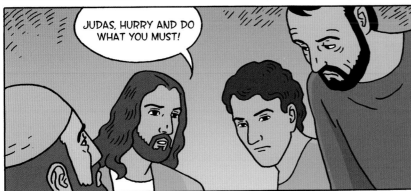

JUDAS, HURRY AND DO WHAT YOU MUST!

I GIVE THE REST OF YOU A NEW COMMANDMENT: LOVE ONE ANOTHER AS I HAVE LOVED YOU.

IF YOU HAVE LOVE FOR ONE ANOTHER, THEN EVERYONE WILL KNOW THAT YOU ARE MY DISCIPLES.

TAKE AND EAT THIS BREAD. IT IS MY BODY, WHICH I GIVE TO YOU. DO THIS IN MEMORY OF ME.

DRINK THIS WINE. IT IS MY BLOOD, WHICH SEALS GOD'S PROMISE, MY BLOOD POURED OUT FOR MANY.

I WILL NEVER AGAIN DRINK WINE UNTIL THE DAY I DRINK THE NEW WINE WITH YOU IN MY FATHER'S KINGDOM.

AFTER DINNER, JESUS WENT, AS HE OFTEN DID, TO THE MOUNT OF OLIVES. THE DISCIPLES WENT WITH HIM.

THIS VERY NIGHT, ALL OF YOU WILL RUN AWAY AND LEAVE ME. THE SCRIPTURE SAYS, "GOD WILL KILL THE SHEPHERD, AND THE SHEEP OF THE FLOCK WILL BE SCATTERED. BUT AFTER I AM RAISED TO LIFE, I WILL GO TO GALILEE AHEAD OF YOU.

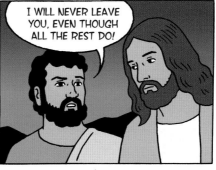

I WILL NEVER LEAVE YOU, EVEN THOUGH ALL THE REST DO!

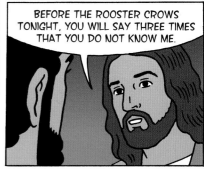

BEFORE THE ROOSTER CROWS TONIGHT, YOU WILL SAY THREE TIMES THAT YOU DO NOT KNOW ME.

JESUS TOOK PETER AND THE TWO SONS OF ZEBEDEE ASIDE

THE SORROW IN MY HEART IS SO GREAT THAT IT ALMOST CRUSHES ME. STAY HERE AND KEEP WATCH WITH ME.

MY FATHER, IF IT IS POSSIBLE, TAKE THIS CUP OF SUFFERING FROM ME! YET NOT WHAT I WANT, BUT WHAT YOU WANT.

THE MAN I KISS IS THE ONE YOU WANT TO ARREST.

LOOK! HERE IS THE MAN WHO WILL BETRAY ME!

TEACHER!

AS THE SOLDIERS STEPPED IN TO ARREST JESUS, PETER GREW ANGRY AND DREW HIS SWORD.

THWACK!

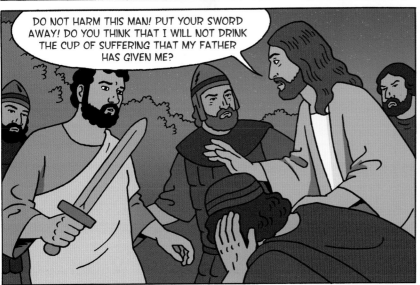

DO NOT HARM THIS MAN! PUT YOUR SWORD AWAY! DO YOU THINK THAT I WILL NOT DRINK THE CUP OF SUFFERING THAT MY FATHER HAS GIVEN ME?

JESUS TOUCHED THE SERVANT'S EAR AND HEALED HIM.

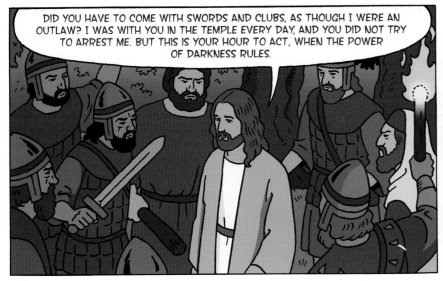

DID YOU HAVE TO COME WITH SWORDS AND CLUBS, AS THOUGH I WERE AN OUTLAW? I WAS WITH YOU IN THE TEMPLE EVERY DAY, AND YOU DID NOT TRY TO ARREST ME. BUT THIS IS YOUR HOUR TO ACT, WHEN THE POWER OF DARKNESS RULES.

THEN, FRIGHTENED, ALL THE DISCIPLES RAN AWAY.

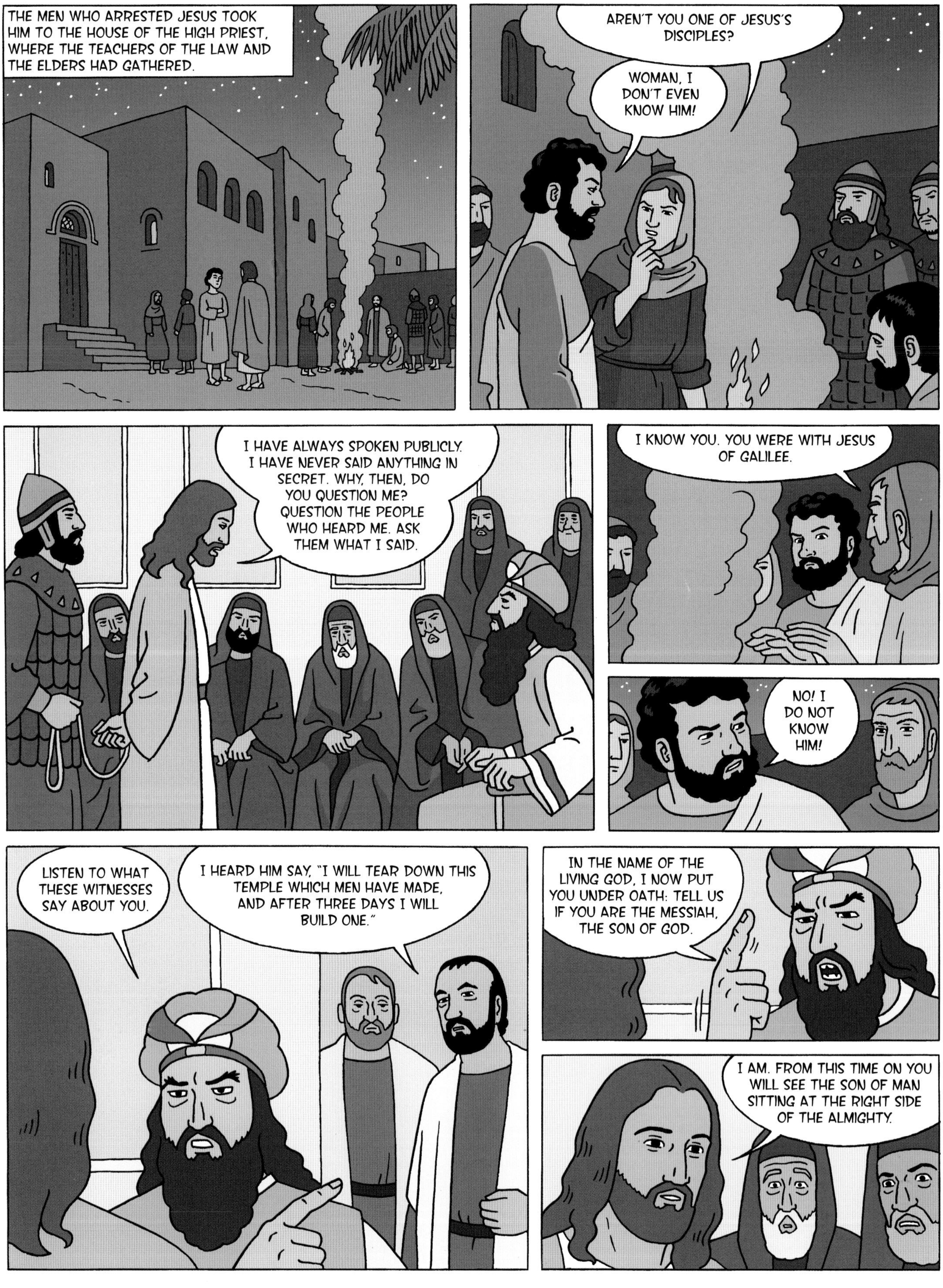
THE MEN WHO ARRESTED JESUS TOOK HIM TO THE HOUSE OF THE HIGH PRIEST, WHERE THE TEACHERS OF THE LAW AND THE ELDERS HAD GATHERED.
AREN'T YOU ONE OF JESUS'S DISCIPLES?
WOMAN, I DON'T EVEN KNOW HIM!
I HAVE ALWAYS SPOKEN PUBLICLY. I HAVE NEVER SAID ANYTHING IN SECRET. WHY, THEN, DO YOU QUESTION ME? QUESTION THE PEOPLE WHO HEARD ME. ASK THEM WHAT I SAID.
I KNOW YOU. YOU WERE WITH JESUS OF GALILEE.
NO! I DO NOT KNOW HIM!
LISTEN TO WHAT THESE WITNESSES SAY ABOUT YOU.
I HEARD HIM SAY, "I WILL TEAR DOWN THIS TEMPLE WHICH MEN HAVE MADE, AND AFTER THREE DAYS I WILL BUILD ONE."
IN THE NAME OF THE LIVING GOD, I NOW PUT YOU UNDER OATH: TELL US IF YOU ARE THE MESSIAH, THE SON OF GOD.
I AM. FROM THIS TIME ON YOU WILL SEE THE SON OF MAN SITTING AT THE RIGHT SIDE OF THE ALMIGHTY.

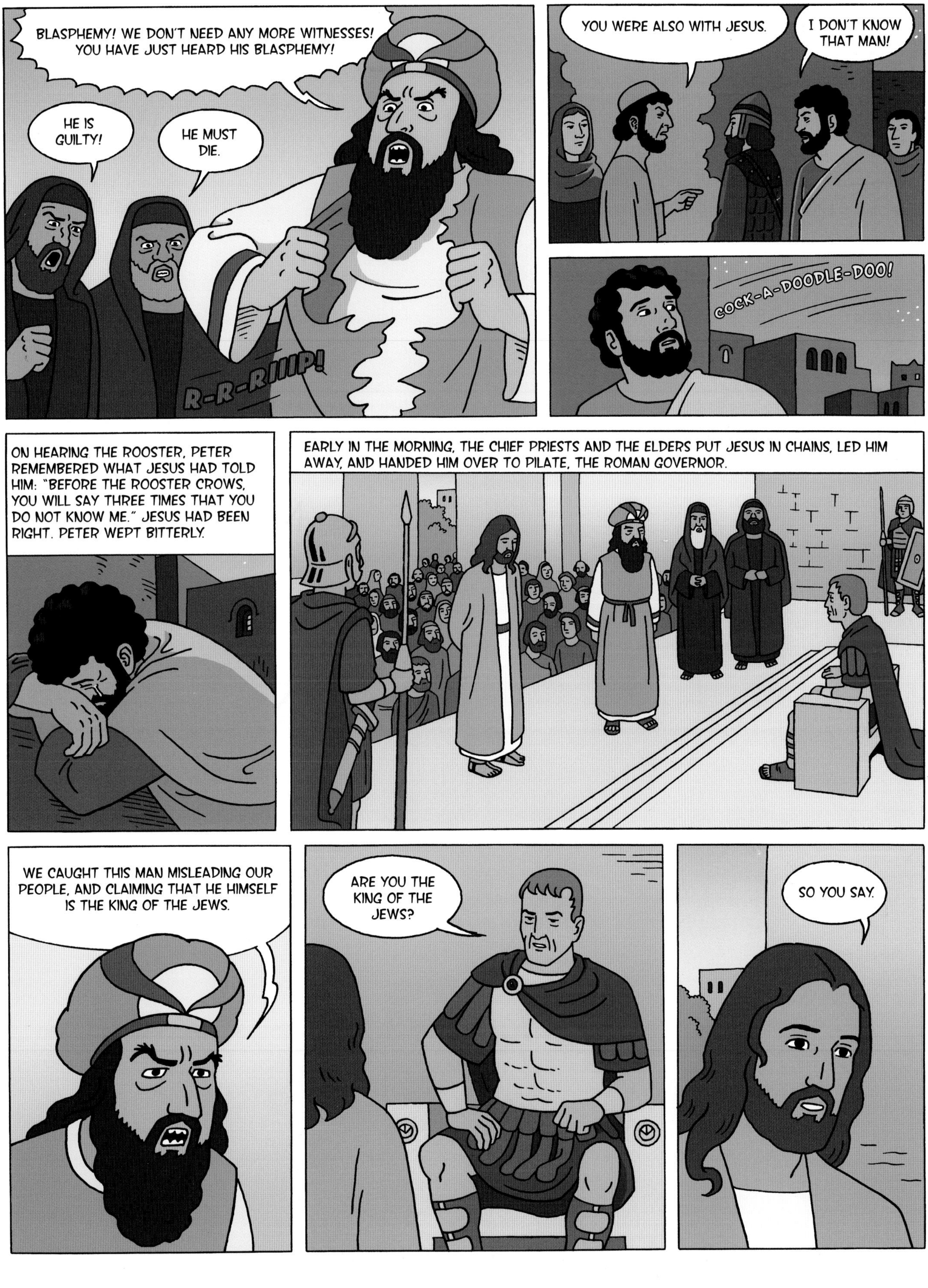
BLASPHEMY! WE DON'T NEED ANY MORE WITNESSES! YOU HAVE JUST HEARD HIS BLASPHEMY!
HE IS GUILTY!
HE MUST DIE.
R-R-RIIIP!
YOU WERE ALSO WITH JESUS.
I DON'T KNOW THAT MAN!
COCK-A-DOODLE-DOO!
ON HEARING THE ROOSTER, PETER REMEMBERED WHAT JESUS HAD TOLD HIM: "BEFORE THE ROOSTER CROWS, YOU WILL SAY THREE TIMES THAT YOU DO NOT KNOW ME." JESUS HAD BEEN RIGHT. PETER WEPT BITTERLY.
EARLY IN THE MORNING, THE CHIEF PRIESTS AND THE ELDERS PUT JESUS IN CHAINS, LED HIM AWAY, AND HANDED HIM OVER TO PILATE, THE ROMAN GOVERNOR.
WE CAUGHT THIS MAN MISLEADING OUR PEOPLE, AND CLAIMING THAT HE HIMSELF IS THE KING OF THE JEWS.
ARE YOU THE KING OF THE JEWS?
SO YOU SAY.

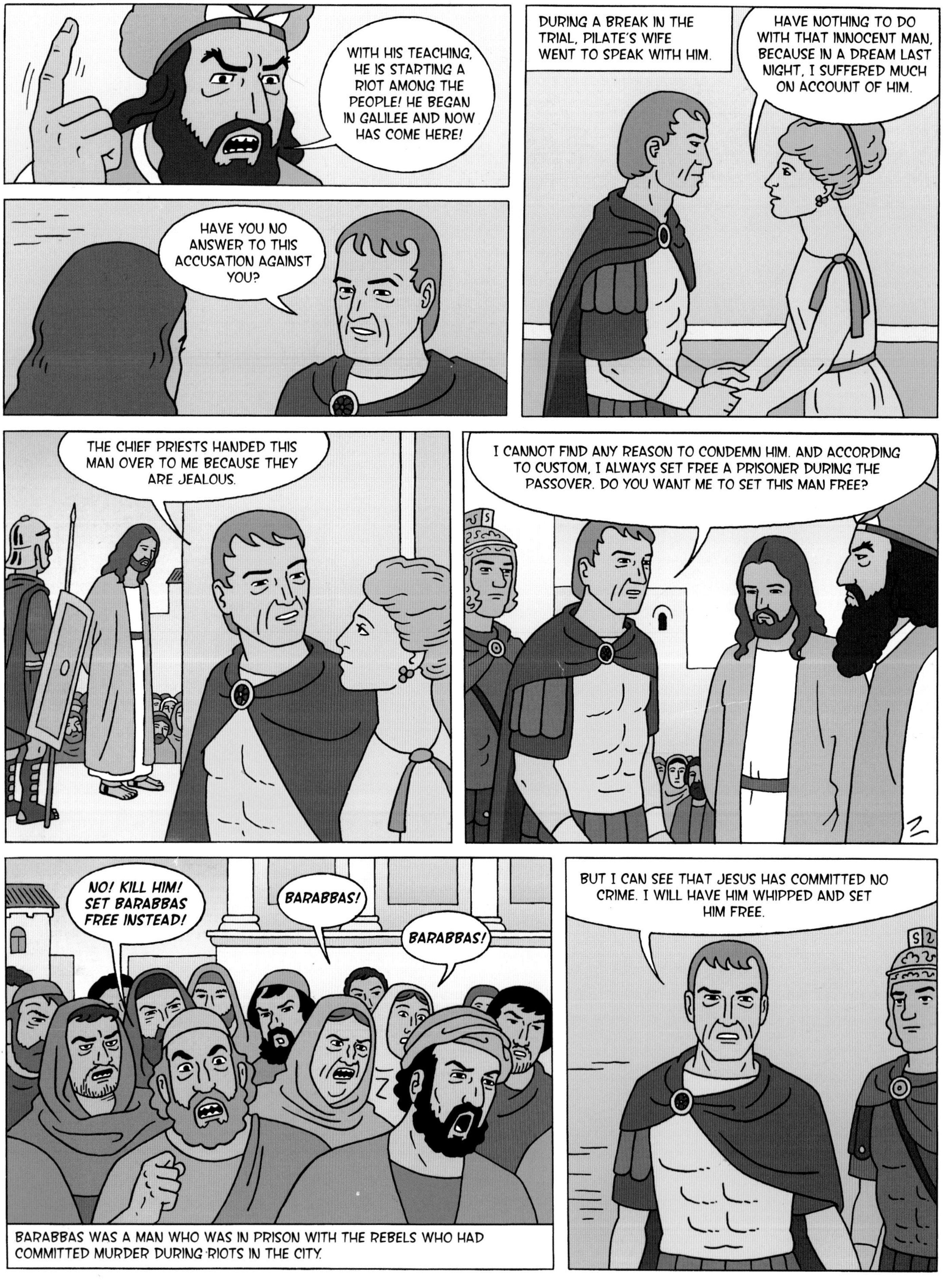
WITH HIS TEACHING, HE IS STARTING A RIOT AMONG THE PEOPLE! HE BEGAN IN GALILEE AND NOW HAS COME HERE!
HAVE YOU NO ANSWER TO THIS ACCUSATION AGAINST YOU?
DURING A BREAK IN THE TRIAL, PILATE'S WIFE WENT TO SPEAK WITH HIM.
HAVE NOTHING TO DO WITH THAT INNOCENT MAN, BECAUSE IN A DREAM LAST NIGHT, I SUFFERED MUCH ON ACCOUNT OF HIM.
THE CHIEF PRIESTS HANDED THIS MAN OVER TO ME BECAUSE THEY ARE JEALOUS.
I CANNOT FIND ANY REASON TO CONDEMN HIM. AND ACCORDING TO CUSTOM, I ALWAYS SET FREE A PRISONER DURING THE PASSOVER. DO YOU WANT ME TO SET THIS MAN FREE?
NO! KILL HIM! SET BARABBAS FREE INSTEAD!
BARABBAS!
BARABBAS!
BARABBAS WAS A MAN WHO WAS IN PRISON WITH THE REBELS WHO HAD COMMITTED MURDER DURING RIOTS IN THE CITY.
BUT I CAN SEE THAT JESUS HAS COMMITTED NO CRIME. I WILL HAVE HIM WHIPPED AND SET HIM FREE.

CRACK!

CRACK!

IT IS NOT ENOUGH!

CRUCIFY HIM!

CRUCIFY HIM!

CRUCIFY HIM!

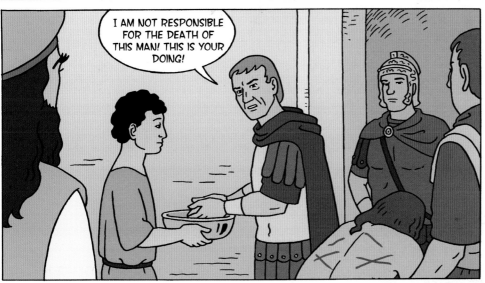

I AM NOT RESPONSIBLE FOR THE DEATH OF THIS MAN! THIS IS YOUR DOING!

IF YOU SET HIM FREE, THAT MEANS YOU ARE NOT THE EMPEROR'S FRIEND! ANYONE WHO CLAIMS TO BE A KING IS A TRAITOR AGAINST THE EMPEROR!

DO YOU REALLY WANT ME TO CRUCIFY YOUR KING?

THE ONLY KING WE HAVE IS THE EMPEROR!

ALL RIGHT, THEN. SO BE IT. CRUCIFY HIM.

149

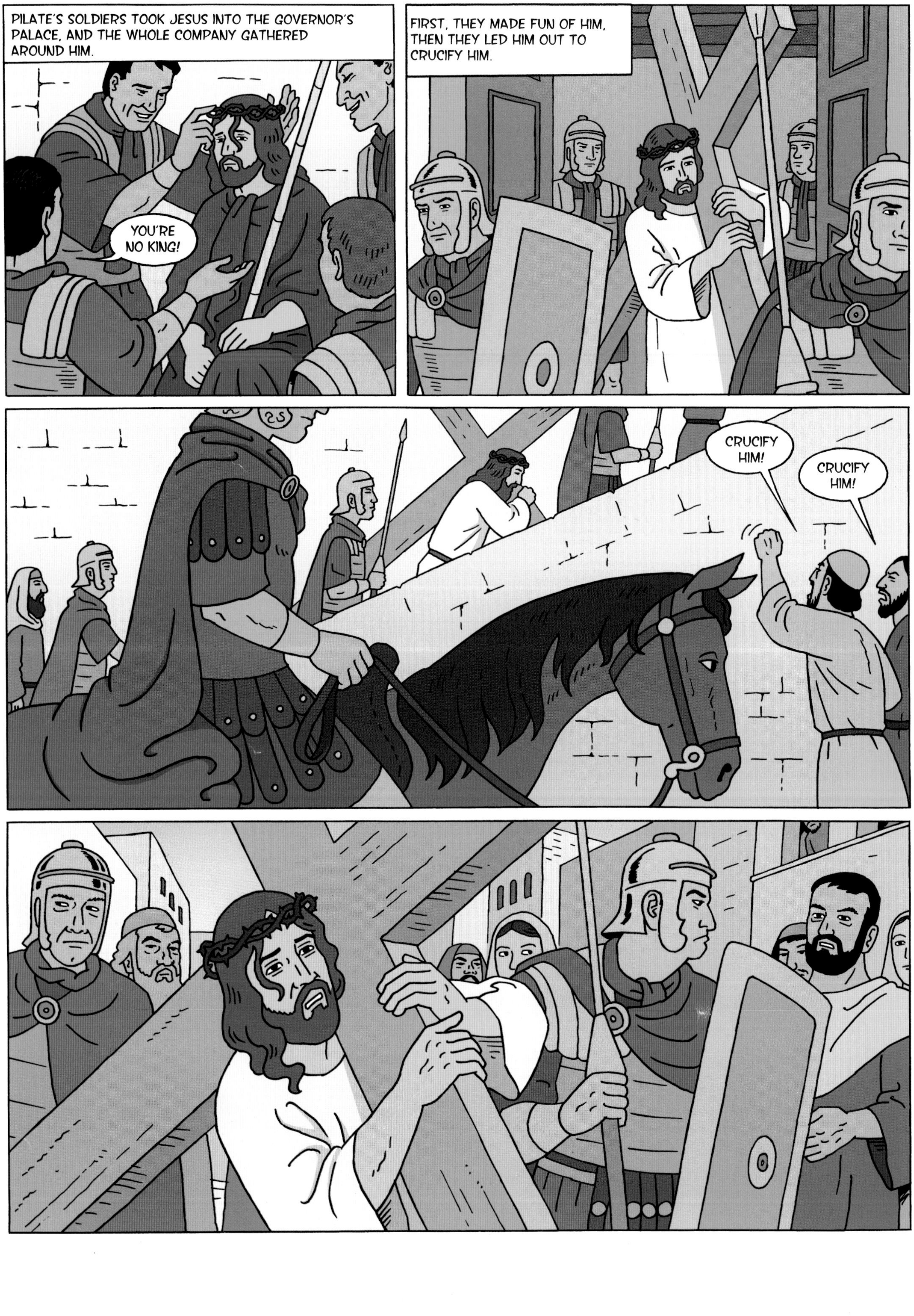
PILATE'S SOLDIERS TOOK JESUS INTO THE GOVERNOR'S PALACE, AND THE WHOLE COMPANY GATHERED AROUND HIM.
YOU'RE NO KING!
FIRST, THEY MADE FUN OF HIM, THEN THEY LED HIM OUT TO CRUCIFY HIM.
CRUCIFY HIM!
CRUCIFY HIM!

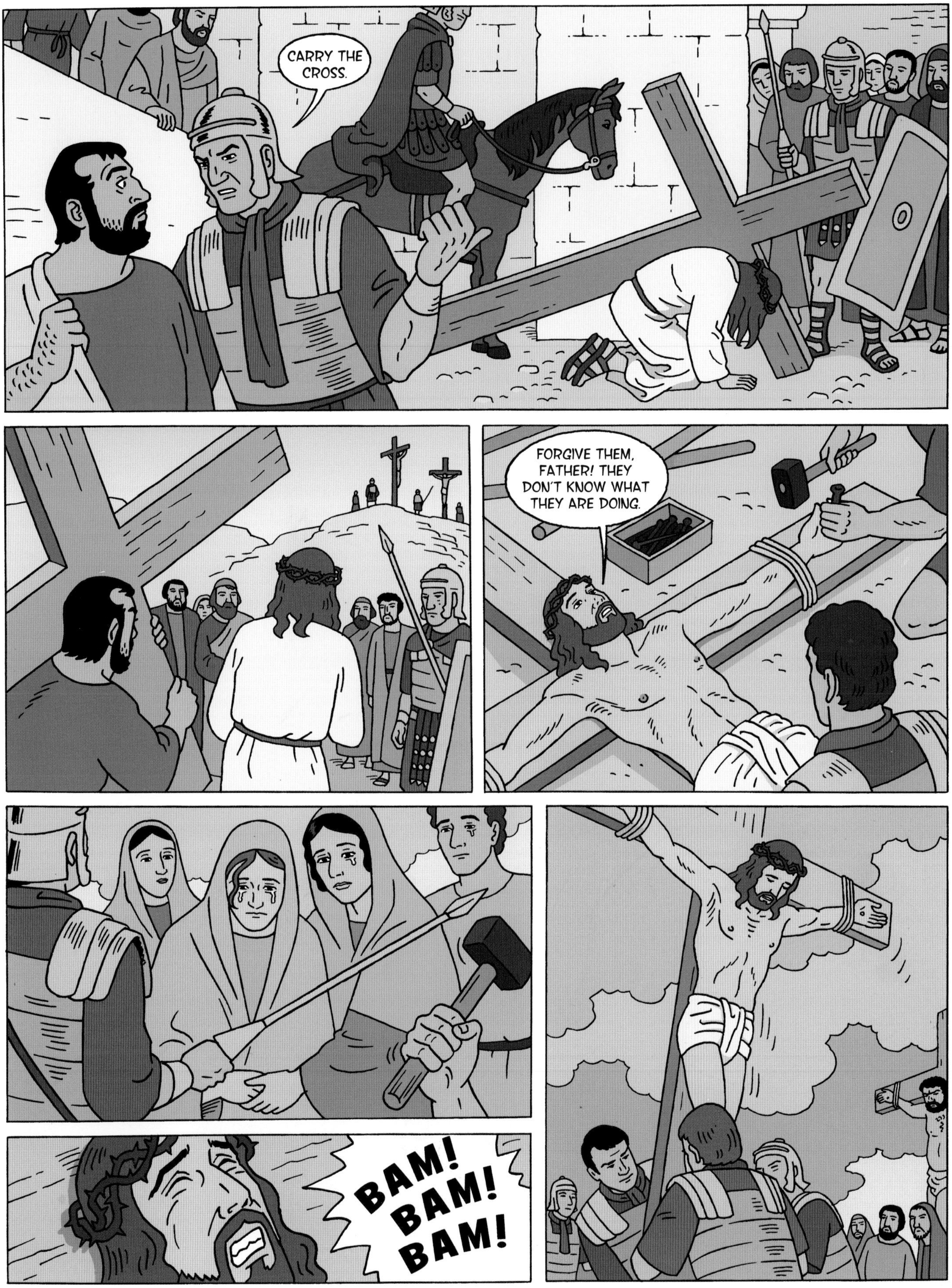
CARRY THE CROSS.
FORGIVE THEM, FATHER! THEY DON'T KNOW WHAT THEY ARE DOING.
BAM! BAM! BAM!

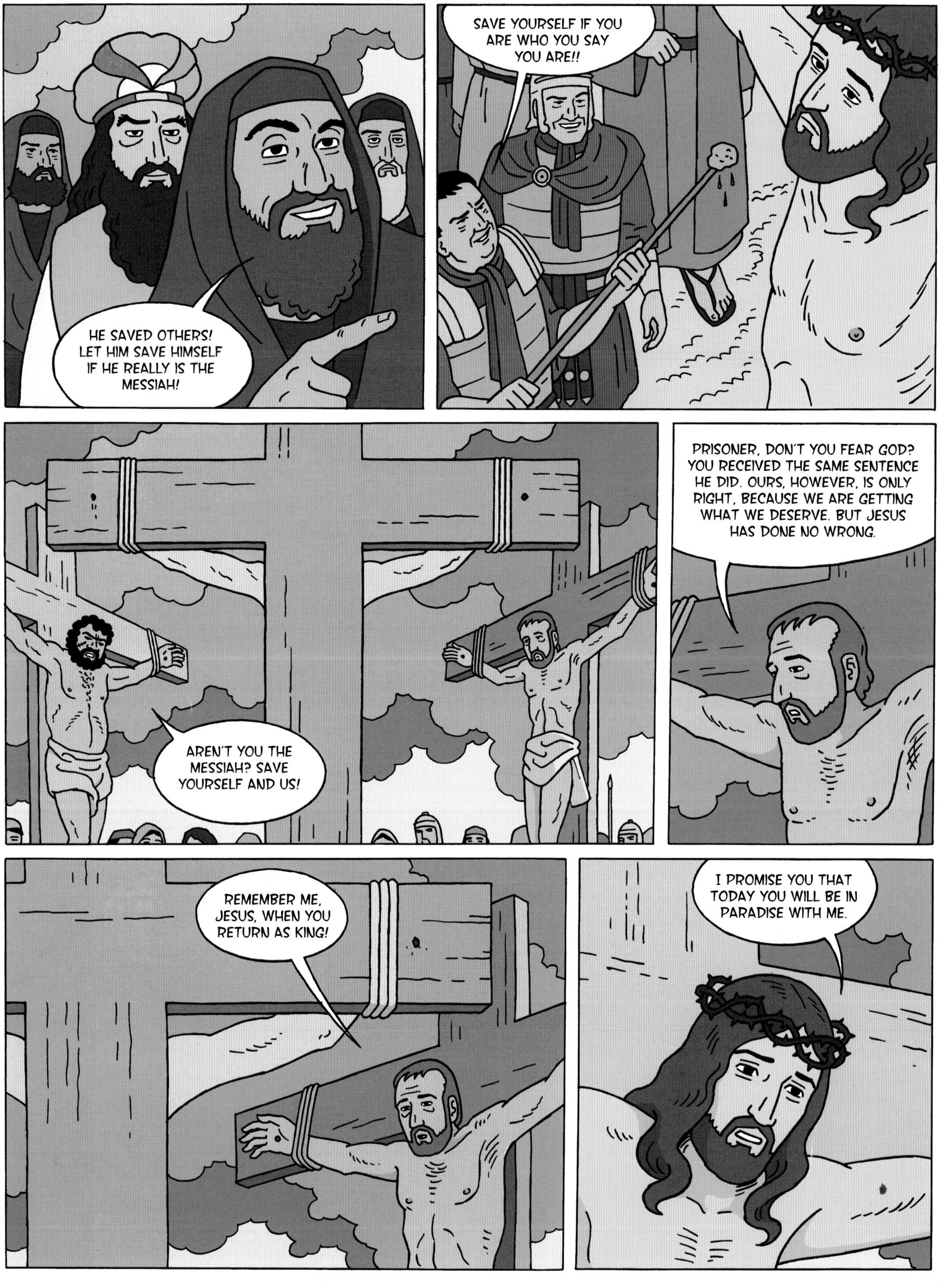
HE SAVED OTHERS! LET HIM SAVE HIMSELF IF HE REALLY IS THE MESSIAH!
SAVE YOURSELF IF YOU ARE WHO YOU SAY YOU ARE!!
AREN'T YOU THE MESSIAH? SAVE YOURSELF AND US!
PRISONER, DON'T YOU FEAR GOD? YOU RECEIVED THE SAME SENTENCE HE DID. OURS, HOWEVER, IS ONLY RIGHT, BECAUSE WE ARE GETTING WHAT WE DESERVE. BUT JESUS HAS DONE NO WRONG.
REMEMBER ME, JESUS, WHEN YOU RETURN AS KING!
I PROMISE YOU THAT TODAY YOU WILL BE IN PARADISE WITH ME.

MOTHER, MY DISCIPLES ARE ALSO YOUR SONS.

FATHER! IN YOUR HANDS I PLACE MY SPIRIT!

HE REALLY WAS THE SON OF GOD!

THAT EVENING, A RICH MAN FROM THE CITY OF ARIMATHEA ARRIVED. HIS NAME WAS JOSEPH, AND HE ALSO WAS A FOLLOWER OF JESUS. HE WENT TO PILATE AND ASKED FOR THE BODY OF JESUS. PILATE ALLOWED JOSEPH TO TAKE HIM.

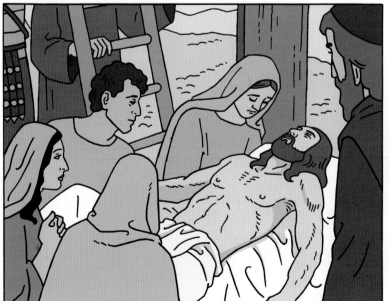

JOSEPH WRAPPED JESUS'S BODY IN A NEW LINEN SHEET AND PLACED IT A TOMB HE RECENTLY DUG OUT OF SOLID ROCK. THEN JOSEPH ROLLED A LARGE STONE IN FRONT OF THE ENTRANCE TO THE TOMB AND WENT AWAY.

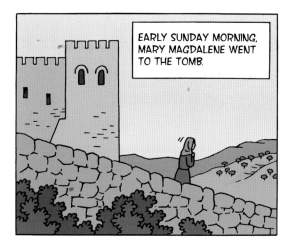

EARLY SUNDAY MORNING, MARY MAGDALENE WENT TO THE TOMB.

SOMEONE HAS TAKEN THE LORD FROM HIS TOMB! WE DON'T KNOW WHERE HE IS!

...!

OH!

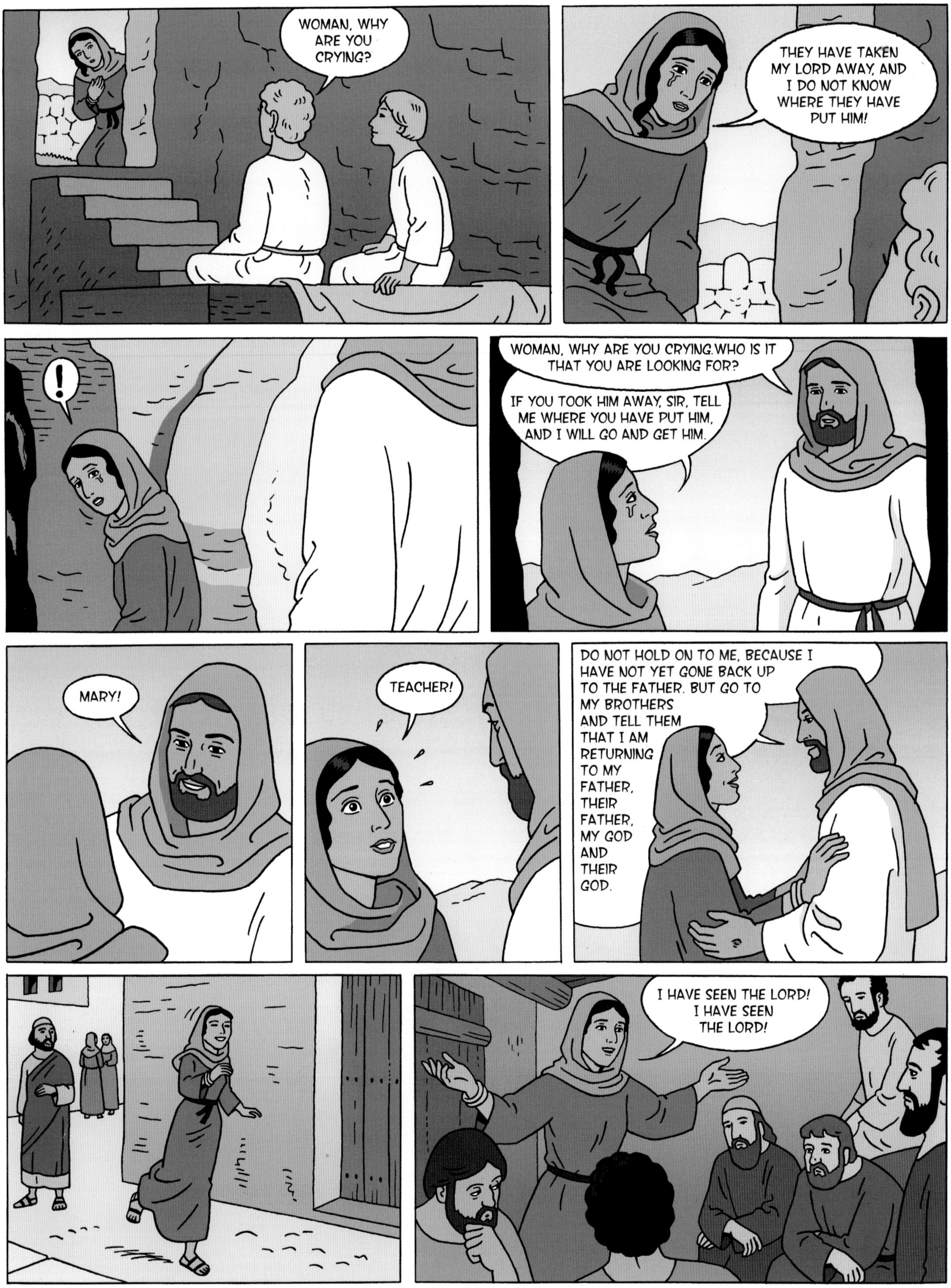
WOMAN, WHY ARE YOU CRYING?
THEY HAVE TAKEN MY LORD AWAY, AND I DO NOT KNOW WHERE THEY HAVE PUT HIM!
!
WOMAN, WHY ARE YOU CRYING.WHO IS IT THAT YOU ARE LOOKING FOR?
IF YOU TOOK HIM AWAY, SIR, TELL ME WHERE YOU HAVE PUT HIM, AND I WILL GO AND GET HIM.
MARY!
TEACHER!
DO NOT HOLD ON TO ME, BECAUSE I HAVE NOT YET GONE BACK UP TO THE FATHER. BUT GO TO MY BROTHERS AND TELL THEM THAT I AM RETURNING TO MY FATHER, THEIR FATHER, MY GOD AND THEIR GOD.
I HAVE SEEN THE LORD! I HAVE SEEN THE LORD!

ON THAT SAME SUNDAY AFTER THE DEATH OF JESUS, TWO OF HIS FOLLOWERS WERE GOING TO A VILLAGE CALLED EMMAUS.

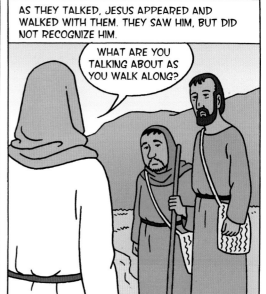

AS THEY TALKED, JESUS APPEARED AND WALKED WITH THEM. THEY SAW HIM, BUT DID NOT RECOGNIZE HIM.

WHAT ARE YOU TALKING ABOUT AS YOU WALK ALONG?

YOU MUST BE THE ONLY VISITOR IN JERUSALEM WHO DOESN'T KNOW THE THINGS THAT HAVE BEEN HAPPENING THESE LAST FEW DAYS!

WHAT THINGS?

WHAT HAS HAPPENED TO JESUS OF NAZARETH, A PROPHET CONSIDERED TO BE POWERFUL IN EVERYTHING HE SAID AND DID. OUR CHIEF PRIESTS AND RULERS HANDED HIM OVER TO BE SENTENCED TO DEATH, AND HE WAS CRUCIFIED.

WE HAD HOPED THAT HE WOULD BE THE ONE WHO WAS GOING TO SET ISRAEL FREE! THREE DAYS HAVE PASSED SINCE IT HAPPENED.

SOME OF OUR GROUP WENT TO THE TOMB AND FOUND IT EXACTLY AS THE WOMAN SAID!

THEY DID NOT SEE HIM.

HOW FOOLISH YOU ARE TO BELIEVE EVERYTHING THAT IS SAID! WAS IT NOT NECESSARY FOR THE MESSIAH TO SUFFER THESE THINGS SO THAT HE COULD THEN ENTER HIS GLORY?

JESUS EXPLAINED TO THEM WHAT WAS SAID ABOUT HIM IN ALL THE SCRIPTURES, BEGINNING WITH THE BOOKS OF MOSES AND THE WRITINGS OF ALL THE PROPHETS.

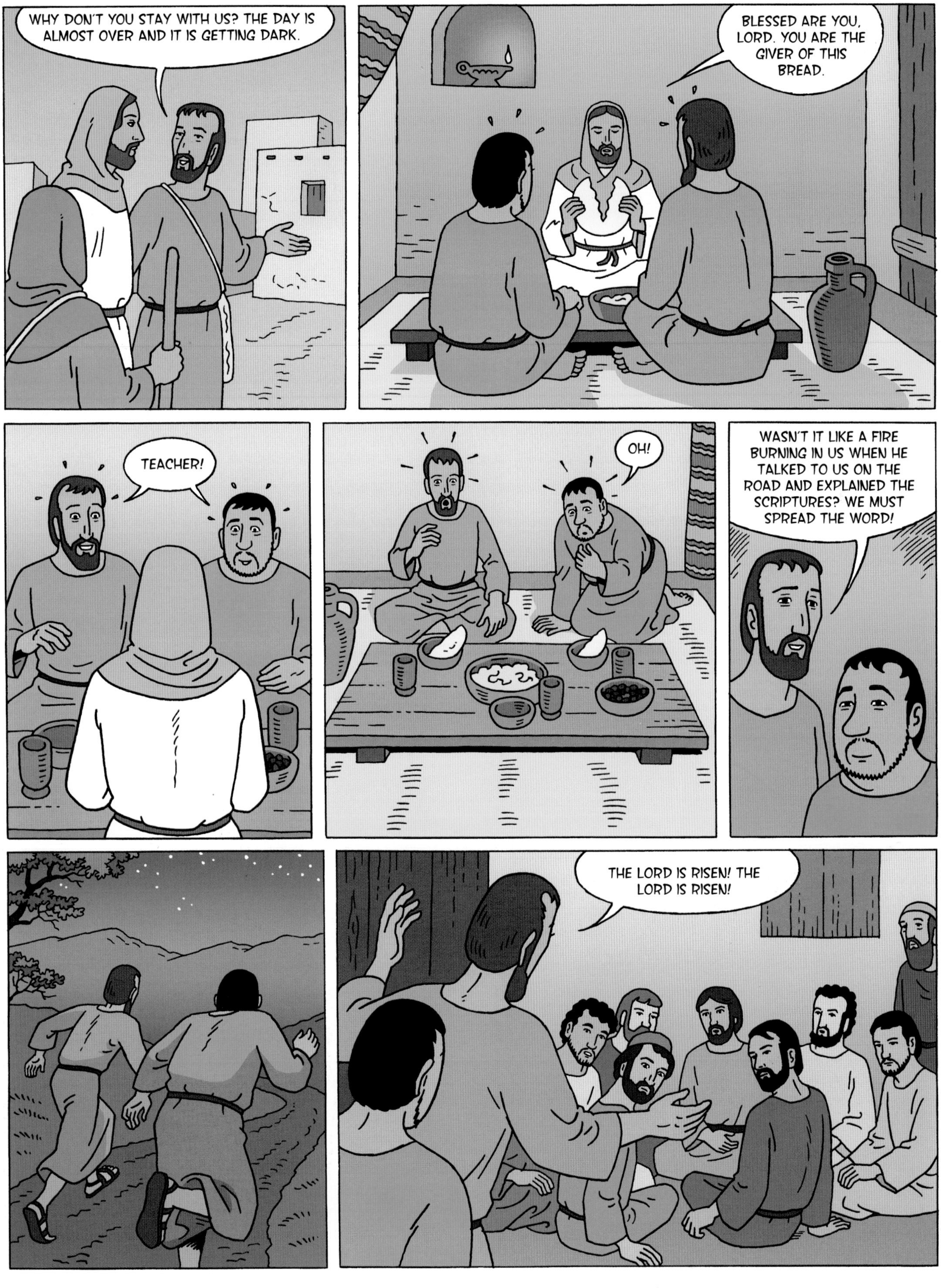
WHY DON'T YOU STAY WITH US? THE DAY IS ALMOST OVER AND IT IS GETTING DARK.
BLESSED ARE YOU, LORD. YOU ARE THE GIVER OF THIS BREAD.
TEACHER!
OH!
WASN'T IT LIKE A FIRE BURNING IN US WHEN HE TALKED TO US ON THE ROAD AND EXPLAINED THE SCRIPTURES? WE MUST SPREAD THE WORD!
THE LORD IS RISEN! THE LORD IS RISEN!

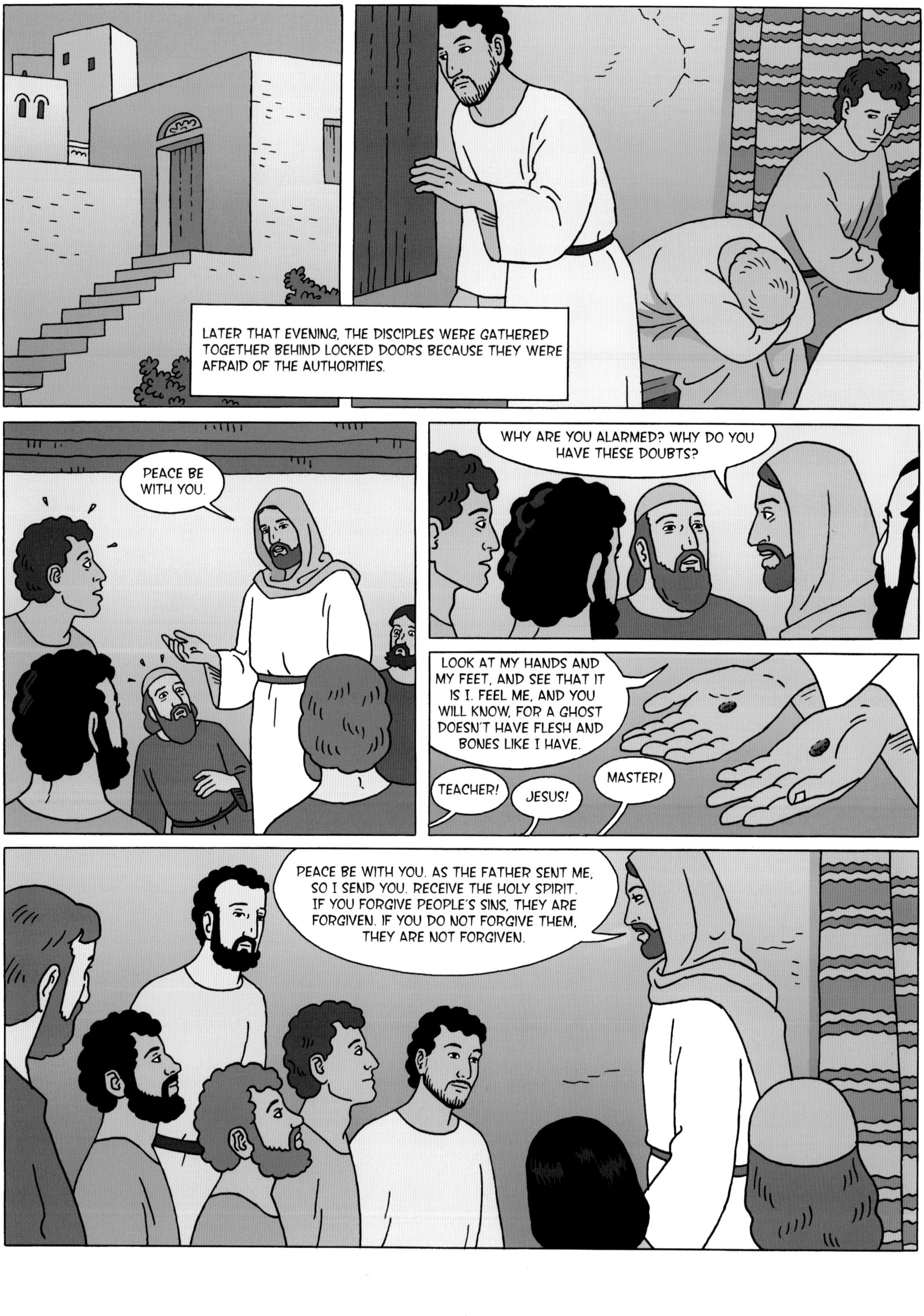
LATER THAT EVENING, THE DISCIPLES WERE GATHERED TOGETHER BEHIND LOCKED DOORS BECAUSE THEY WERE AFRAID OF THE AUTHORITIES.
PEACE BE WITH YOU.
WHY ARE YOU ALARMED? WHY DO YOU HAVE THESE DOUBTS?
LOOK AT MY HANDS AND MY FEET, AND SEE THAT IT IS I. FEEL ME, AND YOU WILL KNOW, FOR A GHOST DOESN'T HAVE FLESH AND BONES LIKE I HAVE.
TEACHER!
JESUS!
MASTER!
PEACE BE WITH YOU. AS THE FATHER SENT ME, SO I SEND YOU. RECEIVE THE HOLY SPIRIT. IF YOU FORGIVE PEOPLE'S SINS, THEY ARE FORGIVEN. IF YOU DO NOT FORGIVE THEM, THEY ARE NOT FORGIVEN.

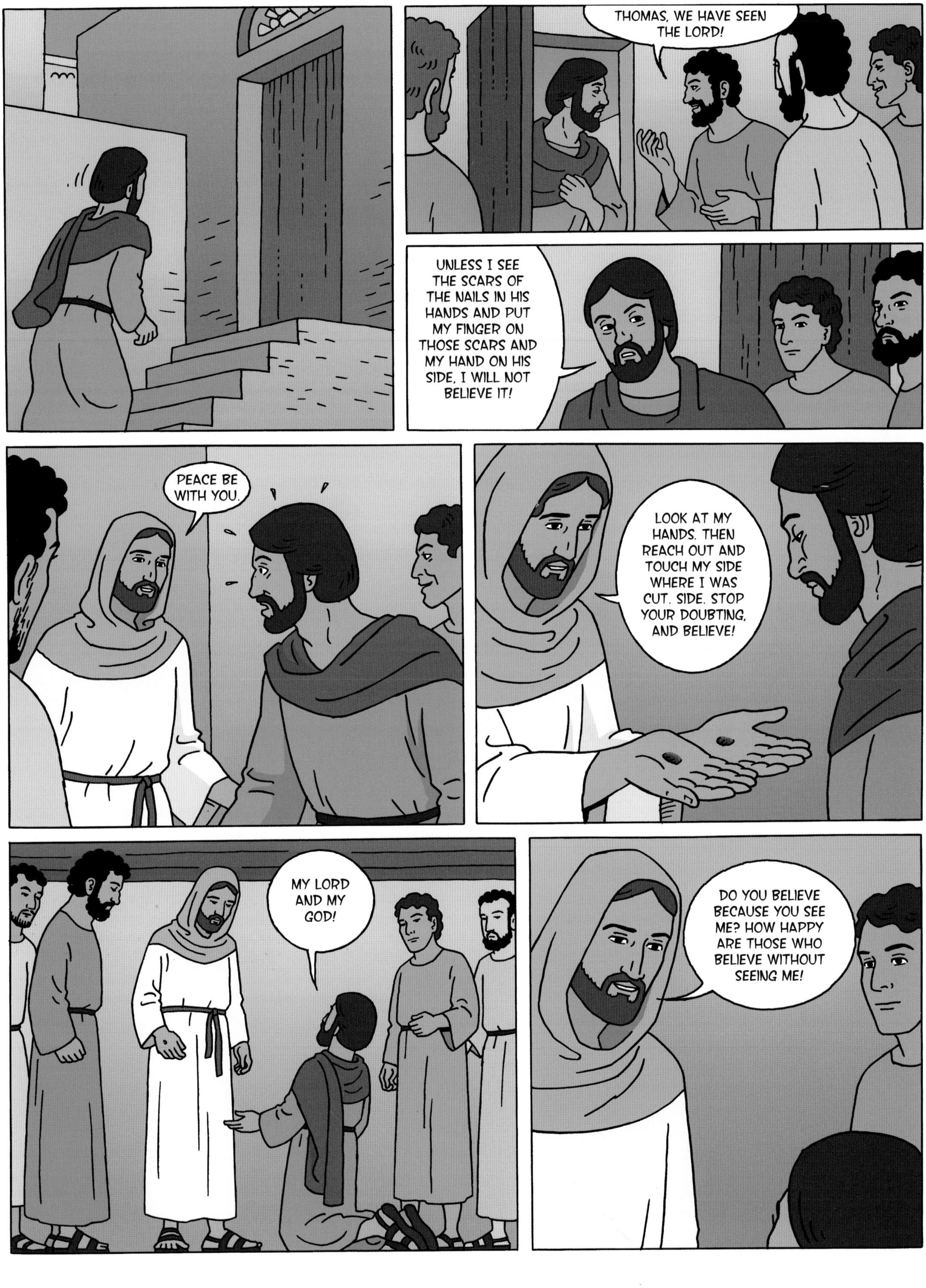
THOMAS, WE HAVE SEEN THE LORD!
UNLESS I SEE THE SCARS OF THE NAILS IN HIS HANDS AND PUT MY FINGER ON THOSE SCARS AND MY HAND ON HIS SIDE, I WILL NOT BELIEVE IT!
PEACE BE WITH YOU.
LOOK AT MY HANDS. THEN REACH OUT AND TOUCH MY SIDE WHERE I WAS CUT. SIDE. STOP YOUR DOUBTING, AND BELIEVE!
MY LORD AND MY GOD!
DO YOU BELIEVE BECAUSE YOU SEE ME? HOW HAPPY ARE THOSE WHO BELIEVE WITHOUT SEEING ME!

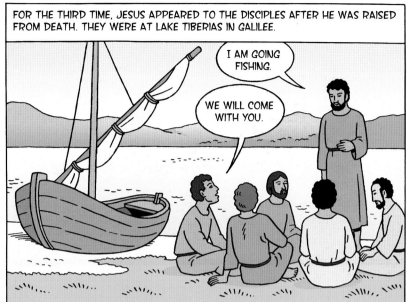

FOR THE THIRD TIME, JESUS APPEARED TO THE DISCIPLES AFTER HE WAS RAISED FROM DEATH. THEY WERE AT LAKE TIBERIAS IN GALILEE.

I AM GOING FISHING.

WE WILL COME WITH YOU.

THERE ARE NO FISH. HEAD TO THE SHORE.

YOUNG MEN, HAVEN'T YOU CAUGHT ANYTHING?

NO.

THROW YOUR NET OUT ON THE RIGHT SIDE OF THE BOAT, AND YOU WILL CATCH SOME.

SO THEY THREW OUT THE NET AND COULD NOT PULL IT BACK IN, BECAUSE THEY HAD CAUGHT SO MANY FISH!

IT IS THE LORD!

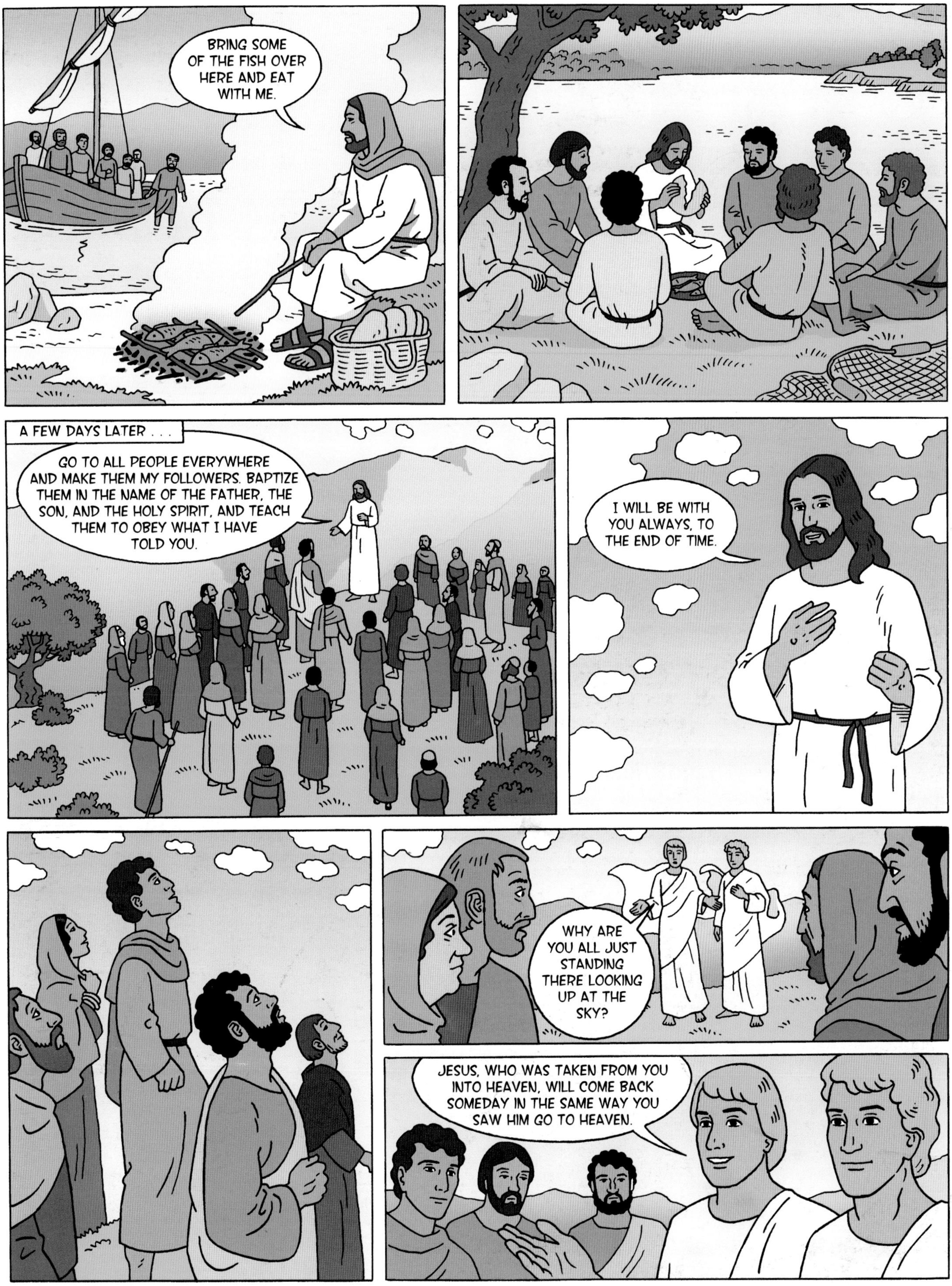
BRING SOME OF THE FISH OVER HERE AND EAT WITH ME.
A FEW DAYS LATER . . .
GO TO ALL PEOPLE EVERYWHERE AND MAKE THEM MY FOLLOWERS. BAPTIZE THEM IN THE NAME OF THE FATHER, THE SON, AND THE HOLY SPIRIT, AND TEACH THEM TO OBEY WHAT I HAVE TOLD YOU.
I WILL BE WITH YOU ALWAYS, TO THE END OF TIME.
WHY ARE YOU ALL JUST STANDING THERE LOOKING UP AT THE SKY?
JESUS, WHO WAS TAKEN FROM YOU INTO HEAVEN, WILL COME BACK SOMEDAY IN THE SAME WAY YOU SAW HIM GO TO HEAVEN.